Images of the Journey in Dante's *Divine Comedy*

Images of the Journey in Dante's *Divine Comedy*

Charles H. Taylor and Patricia Finley

An illustrated and interpretive guide to the poet's sacred vision, with 257

annotated illustrations selected from six centuries of artistic response to the poem

Yale University Press New Haven and London

In Memoriam H. L. 1904–1995

Published with assistance from Robert A. Lawrence
Copyright © 1997 by Yale University
All rights reserved
This book may not be reproduced, in whole or in
part, including illustrations, in any form (beyond
that copying permitted by Sections 107 and 108 of
the U.S. Copyright Law and except by reviewers for
the public press), without written permission from
the publishers

Designed by Sonia L. Scanlon
Set in Optima type by Amy Storm
Printed in Hong Kong by C&C Offest Printing CO., LTD.

Taylor, Charles H., 1928–
      Images of the journey in Dante's Divine
comedy / Charles H. Taylor and Patricia Finley.
            p.   cm.
      "An illustrated and interpretive guide to the
poet's sacred vision, with 257 annotated illustra-
tions selected from six centuries of artistic response
to the poem."
      Includes bibliographical references and index.
      ISBN 0-300-06834-4 (cloth : alk. paper)
      1. Dante Alighieri, 1256–1321. Divina comme-
dia—Illustrations. I. Finley, Patricia, 1925–
II. Title.
PQ4329.T39 1997
851'.1—dc21 96-37241
CIP

A catalogue record for this book is available from
the British Library

The paper in this book meets the guidelines for
permanence and durability of the Committee on
Production Guidelines for Book Longevity of the
Council on Library Resources

10 9 8 7 6 5 4 3 2 1

Contents

LA DIVINA COMEDIA
di
DANTE ALIGHIERI
cioè
L'Inferno, Il Purgatorio, ed Il Paradiso
Composto da Giovanni Flaxman Scultore Inglese ed inciso da Tommaso Piroli Romano.
1793

In possesso di

Tommaso Hope Scudiere, Amsterdam

Preface

This book is meant above all to be an encouragement to read Dante's great poem with pleasure and enthusiasm, or to read it again with renewed appetite and appreciation for the depth of its insight into the essential human journey. More than two hundred and fifty illustrations from six centuries of artistic response to the poem—in color whenever the originals are—provide a vivid and structured outline of the poet's imagined journey through the interior depths of Hell, the atoning suffering of Purgatory, and the experience of sacred vision in Paradise. Accompanying captions illuminate the artistry both of Dante's poem and of those who have interpreted it through art, especially in relation to the inner darkness, suffering, and quest for deeper meanings of our own time. Finally, twenty short essays, interspersed among the illustrations, examine the poem as a psychological journey from the dark wood of depression, through the painful purgations achieved in reflection and dreams, to the maturity of objective love and inner vision that are grounded in feminine compassion. The parts form a whole: the visible images of the illustrations provide the skeleton that supports the body of the interpretation, always with ultimate reference to the inexhaustible riches of the *Divine Comedy*.

The *Commedia* of Dante Alighieri (1265–1321) became popularly known as the *Divina Commedia*, or *Divine Comedy*, as its reputation grew after its appearance in the fourteenth century. It is experienced by most readers not only as the foremost poem of Christian passion but also as one of the most powerful expressions of sacred imagination in all literature. To T. S. Eliot, Dante was "the most universal of poets in the western languages" and shared the pinnacle of greatness only with Shakespeare ("Dante," in *Selected Essays*, 200). Modern readers need be neither Christian nor consciously religious to feel the impact of the *Commedia*'s narrative structure and dramatic imagery.

Dante's imagination sketches pictures for his reader's inner eye so vividly that his word-images have invited illustration from the days of the earliest manuscripts to the present. Pictorial responses began to appear in the first illuminations of the text within two decades of the poet's death in 1321. Through the centuries, the depiction of the action and characters of the *Commedia* has preoccupied not only many wonderfully naive yet powerful medieval illuminators but also later artists as notable and diverse as Sandro Botticelli and Giovanni di Paolo, William Blake and Gustave Doré, Renato Guttuso and Leonard Baskin. Many of these artists spent years immersed in a passionate dialogue with Dante's vision. As Dante's art has provoked the art of others, one can imagine him having at least as much right as Falstaff to assert, "I am not only witty in myself, but the cause that wit is in other men."

In our desire to illuminate both Dante's own vision and its meaning for us today, we have selected illustrations that are of narrative interest and close to the text, artistically lively, and in a diversity of styles. We have generally not represented those artists who use the poem primarily as a jumping-off point for a personal artistic response that bears little relation to the text. The illustrations touch every level of the pilgrim's journey: circling down into the depths of Hell, climbing up the terraces of the Mountain of Purgatory, and ascending through the spheres of Paradise. Because film and television have made the visual medium for the presentation of story as important again in this century as it was before the invention of the printing press—when, for example, the great cathedral windows of stained glass were primary sources of education—we hope that these illustrations will entice readers to Dante's poem.

We approach the art and the poem from the perspective of Jungian psychoanalysts trained, respectively, in literary criticism and visual art. The power of Dante's poem to move a contemporary generation was first brought home to one of us by teaching the *Inferno* to beginning students of literature in a public university forty years ago. The images affected some students so strongly that they thought Dante actually believed that the horrors he describes in the interior of the earth were what he would have seen if he had drilled a deep enough hole into the ground beneath Jerusalem. The need to communicate a symbolic attitude in approaching the poem, so evident then, became decades later an opportunity to read the poem symbolically at many levels with candidates well into their development as Jungian psychoanalysts. Leading a joint seminar together, we amplified our reflection on the narrative as a journey into the interior of human pathology, suffering, and the enduring quest for sacred meaning through the use of historic illustrations. Responses to those and other presentations encouraged us to give our approach an embodied form, and this book is the result. In our seminar we naturally emphasized the parallels between the pilgrim's experiences and observations and clinical practice with individual patients today. In this book we have favored common discourse over clinical terminology but have tried to communicate faithfully the psychological subtlety of Dante's vision.

Sigmund Freud and Carl Jung shared a keen interest in the artifacts of ancient cultures, but for Freud the manifestations of religious concern and activity derived essentially from illusions created to defend humankind against a full acceptance of the tragedy of mortality. For Jung, the rituals and artifacts of sacred devotion not only revealed a universal need to explore the meaning of the human condition but also contained much of the accumulated wisdom of human experience. He understood the expression of interest in sacred symbolism over thousands of years to be an archetypal human activity, manifest in almost every culture. Jung's lifework demonstrates that conscious attention to the sacred is a recurring and continuing element in the history and psychology of human awareness. Such a view of the significance of sacred energy looks not for the objective reality of the deities imagined but rather for the subjective meaning of these images as they appear in vivid art and ritual throughout prehistory and history. For this reason, Jung's approach to the artistic renderings of religious experience, both visual and verbal, is sympathetic to their deepest psychological meanings, without either a commitment to or an insistence on any particular doctrine's objective reality or truth.

Far from having a cultist's attachment to one sacred tradition or person, the passion in such a view of sacred imagery is devoted precisely to openness and a symbolic attitude rather than to exclusiveness and fundamentalist certainty. Examination of the art of the *Commedia* and its word-pictures, while remaining sympathetic to its Christian point of view, as toward any other religious tradition, is particularly appropriate to a search for the elements of the poem's action and images that are most meaningful to readers today. Because the richness of Dante's sophisticatedly reflective religious thought becomes more expressive of the mystical and visionary strain in medieval Christianity as the poem progresses, we believe that our reading is in tune both with the essentials of the poem and with its still meaningful vision of the movement into psychological maturity toward which the pilgrim's journey is directed.

Throughout, we have sought to tie our observations to the text and illustrations and point to parallels we have noted when working in depth with persons seeking psychological growth. Because our approach elucidates the journey as a symbolic model of psychic development, we hope that the more familiar images of the *Inferno* will gain deeper meaning for many readers by exploration of how they relate to the inner condition of modern individuals. We believe, moreover, that appreciation of the *Purgatorio*'s images of meaningful suffering and, especially, apprehension of the *Paradiso*'s emphasis on the interiority of divine reality and its lively rendering of the interactive relation between devoted love and encompassing vision will give the two less-often read parts of the poem new life for modern readers. Western artistic efforts to imagine the paradisal condition as a metaphor for human wholeness and psychic maturity rarely achieve the complex appeal of Dante's unfolding vision. Almost seven centuries after its conception, the poem continues to be relevant to the psychological and spiritual journey of every individual.

The captions locate the illustrations in the flow of the narrative and relate them to the primary meaning of the action at the place depicted. We try to provide enough information and observation about the pictures so that a reader who knows the text, or reads along in an annotated translation, can easily get its point. In quoting from the *Commedia*, we have used the version of Allen Mandelbaum, poet and translator of Virgil, for the excellence of his verse and its faithfulness to the original meaning. His translation is also unforced by Dante's rhyme scheme, which is natural for Italian but difficult to execute in English. (Other versions, such as those by John Ciardi, Dorothy Sayers, and Charles Singleton have their particular virtues and may be preferred by individual readers.) We also make many modest and occasional substantive observations about the historical context of an illustrator's work and its comparative style in relation to the work of other illustrators, especially when artists of greatly divergent dates or styles offer versions of the same scene. In the interest of maintaining the poem's flow of action, we have erred on the side of brevity. We comment more broadly on the development of illustrative style and its relation to interpretation of the poem in the next section, "On the Illustrations." Our observations there are supported by our notes on specific illustrations.

The essays that are interspersed with the illustrations are intended to suggest how deeply the poem explores the stages of moral and spiritual development in images that are psychologically acute for people today. In addition, in the Introduction and Conclusion we examine the creation of the poem in the context of Dante's own development, especially in relation to a remarkable early dream that has received little modern attention. We hope also that our observations on the three dreams the poet invents in the *Purgatorio* will illuminate what is taking place within the pilgrim's character as he participates in the symbolic journey up the Mountain of Purgatory. That the poet can devise such telling dreams for his protagonist is further evidence of his profound connection to the deeper reaches of the psyche.

Although Jung had great respect for the *Commedia*, referring occasionally to it in his texts and notes (to the three-faced image of Dis, or the Devil, as a shadow-reflection of the triune godhead of the Christian Trinity, for example) and although he clearly understood the pilgrim's journey as a psychological one with Beatrice at its center, he never explored that understanding at length, as he did, for example, with Goethe's *Faust* as well as many ancient sacred and literary texts, In our effort to suggest how the *Commedia*'s psychological and sacred themes reveal inner realities shared as much by modern readers as by its medieval audience, we wish to acknowledge Helen Luke's *Dark Wood to White Rose* (1975; reprinted by Parabola Books in 1989). However, whereas Luke retells the essentials of Dante's narrative to provide the frame for her interpretation of psychological maturation, we have allowed our large selection of illustrations to reflect much of the narrative action and then focused intently on a limited number of evolving images or nodal actions for exploration in depth. Others whose work we have consulted include particularly William Anderson and John Freccero, as well as the translators and scholars mentioned above and the works from which we have drawn our illustrations—especially those edited by Peter Brieger and colleagues, Kenneth Clark, Milton Klonsky, and John Pope-Hennessey (see "Works Cited"). We make no claim to command the massive Dante scholarship and know that many of our comments have been anticipated in the language of the Christian and literary traditions, though we believe that our psychological commentary looks inward in a way that may enlarge the awareness of our readers.

Dante's depiction of many individuals—imagined in their post-mortal essence as inhabitants of Hell, Purgatory, and Paradise—captures the highly personal nature of religious experience, experience that may at one time be refused in opaque denial and at another be received in numinous awe. His characterization of Beatrice, by frequent allusion in the first half of the poem and in her own person in the later cantos, presents a guide at once human and transcendent. She is the most developed of Dante's many images of the divine, presented as an interior reality. In Beatrice we see the rich completion of an inner figure who had lived and grown within the poet from the age of nine until his death. Examination of the first dream the poet reports in response to an early encounter with Beatrice will set the psychological context within which his great life's work unfolded. But first, it is appropriate to describe in more detail why we chose particular illustrators and to suggest from a wider angle of vision how their cultures condition the orientations of the artists whose work is represented.

A note on citations: sources of quotations are indicated in the text by author and title initially, with full references in "Works Cited." Unless otherwise noted, all quotations from the *Commedia* are from Allen Mandelbaum's translation (New York, 1984). Biblical quotations are from the Jerusalem Bible, and references to the writings of Carl Jung, abbreviated as *CW*, volume number, paragraph number, are to *The Collected Works of C. G. Jung*, ed. Herbert Read et al., 20 vols. (New York, 1953–1979).

On the Illustrations

The illustrations presented in this book relate to the narrative and symbolic movement of the poem as it unfolds. Accompanying remarks set them in context, comment on their artistic qualities, and compare them with other illustrations of the same action in the poem. Whenever pertinent, we point out how artists have reflected the issues of psychological growth, the inner experience of transpersonal reality, and the consequently viable meanings for readers today. Dante's image journey has engaged the devoted energy of countless illustrators for more than six centuries since it appeared, providing evidence that his poem, by means of its extraordinarily specific narrative and visual detail, has indeed activated passionate responses from the deepest levels of our common humanity.

Some illustrators, like Sandro Botticelli, stay very close to the images Dante describes; others inspired or aggravated by the poem, like William Blake, pursue their own images. But in accord with the *Commedia*'s basic command to "Look! Look well!" the artist's task is to pay full attention to the emotional reality of the imagery he seeks to elucidate by clearly responding to it, whether by concurring, enhancing, or opposing. Most of the artists whose works we have chosen fulfill this command, but some have been selected because they miss the poet's point and thereby highlight it. We have not included those modern illustrations that are either too abstract or too personal to be readily identifiable in their relation to the poet's text. Dante's images leave ample room for interpretation and abstraction without losing their referents.

In addition to closeness to the meaning of the text, we have sought artistic diversity. Artists' visual approaches to the two-dimensional form of the book or manuscript page vary. Some seek to design the whole page as a unity; others let their pictures stand out from the typography, especially in the centuries after printing and a variety of illustrators' crafts—lithography, engraving, etching—became common. Some illustrators exploit the page through the interaction of dark and light patterns and flattened perspective; others use every trick of perspective to give the impression of three-dimensionality.

We have enjoyed discovering the counterpoint between medieval and more recent styles. The sense of hieratic simplicity and unself-conscious candor of the earliest illuminations is followed by the more sophisticated linear perspective of the Renaissance and later periods; modern artistry then returns to a conscious use of degrees of flatness for the exploration of symbolic expression. The incarnate world can be used to communicate the symbolic realm in many ways. The medieval attitude of spontaneous humility before God's creation cannot be duplicated today, but a living sense of the numinous in this world remains a significant aspect of contemporary experience.

We have also looked for what gives an artist's work a presence—not as a realistic copy of an outward form but with a sense of being alive as natural forms are alive. Thomas Aquinas put it as imitating nature in its manner of operation. The most effective illustrations evoke the emotion and energy of the event depicted. The artist's technique, rather than drawing attention to itself, usually facilitates the sense of aliveness that comes through the forms. Blake provides two particularly vivid examples of this in his focus on the doubled-back swirling shape that conveys the sensation of being swept away by compulsive lust in the winds of the Inferno's second circle (see fig. 22) and in his equally apt rendering of the upreaching, transforming fire that purges the lustful on the top terrace of the Mountain of Purgatory (see fig. 167). Medieval illuminators often comment with straightforward pungency and textual precision: the Pisan's pilgrim and guide (see fig. 124) clearly climb laboriously and sit solidly in discourse on the sun, while the Paduan's concretization of the impact of Beatrice's glance (see fig. 177) leaves no doubt as to its force. Botticelli's sacred wood (see fig. 170), with its supple trees and lissome guide, gives us an awakening touch, a glimpse of the spiritual feminine power that comes later in the Earthly Paradise. Doré's Celestial Rose manages to suggest some measure of the unspeakable power of light in the *Paradiso* (see fig. 247).

Cultural attitudes change through history, and our illustrations reflect these shifts. Many of the illustrations come from the medieval manuscripts that began to appear shortly after Dante finished his poem in 1321. Medieval artists and writers shared an unusually integrated set of values contained in the relationships among God, humankind, and the concrete world of nature. As a result, they often created a unity of effect by composing the illustrated page as a whole, sometimes even designing the illustration without borders so that it is not separated from the writing. The chief illustration on a page is frequently positioned across its bottom quarter, as if to ground and emphasize one of the actions in the immediately proximate text.

Fourteenth-century illuminators, in their new and delighted study of natural forms, learned to translate the visual principles of growth and volume across media. Their painted human figures and plant forms were made to look not alive as if they were flesh or leaves but as new forms with their own energies, partaking of the order of the cosmos as the artists perceived it. The realm of things seen was assumed to embody truths unseen but even more real, so that these illuminators penetrated beneath the surface to a continuum of meaning to which all could relate. Their mode of expression is at once naive and knowing, sensual and spiritual, concrete and symbolic. The assumption of meaning allows a lighter touch that conveys conviction and a clear-sighted, rather than fanatical, observation of the world as it is.

We have selected a number of illustrations from two fourteenth-century Tuscan manuscripts designated Pisan by Peter Brieger and Millard Meiss and distinguished here by their dates: the manuscript of ca. 1345, located now in the Musée Condé, Chantilly, and the manuscript of ca. 1385, at the Historische Bibliotek des Christianeums, Hamburg. Peter Brieger and Meiss see the illuminator of the Pisan manuscript in Chantilly as a major artist who worked in the style of Francesco Traini and heavily influenced the later artist (or artists). Hans Haupt's commentary accompanying the handsome facsimile edition of the *Codex Altonensis* explores its influences and history and suggests that the painter of the completed illuminations (*Inferno* and part of *Purgatorio*) may have been a student of Giotto. The earlier work presents a more integrated effect and a subtler color palette, but the Codex Altonensis illuminations frequently make up in energy and drama what they lack in aesthetic elegance—as, for example, in fig. 124, noted earlier. Although the styles of the two manuscripts are quite distinct when closely observed, the similarity of subject matter, the arrangement of figures, and the unusual use of copes and tiaras in dressing the pilgrim and Virgil reveal their close connection.

Medieval manuscripts were sometimes illuminated by more than one artist of varying talents and strengths. Such a manuscript is in Venice at the Biblioteca Nazionale Marciana, presumed to have been executed by several Venetians in the late fourteenth century (Brieger and Giulia Bologna agree on this date; Sergio Samek-Ludovici thinks it is later). We have selected a number of examples from its *Paradiso*. Whereas the illuminators of the first two canticles usually permit the bare parchment to provide the atmosphere of the *Inferno* and the *Purgatorio* (from which we have chosen five examples) and draw their figures in great detail, the illustrators of the third canticle generally use a brilliant blue background and often have a cruder touch. Although the figures are sometimes heavy-handed, the blue evokes the *Paradiso*'s joyousness and well suits the feelings conveyed by the characters' lively gestures.

Manuscripts were originally produced by monks for other religious, but as they came to be crafted by workmen in guilds for a lay reading public of courtiers and merchants, illustrators became known by name. The fine work of Vecchietta and Giovanni di Paolo in the mid-fifteenth century maintained the meaningful aliveness and acute attentiveness of previous masters, but by Gugielmo Giraldi's time (1480), a degree of separation from the poem in feeling and a self-conscious elaboration appeared. His was the last illuminated manuscript of the *Commedia* before the printing press took hold.

In many ways, the illuminators who shared Dante's time are best able to communicate his meaning, accessibility, and economy of expression, but there is something to be said for distance and objectivity. Botticelli, more than a century later, was able to learn from many great painters since Cimabue and Giotto had begun the movement away from Byzantine stylization toward more earthy solidity. He was a student of Christoforo Landino, whom Kenneth Clark has called the king of Dante commentators, and his friend Antonio Manetti was a famous Dante scholar. Botticelli's work remains within the medieval tradition of educating through pictures, with clarity and precision of detail, but raised to a point of great complexity—except where he used simplicity to express deep meanings, as in his decision to confine most of his illustrations for the *Paradiso* to the relationship between Dante and Beatrice.

Botticelli's very large drawings, thirty-two by forty-seven centimeters, in silverpoint (unfortunately faded) and ink on vellum were initially made for Lorenzo di Pierfrancesco de' Medici but not printed until 1887 because of their large scale (see Clark, ed., *The Drawings by Sandro Botticelli*, 7ff.). As works of art, however, their obedience to Dante's spirit protects them from any hint of self-aggrandizement. Yet other illustrators of Botticelli's time, such as Giraldi, were seduced away from Dante's meaning by a rich and decorative formalism and lost vitality in the process.

There is a dearth of fine illustration during the years of the Enlightenment, corresponding to a reduced interest in Dante, but we find an intriguing threesome in London in the 1820s: John Flaxman, Henry Fuseli, and William Blake. Blake noted with appreciation the influence of Fuseli's dramatic wash drawings and oil paintings but claimed in 1809–10, long before he did his own illustrations (*Public Address*; see Klonsky, *Blake's Dante*, 18, 148), that Flaxman had used many of his ideas without acknowledgment, presumably because they had talked about the *Commedia* early in their long friendship. Whatever the cross-influences, they appear to have heightened each others' fascination with the poem. Blake is the illustrator most at odds with Dante's image of divine retribution and the condemning deity of the *Inferno* (see Milton Klonsky, Albert Roe, and David Bindman for discussions of this and other facts of Blake's attitude). Yet Blake seems to underappreciate the increasingly visionary, internalized image of deity presented in the upper reaches of Purgatory and, especially, in the *Paradiso*. In contrast, Botticelli honors the Christ image—as "a sun above a thousand lamps" (XXIII, 28) in the realm of the Fixed Stars, for example—but in the *Paradiso* generally keeps the focus on Beatrice and Dante, the human mediators, perceivers of divine reality. Blake has a visionary's liberal-humane image of godhead and is furious with the old Yahweh, but does not see clearly how the work of meaningful suffering in Purgatory leads to Dante's most profound visions. Perhaps because he was ill and unable to work extensively on the later parts of the poem, he does not fully recognize the poet's development.

Doré had a huge investment in the *Commedia*: he paid to have his first illustrations published (see comments at fig. 36), and he was one of the few artists to attend to the major parts of each canticle. In general, he pays close attention to the text, but he was famed for the speed with which he worked, keeping a small stable of experienced engravers of his own choice busy doing the wooden plates on which he did his drawings directly. Since this was his usual practice, it appears to explain why few original drawings for his illustrated works have survived. (See, for example, Lehman-Haupt, *The Terrible Doré*, 20, and Rose, *Gustave Doré*, 24.) The first edition of his illustrated *Inferno* was published in Paris in 1861 and became vastly popular. In 1868 the *Purgatorio* and *Paradiso* were published together with the *Inferno* in a two-volume set, but the latter canticles never achieved the same fame. W. B. Yeats wrote in 1897 expressing his great appreciation of Blake's achievement but dismissing Doré's work as "a noisy and demagogic art"—though he acknowledged in the same paragraph John Addington Symonds's approval of Doré's "very effective sense of luminosity and gloom" ("Blake's Illustrations to Dante," in *Essays and Introductions*, 140–141). Blake's engagement with Dante's visionary depth is obvious, but Doré has much to offer both in continuing the line of teaching through images and in his nineteenth-century conception of space and light. However, his diminished and stereotyped figures of Dante and Beatrice in Paradise suffer in comparison with Botticelli's differentiated pair.

Arriving at the 1960s and 1970s, we find another kind of contrast in the way Renato Guttuso's straightforward storytelling compares with Leonard Baskin's and Rico Lebrun's visionary depth. Guttuso often provides acute renderings of how the damned might have suffered in each location in Hell, whereas Baskin's powerful draftsmanship and psychological understanding facilitate an unusual degree of "penetration beneath surfaces," as he himself describes the goal of art, "to the true meanings of things in their relation to life" (quoted in Jaffe, *The Sculpture of Leonard Baskin*, 34). Rico Lebrun pressed more insistently still into the meaning of deliberately chosen evil in his impressive drawings, limited to the lower circles of the Inferno. This sense of an individual artist's conscious return to values of Dante's time, to the search for the underlying truth of experience, brings us full circle. Contemporary artists' feelings of responsibility to the truth of painful events—Lebrun and Baskin have both explored deeply the imagery of the Holocaust—underlie their commitment to a symbolic inwardness, a depiction of states of being, that resembles Dante's own conception (see figs. 80, 81).

Readers will see that illustrators are represented neither equally in our book as a whole nor equally through the three canticles of the poem. In part this has to do, as we have mentioned, with the aptness of each image to the stage of the poem's development or to the actions being illustrated. Yet artists also varied widely in the amount of work they put into the different parts of the *Commedia*. A few, like Botticelli and Doré, created many illustrations of each canticle, but others put much more energy into depicting the *Inferno* (by far the most frequently illustrated) or the *Purgatorio* than the *Paradiso*. Some of those most attuned to the *Inferno* were not as open to the *Paradiso*, which is psychologically more distant from everyday experience.

William Blake not only had marked sympathy for the souls in darkness but was too ill to complete the demanding project and therefore left many illustrations partially unfinished, as well as fewer for the *Paradiso*. Some artists, such as the Pisan illuminator, created few or no illustrations for the *Paradiso*, and we do not know whether they ran out of time and energy or patronage or were reluctant to take up the challenge. Only rarely, as in the allocation of one manuscript to two illuminators, did one artist work on the *Paradiso* (Giovanni di Paolo) and not on the other two canticles (Vecchietta). Kenneth Clark, in fact, considers this whole fifteenth-century Sienese codex (designated Yates-Thompson in the British Library) to be the most beautiful illustrated *Commedia* in existence in its inventiveness, radiant color, and poetic quality. Clark believes Priamo della Quercia was the painter of the first two canticles, but Pope-Hennessey (*The Illuminations to Dante's Divine Comedy*, 14–17) has later concluded that Vecchietta was the artist; we accept his judgment, which he supports with qualitative comparison of the two artists' work.

The *Inferno* has held an overwhelming fascination for readers in nearly every century. That is understandable, since most of us know best the early part of the journey. The burdens of the *Purgatorio*—carrying one's cross and being responsible for one's negative qualities—are known in some measure to us all, but to different degrees. Intimations of Paradise, a wholeness rarely achieved, and never arrived at without qualification, daunts even those artists whose attitude toward the sacred approximates Dante's. In our time, the poet's great work remains, as it has for almost seven hundred years, a unique guide to an interior vision of the divine.

Introduction **Beatrice the Heart-Eater**

Near the beginning of his first work—the youthful autobiography he called *La vita nuova*—Dante reports a dream that reflects the powerful impact of a courteous greeting from his beloved Beatrice. Having first seen and been seized by love for her at the tender age of nine (she was eight), he came upon her nine years later in the company of two older women, and she spoke to him for the first time. "And such was the virtue of her greeting that I seemed to experience the height of bliss" (trans. Barbara Reynolds, 31). He continues,

> I was filled with such joy that, my senses reeling, I had to withdraw from the sight of others. So I returned to the loneliness of my room and began to think about this gracious person. As I thought of her I fell asleep and a marvelous vision appeared to me. In my room I seemed to see a cloud the color of fire, and in the cloud a lordly figure, frightening to behold, yet in himself, it seemed to me, he was filled with a marvelous joy. He said many things, of which I understood only a few; among them were the words: *Ego dominus tuus* ("I am your Master"). In his arms I seemed to see a naked figure, sleeping, wrapped lightly in a crimson cloth. Gazing intently I saw that it was she who had bestowed her greeting on me earlier that day. In one hand the standing figure held a fiery object, and he seemed to say, *Vide cor tuum* ("Behold your heart"). After a little while I thought he wakened her who slept and prevailed on her to eat the glowing object in his hand. Reluctantly and hesitantly she did so. A few moments later his happiness turned to bitter grief, and, weeping, he gathered the figure in his arms and together they seemed to ascend into the heavens. I felt such anguish at their departure that my light sleep was broken, and I awoke. (31–32)

Soon afterward he circulated a sonnet describing the dream to "a number of poets who were famous at that time" and asked them to interpret his vision. The responses expressed diverse opinions; yet, wrote Dante some years later, "the true meaning of the dream was not then perceived by anyone, but now it is perfectly clear to the simplest reader" (33). That true meaning was the foreshadowing in his dream, at eighteen, of the death of Beatrice when he was twenty-five, which a few years hence, he sees clearly is the meaning of Love's weeping ascent "into the heavens" with his lady in his arms. Later commentators have generally accepted Dante's interpretation.

Yet the action of the dream deserves further exploration, for it conveys important insight into the poet's inner condition. That he writes at length about the dream nine years after he had it underscores its power for him, as indeed we might infer from the striking images present in the dream.

The dream commences with the dramatic appearance in the poet's room of "a cloud the color of fire, and in the cloud a lordly figure, frightening to behold." We are reminded of the images of cloud and fire in which the Lord appears to the Israelites in *Exodus*: "For the cloud of Yahweh rested on the tabernacle by day, and a fire shone within the cloud by night" (40:38, Jerusalem Bible). But the lord in Dante's dream is "Amor," Love, announcing in numinous splendor and unequivocal terms the dominating ruler of the poet's life and imagination. Yet, for all his terrifying power, the figure comes at first "filled with a marvelous joy," bearing the message that Love is his master and carrying the naked sleeping body of the beloved, wrapped only in "uno drappo sanguigno," a crimson or, literally, "blood-red" cloth. The color suggests the vitality, passion, and suffering that will surround Beatrice's image for the dreamer throughout his life.

Using Latin rather than the vernacular, as Dante often does to emphasize a point, Amor not only pronounces "Ego dominus tuus" but also asserts that the flaming object in his hand is the dreamer's heart. "Vide cor tuum," he says, as if to ensure that Dante will heed the significance of the action that follows. Amor then proceeds to make Beatrice eat this flaming heart, requiring her to incorporate what she is reluctant, even fearful, to consume (she eats it "dubitosamente"). Even though the eaten heart is not an unusual medieval metaphor for a devouring passion, here the forced nature of the assimilation and the beloved's uneasy reluctance illuminate the psychological danger inherent in the image. Eating another's heart may benefit the eater, as it is imagined to do in primitive rituals of acquiring an enemy's valor, but it kills the donor.

Were a modern man to present us with an image of a woman eating his heart, we might well fear that the dreamer's life force will be consumed and assimilated by the object of his projection. If the dreamer's inflamed heart, fed by the god of love to his beloved, is presented as remaining within her interior body, we might infer that his psyche risks dying as an independent being. To be eaten alive, even by one's beloved, is no less a death than to be consumed by the dragon in its cave, the monster in his lair, or the witch in her hut. If not his whole psyche, at least his feeling function, the domain of the heart, is at risk of loss or regression into the unconscious. Yet the dream says that the devouring occurred; it is a fact of psychic history, and it is important to bear this in mind as we observe the progression of Dante's life and work.

Returning to the dream: "A few moments later his [Amor's] happiness turned to bitter grief, and, weeping, he gathered the figure in his arms and together they seemed to ascend into the heavens." The dreamer then wakes with an anguished start. Dante asks his fellow poets to interpret the dream but gains no insight for several years. Meanwhile, he continues to worship his lady, mostly from afar, and for a long time attempts to conceal her identity. He expresses his passion through verse, seeming to know intuitively that his devotion to Beatrice is meant to motivate his inner creativity rather than to seek fulfillment in an embodied personal relationship. (Dante's deep childhood attachment to Beatrice may well have arisen in part as compensation for his mother's death when he was young, between five and eight. Such an early loss may focus a child's need for nurture on an idealized person, even when there is little direct contact with that individual. Although Dante does not speak of his reaction to this loss, we can examine the relationship of his later work to what he does tell us about his feelings for Beatrice, including his description of this vivid dream.)

After a time Beatrice's father died, and Dante had premonitions, heightened by a serious illness of his own, that Beatrice's death would soon follow. In response, he writes a long poem describing these premonitions and his feeling of sorrow, whereupon Love visits him inwardly, corrects his feeling, and restores him to joy, saying, "Bless now the day I took you in my power" (70). He then has the first vision of Beatrice that explicitly compares her with the figure of Christ, an analogy that grows organically within him for many years thereafter.

In his vision, the poet sees his best friend's lady, whose name is Joan but whose nickname is Primavera (Spring), coming toward him, followed by Beatrice a bit behind. Again Love speaks in his heart to explain that Joan's nickname is Primavera because it "means that she will come first (*prima verra*)" and continues that Joan's given name also "signifies 'she will come first,' for Joan comes from John, who preceded the True Light, saying *Ergo vox clamantis in deserto: parate viam Domini*" (71)—that is, her name comes from John the Baptist, who cried out in the wilderness to prepare the way of the Lord.

Furthermore, Love points out, "Anyone who thought carefully about this would call Beatrice Love because of the great resemblance she bears to me!" (71). Here, as elsewhere, the poet plays on Beatrice's name, which means the "one who blesses." But even more boldly, Beatrice in this passage is compared explicitly to Christ, for she follows Primavera/Joan as Christ followed John the Baptist. Dante's urge to make of Beatrice a Christlike figure is apparent from this moment when he first contemplates and feels the grief of her possible death.

Not much later, when Beatrice in fact dies, there is no further question of the poet acting out his love in this world. Dante mourns grievously, but characteristically he decides, when tears can no longer relieve his sorrow, "to give vent to it by a sorrowful composition" (81). He does not fall into hopeless despair (surrendering his heart to the digestion of his lady) but turns again to internalization through his poetic craft as the way to salve his wound.

A year passes and he is briefly "gladdened overmuch" by the company of a compassionate lady who distracts him temporarily from his devotion to Beatrice. He lives for a time in inner conflict until Beatrice appears to him in a vision, "in glory, clothed in the crimson garments in which she first appeared before my eyes" (94). Contemplating this vision, the poet rededicates himself to Beatrice and composes some further sonnets. Then one day he has a final powerful vision that makes him decide to say nothing more of her until he can do so "more worthily." If God will give him life enough, he says, "I hope to compose concerning her what has never been written in rhyme of any woman" (99).

Thus already, at about twenty-eight, the poet imagines the masterwork that will manifest the transformation of his eaten heart. It will be many years before he actually begins the great work that fulfills his vision, and it will be almost his life's end before he fully realizes the image in which he sees Beatrice following Joan as Jesus did John the Baptist. The confident character of Dante's inward imagination is marked from his youth, as he determines to keep his own counsel until he is ready to make Beatrice his image of divine interiority—and to do it so convincingly that he earns his place with the great poets of antiquity. Few are the examples in human history of an artist or prophet who felt called so early by such a deep inner figure and knew so assuredly the reality of the transpersonal level from which the vision came.

Because Dante knows that a god has determined his fate and recognizes that Beatrice is a figure who, for him, carries the authority of Christ, he sets out to make her consumption of his heart the incentive to assimilate this numinous experience in his life and work. It is his ability to turn to creative account the enormity of his desire that saves him from being devoured by this love.

Further confirmation of the creative power that lies behind his dream is the fact that Love himself, despite his authority as master, weeps grievously for the death of Beatrice in his arms. This death is patently not of his choice; it appears that a larger power rules both the poet and the poet's personal god. This transpersonal power "arranges" events so that the poet can never claim his love in this world, in mortal time and earthly union. We might call the larger power the universal force that expresses itself in the poet's calling. Whether we describe this in cosmic terms as being "the Love that moves the sun and the other stars" or, in more psychological language, as what Jung might call the center of the larger personality, this force rules the developmental unfolding of human natures. It guides the ego, sends the dreams, and ultimately rules even the god of personal love.

Although Dante has intimations from the beginning of the symbolic nature of his love—always keeping it at a distance, making it the stimulus of poetry rather than of action—permanent interiority is enforced by the death of his beloved. This event soon begets his determination to write of her what has never been written of a mortal woman. Through the poet's artistry, Beatrice becomes immortal, while in turn her image works in the poet's soul to bring him immortality, too. The eater of his heart becomes the one who nourishes his soul; we could say that each devours and transforms the other.

In death, Beatrice becomes the agent of transformation for the poet as he allies her image with the agent of transformation for all humankind. The loss of her incarnate being fosters an imaginative process that parallels in its meaning the nurture of Christians by the eucharistic flesh and blood of the sacrificed savior. But because she is feminine in her nature, the figure of Beatrice also evokes the nurturing goddess who lies behind all sacred rituals of feeding and nourishment. This is what Dante achieves, after he resolves that the goal of his life will be to move from a love that is heart-devouring to a love that will make his soul welcome in Paradise when it is released from mortal flesh. The poet's vehicle becomes the invention of a journey whose images feed multiple generations of spiritual seekers, from medieval to modern times.

In reviewing the illuminations, drawings, and paintings that Dante's imagination has evoked in the artists who read his poem, we are reminded of the alchemical image of *multiplicatio*, the generative power of the consummation of the process when sacred wholeness is touched. The poem gives rise to multiple illustrations and commentaries, nurturing the sacred vision of artists and readers much as the second person of the deity—who is at the core of the *Commedia's* final vision—multiplied loaves and fishes in the Gospel story.

For Dante, the figure who stands behind Beatrice throughout the poem is that part of the God-image who, in the poet's wondrous vision of the Trinity at the end of the poem, bears within him "la nostra effige," our (human) effigy (*Paradiso*, XXXIII, 131). This vision, like the circle that cannot be squared, fills the poet with unresolvable perplexity. Although Dante clearly refers in part to the mystery of the Incarnation, when the spirit of God entered the mortal body of Jesus, this image is so well understood that his great perplexity is somewhat hard to grasp. For us as modern readers, his consternation in facing an image of the "human effigy" in his ultimate vision of God's essential nature reveals a profound psychological truth that we shall seek to illuminate in the essays that follow.

one Hell

Depression and Despair (The *Inferno*)

The Dark Wood at the Beginning   Images 1–8   Dante opens his poem with an image of himself as a person stuck in the middle of his life—he was thirty-five in the year 1300—in the midst of a dark and terrifying wood (see figs. 1, 2). This wood may be seen as the personal depression that accompanies a midlife crisis, a fearful sense of meaninglessness that forces one to reassess everything. Of this condition Dante observes, "Death is hardly more severe" (I, 7), and it is indeed the psychological condition from which either suicide (or perhaps a substitute, such as the death- in-life of alcoholism or drug addiction) or rebirth earned through conscious suffering may ensue. The pilgrim enters the wood "full of sleep" (11), of unconsciousness, and at first hopes to escape his depression by an easy and direct ascent up the little hill whose crest is appealingly illuminated by heavenly sunshine. It seems at first only a negotiable distance away.

But the fierce animality of human nature won't allow it, for, as Jung remarks, psychic reality does not permit us to "jump over the shadow" of lust, egocentric pride, and greedy desirousness, the instincts with which we are physically endowed, here symbolically represented by the leopard, the lion, and the she-wolf. These rush down the hill at the traveler, block his way, and push him back into the wood of his depression (see figs. 5–8). Unable to rise out of his depression directly, he is instead drawn deeper into the underworld. Here the darkness, which permeates the Inferno, is palpable, as Gustave Doré especially (fig. 1) makes clear, and even seems to reach out to entangle us, as Renato Guttuso (fig. 2) suggests. We have been thrust "back to where the sun is speechless" (60) and our defenses crumble; perhaps, as moderns, we make our way despondently to the therapist's or counselor's office. Dreams at this time may well present a fearful forest with no visible path, overgrown and ominous in its disorienting shadows.

If we surrender reluctantly to our need for help, doing so may feel as unchosen as Virgil's appearance in the wood, for we would not have sought guidance except under extreme duress. And the guide asks Dante, "Why not climb up the mountain of delight, / the origin and cause of every joy?" (77–78), as if wishing to make certain, as a therapist might, that the suffering client realizes that he or she cannot escape the depression through ego-centered efforts alone. The pilgrim does not respond, tacitly acknowledging his helplessness in the face of the three beasts, and so Virgil assures himself that Dante is ready to join the journey he will lead him on, unwelcome as his— or ours—may be in its particulars. The process of descending into the underworld in order to be reborn, or of entering the belly of the whale to be belched out into the service of God as Jonah was, or of discovering the meaning of commitment by surviving forty years in the Wilderness such as the Israelites endured, requires submission of the ego to a time of profound suffering.

So it is that Virgil lets Dante know what he knows: it is not in the nature of the situation for him to be able to make the direct ascent; first he must descend through Hell. Virgil understands that the dark examination of personal pathology and the shadow side of human nature is a required part of the healing journey. "It is another path that you must take," he says, ". . . if you would leave this savage wilderness" (91, 93).

1

Dante's contemporary readers well understood that his description of Hell was not to be taken literally, as if it were a documentary. Thinking in pictures or in symbolic actions came naturally to the medieval mind, and even naive readers knew that the poet was depicting the living condition of those in a state of sin as well as exploring what life in the afterworld might hold. "Sin" is as much the psychological state that gives rise to the acts of desirousness, violence, and betrayal that violate the commandments as it is the deeds themselves, and Dante's images, as we shall see, always go beyond the external action to assess the inner condition. Many "sinners," as defined by action, will be found among the saved in Purgatory and Paradise, making it necessary to examine the subtleties of inner reality the poet presents in the course of the journey.

2

Christian teaching, which allows sinners who repent before their death to be saved, even at the last moment, makes it clear that it is finally the issue of inner awareness that determines one's fate. The depth and modernity of Dante's imagination becomes manifest as we approach the scenes he visualized from a psychological point of view.

Along the path through the Inferno, sinners are found deeper the more deeply their sin involves specifically human capacities of mind and heart—the fraudulent and the betrayers are located in the lower levels, whereas the indulgent of appetites dwell in the upper circles. Sins of aggression and violence, being more intentional and harmful than those of indulgence and yet more natural to the animal root of humanness than those of treachery, are placed in the middle levels (see figs. 3, 4). In modern parlance, we might say that the descent is ordered in terms of increasing injury and unrelatedness to others, especially in the degree that the specifically human capacity for conscious loving relationship is violated.

Only after descending through the infernal regions can the pilgrim move on to discover the nature of meaningful suffering and hope for a connection to the transforming energies of the transpersonal realm. Once at that higher level, Virgil tells Dante in the very first canto, "a soul more worthy than I am will guide you" (122), much as a therapist might defer to the guide who comes forward within the sufferer's soul and alone makes possible the later stages in the development of a larger personality. Even at the bitter beginning of his dark and painful downward journey, the poet conveys his knowledge that the ultimate guide for the process, which requires at first all the knowledge and experience human learning can muster, comes from a level that transcends the ego not only of the patient but of the therapist as well.

Heraclitus says, "The way up and the way down is one and the same," but for most of us the way down is the only way up. Dante's imagination of the journey corresponds to the human reality that requires our participation in the process of descent even as we perceive the metaphysical possibility of a direct ascent. We know, as it were, that although it is in theory possible to ascend the mount of enlightenment without passing through the dark night of the soul, in real life it never happens that way. In describing a dream, one man put it with the homely economy of commentary from the personal unconscious: "I see a large and attractively furnished house that I am meant to occupy, but the only entrance is through the dark and filthy coal bin, where I am loathe to go and will surely be soiled. But there is no other way." For all its dirt, the coal bin in the cellar contains the fossil energy (in this case, also the fuel of the dreamer's grandparents) whose transformation will make it possible to live in the house above.

3   Sandro Botticelli's consistently faithful rendering of Dante's descriptions includes even this detailed cross-section of the infernal funnel-shaped pit. We see the great dividing bands of water, blood, and stone, the two frightening woods, and the two gates.

Below the seven-walled castle of Limbo lie the circles of instinctual weakness indulged (lust, various forms of greed, rage), depicted in images of overpowering wind, slush, and mud, all symbols of uncontrolled desirousness and affect.

At the Gate of Dis, at circle six, images of fire begin. Below the Heretics, who burn in their tombs, the Violent Against Others, Self, and Nature suffer eternally in boiling blood, in bleeding trees, in fiery rain, or on burning sands. Between the bloody river and the fiery rain there is the second, more terrible dark wood of the suicides. At circle eight, with ten subdivisions, intentional fraud or malice is variously represented and each state of soul is specifically depicted. There are pits of boiling pitch or excrement, heads are set backward on bodies, disease erupts in constant sores—when there are enforcers of the torments, they are demons. At circle nine, with four degrees of increasingly profound betrayal, the ice of Cocytus is kept frozen by the wind from the six wings of Dis.

4   This chart, funnel-shaped like the Botticelli painting, is from Dorothy Sayers's translation. In the modern way, it reveals the logic of Dante's structure more clearly than Botticelli, though it loses his graphic power.

4

3

5

5   This heavily damaged early illumination from Siena, ca. 1340, evokes a sense of space that is unusual in medieval manuscripts. More typical is the convention of repeating the principle figures as the action unfolds, as in an instructive cartoon strip. The pilgrim wakes in the dark woods and starts to ascend the little hill, where he sees the sun (and, here, the moon) and encounters the three beasts.

6   Wild beasts appear as threatening barriers to the pilgrim's
—or, in psychological terms, the ego's—desire to progress upward directly toward the
light. The leopard, the lion, and the she-wolf of instinctual desire and aggression (and
probably also of fraud, of pride, and of greed) are hungry and cannot be pushed aside.
Aware of his helplessness, the pilgrim turns back, whereupon his guide appears. Virgil
offers to take him through an eternal place where he will see "ancient spirits in their
pain," then to a realm of "souls who are content / within the fire" (I, 116, 118–119);
after that, says Virgil, a more worthy soul will guide him.

    Milton Klonsky points out that for William Blake (whose illustrations were
made between 1824 and 1827), the pilgrim's red robe signified emotion, the guide's blue
robe imagination. Blake's three-dimensional animals have greater emotional vigor than
those in the manuscripts.

6

7

7   The sense of light in a Neapolitan version (ca. 1370) of the same scene seems to have gone from the sun into the guide, who appears in a mandorla such as often contains the figure of Christ in medieval art. The stag on the right, entirely the illuminator's idea, is a medieval symbol of Christ, a hint in animal form of the large vision of the journey and an affirmation of the importance of the animal level of the psyche. The image of Virgil here expresses the projection of transpersonal value upon the guide in the pilgrim's full-fledged transference at the start, even though Virgil warns that he should not be overvalued. But the miraculousness of such a guide's appearance elicits the enormous relief one feels in the discovery that guidance out of one's inner darkness may really be available.

8   The sun's light in this Pisan manuscript of ca. 1385 has become a star, perhaps a star of individual destiny. The medieval appreciation of symbolic values is strongly evident in these illustrations. In the early stages of inner work we naturally are encouraged by images of light and guiding figures in dreams or fantasies and may be concerned if we do not encounter them.

        This Pisan manuscript appeals to the modern taste for an interplay of relatively flat shapes that maintain the page surface and yet are solidly realized. The strong, clear shapes are arranged in patterns of controlled visual liveliness, as we shall see again in other illustrations from this manuscript.

8

9   In the same Pisan manuscript, Virgil now reveals the weighty feminine compassion behind his presence. He puts it that Mary called upon Lucia, who came to Beatrice, who came to him. It is a nice touch that Beatrice has the courtesy to persuade rather than command Virgil to help (see "Beatrice, Lucia, Mary," below).

    The circular frame that surrounds the naturalistic rendering of each feminine figure Virgil points to emphasizes the symbolic other-worldliness of this iterated feminine intervention. The hands of each feminine figure reach out receptively as if to image the breaking of the normal frame that their special concern for the pilgrim represents. Through this device, the illuminator conveys visually what Dante is at pains to reveal in his text.

    Modern psyches, bearing centuries of patriarchal repression, at first examination in depth often appear to contain only the more negative nonhuman images of the feminine power. Sometimes these do indeed come in the form of such predatory animals as leopard, lion, and wolf—for Dante, the she-wolf, the last and most fearful, thrusting him back into the wood, is explicitly female. Yet already at the beginning of his poem the female characterization of repressed or abused elemental instinct is counterbalanced by images of the caring intervention of feminine authorities.

9

THROUGH ME THE WAY INTO THE SUFFERING CITY,

THROUGH ME THE WAY TO THE ETERNAL PAIN,

THROUGH ME THE WAY THAT RUNS AMONG THE LOST.

JUSTICE URGED ON MY HIGH ARTIFICER;

MY MAKER WAS DIVINE AUTHORITY,

THE HIGHEST WISDOM, AND THE PRIMAL LOVE.

BEFORE ME NOTHING BUT ETERNAL THINGS

WERE MADE, AND I ENDURE ETERNALLY.

ABANDON EVERY HOPE, WHO ENTER HERE. (III, 1–9)

The eternal hopelessness that is the condition of the damned reflects their refusal in life to acknowledge their evil (see "A Contention for the Soul," below).

This Pisan manuscript by the earlier master (see "On the Illustrations," above) depicts a more personal experience of the entrance—focusing on the doorway—than the Blake watercolor, although it hints at archetypal energies in the owl and the bats (not mentioned by Dante). The medieval manuscripts are compelling; though they sometimes strike modern viewers as amusing in their homely imagery, they do convey a sense of the pervasive assumption of the transpersonal dimension in the everyday.

10

HELL Canto 3

11

11   Hellgate is wide open (unlike the gate of the City of Dis). Blake shows forms that rise up, rather than descend, perhaps suggesting the stenches and vapors and smoke that Dante describes at various levels. Blake often took liberties with the text of the *Commedia*. He also took exception to Dante's view of God as he understood it and was fascinated with the darker energies; one can feel the passion of his wrestling. In the last three years of his life, Blake was obsessed with his work on this poem, painting the watercolors in bed during his final illness and leaving more than a hundred illustrations in various stages of completion. Although his work reveals, as this illustration does, a control of perspective not available to the medieval illuminators, Blake often foreshortens his images as if to accommodate both his visionary style and his awareness of the book as a medium.

nfpuofe diceroli molto breue
Qneſti non áno ſperança dimorte
et lalor cieca uita etanto buſſa
chenuidioſi ſon dognaltra ſorte

Fama dilor ilmondo eſſer nö laſſa
miſericordia giuſticia glidiſdegna
nö ragionar dilor maguardepaſſa
E io chenguazdai ridunanſegna
che guando corea tanto racta
che dogni poſa mipareandegna
E dietro luueniua ſi lunga tracta
digéte chio nö auria creduto
chemorte tanta nauteſſe diſſacta

iſinalfiume diparllar mitraſſi
E decchouerſo noi uenir pnaue
un uecchio bianco per antico pelo
gridando guai auoi anime praue.

Non iſpate mai uederlocielo
io uegno pmenarui alaltra riua
netenebrettene uicaldo engielo
E tu chese coſti anima uiua
partea dacoteſti che ſon morti
ma poi cheuide chimonö partiua
Diſſe per altre uie per altri porti
uerrai apiaggia nö g per paſſare
pioleue legno cöuien chea porti

12

12   Many of us may recall dreams in which there are swarms of stinging insects and snakes or worms underfoot. These undecided souls in the later Pisan manuscript rush about in an eternally transitional space, wailing and swearing and bleeding, following the banner of the moment. One senses that some of them are wondering whether to attach themselves to the pilgrim, who is being hurried out of the scene by his guide. They are the uncommitted, denied access even to Hell.

13   Blake shows us the entire scene on the shores of the River Acheron, where "these wretched ones, who never were alive" (III, 64) waver forever. (Modern references to Limbo seem often to refer to this state rather than to Dante's view of that realm, as we shall see.) In therapeutic circles nowadays there is much talk about the "borderline condition," imaged vividly here in the inability of these souls to commit themselves to one side or another of life's many conflicts. Dante's scorn for those who are unable to make moral choices, whether for good or ill, is reflected in his image of their rejection by both Heaven and Hell. Those angels undecided at the time of Satan's challenge to God are depicted across the top of the watercolor.

13

14, 15   It is perhaps unfair to Gustave Doré to present the crossing of the Acheron from Michelangelo's Last Judgment next to his version. The weighty power and life of Michelangelo's wonderfully articulated large compositional shapes make Doré's look less substantial. This scene from the Sistine Chapel frescoes (completed in 1541) is not strictly an illustration of Dante's work—its subject matter is more general and inclusive than the Acheron scene—but we know that Michelangelo revered Dante's poem and was probably influenced by it. (There is a legend that Michelangelo drew illustrations in the margin of a manuscript of the *Divine Comedy* that was later lost in a shipwreck.) Doré's genius lies in his capacity to render, in a scale attuned to the page of a book, the great dark spaces that Dante and Virgil traverse.

14

15

16   In vivid contrast to Doré's distance, Renato Guttuso brings us into the immediate experience of peering down the dark slope, into the tangle of bodies, where Charon's lifted oar threatens us with worse if we do not go with him. We feel the modern emphasis on the foreground of personal experience, yet here the artist also looks deep into the fearsome darkness of eternity. At this place the pilgrim recognizes the perverse determinedness of disordered energy, is overwhelmed by terror in the whirlwind that "crackled with a blood-red light" (III, 134), and then awakens to find himself in the first circle.

17   In Blake's view of Dante's Limbo, the realm of the virtuous pagans, women and children float in their unlighted, unbaptized state, but there is a beautiful open meadow and the great poets of antiquity stroll under noble trees. As they approach this first circle, where Virgil himself dwells, Dante mistakes his guide's pallor for fear, but Virgil corrects him, saying, "The anguish of the people / whose place is here below, has touched my face / with the compassion you mistake for fear" (IV, 19–21). Although these souls have lived virtuously, Virgil continues, they have not known "the portal of the faith that you embrace" (36), and so "we have no hope . . . yet we live in longing" (42). David Bindman suggests that the dark cloud above the scene is Blake's way of emphasizing the pagans' "distance from the higher reaches of the imagination" (*William Blake*, 180).

     The celebrated poets of antiquity, Homer, Horace, Ovid, and Lucan as well as Virgil, reside here in "sorrow without torments" (28) but in great dignity. Dante, with the pride he will later acknowledge, is invited to "join their ranks" and names himself "sixth among such intellects" (IV, 101–102) at the start of the poem that will make him so!

17

18

18   This image of ca. 1445 by Vecchietta includes the pilgrim swooning in fear before he is transported across the river and is faithful to Dante's textual image of Limbo: the moat-defended, seven-walled castle. If we look for modern examples of this kind of walled-off intelligence, we might find an arrested development of the whole person owing to a lack of relation to the transpersonal dimension. Limbo is depicted by Dante not as a terrible state, for there is no inflicted pain, but as a sad and meaningless separation from the numinosity of the divine.

19   At the beginning of the part of the journey where "no thing gleams" (IV, 151), Minos, the "connoisseur of sin" (V, 9), sorts the souls as they enter, indicating the level they require by the number of times he wraps his tail around himself. Blake and Guttuso give us two versions of this lurid image of a malevolent aspect of the archetype of judgment. Their treatments of this subject have a similar use of massive shapes and distribution of heavily contrasting light and dark, but Blake sets the scene more inclusively, whereas Guttuso provides a modern screen-filling view.

20   Guttuso's version is closer than Blake's to Dante's dreadful Minos, who gnashes his teeth as he examines and judges. The mythological Minos was king of Crete, both wise and fierce in judgment. Each sinner's previously rejected capacity for self-knowledge, a neglected conscience, is suggested by the verbal confession he or she makes here to Minos, on which he bases his assignment. Guttuso also renders explicitly the monster's use of his tail to appoint the depth of the sinner's descent.

21

22

23

21, 22, 23　　　　　The manuscript illumination characteristically repeats the figures of pilgrim and guide as they progress through the various events, rather like sketches for an animated cartoon. At the circle of the Lustful, the pilgrim faints out of pity for the storm-tossed couples who are swept around in a whirlwind as they were swept away in the passion of unconscious merger. Vecchietta and Blake render more graphically than Doré the pilgrim's distress in the face of torment for a sin to which he knows he is susceptible, while the poet who structures the journey is ruthless in his vision.

All three artists communicate, in varying degrees of intensity but with remarkably similar pictorial approach, the sweeping power of an experience of instinctual weakness indulged. The fatal affair of Paolo and Francesca, whose telling by Francesca causes the pilgrim to swoon, is portrayed in the joined couple who present themselves to the travelers in each illustration. Blake also includes, above the figure of Virgil, a luminous sketch of the tender embrace that was provoked by the couple's reading of the romance of Lancelot and Guinevere and for which they were killed when discovered by Francesca's husband. Dante's image of the whirlwind powerfully portrays the couple's loss of objectivity in erotic projection.

luuctr alargo qunghiate lemany
graffia glifpiti i goia ausquatra
rllar glifa lapioggia come cam
cellun celati fann allaltro fclxemo
uolgofi fpeffo imuseu profani

pla dinofa colpa dela gola
come tu uedi ala pioggia mi fiacco
Et io aia trifta no fon fola
clx tuete qifte afimil pena ftanno
pfimul colpa qpin no fe parola.

24   In the third circle lie the Gluttonous, pelted by freezing and filthy rain and flayed by the claws of the barking beast Cerberus. The essence of gluttony, the indulgent consumption of more food than the metabolism of warm flesh requires, is here conveyed by the barrenness of frozen slush. In modern terms, we may see the torment as reflecting the sterility of consumption for its own sake.

As in the two depictions of Hellgate, this Pisan version (ca. 1385) of the ancient mythic guardian of Hades is more realistic than Blake's, but both are monstrous —the Pisan more tense, the other slouching.

25   Blake shows Virgil feeding dirt to Cerberus, adding for good measure a shark- or flame-toothed cave mouth in the background. Although in the *Commedia* Virgil throws dirt into Cerberus's mouths, in the *Aeneid* the sibyl tames him with honeycakes. From a modern point of view, Dante's use of dirt for distraction underscores the unnourishing character of Cerberus's realm, whereas Virgil's poetic imagination suggests that sweets are the narcotic core of many eating disorders.

25

26   Among the Avaricious, at the fourth circle, Virgil curses Plutus, who has threatened to get in the way: "Let your vindictiveness feed on yourself!" (VII, 9) he shouts, and Plutus collapses like sails on a broken mast. Two groups of souls push weights with their chests in opposite semicircles, and as they meet each other reverse directions, one group yelling, "Why do you hoard?" while the other cries, "Why do you squander?" (30). Vecchietta's rendering of their identical burdens emphasizes that the hoarders and the spendthrifts are each equally obsessed with materiality and that this obsession is its own torment.

27 The Wheel of Fortune (depicted here in a Florentine manuscript of ca. 1440) is a familiar medieval image that stresses the timelessness of the turns of fate and the importance, therefore, of one's attitude toward it in all its phases. Virgil describes Fortune as God's appointed minister, an elemental, impersonal feminine force who serves divine wisdom and fairness by guiding the reversals of worldly goods and power "in ways that human reason can't prevent" (VII, 81). We may see this as an image of the tendency of any pronounced condition to constellate its opposite in the unconscious, so that it eventually finds expression.

27

28   In the fifth circle, Blake depicts another level of the self-indulgent, the Wrathful and Sullen, who rage in the swampy, dark waters of the River Styx. The Wrathful are visible in the slime but the Sullen are hidden beneath it; only muddy bubbles breaking the surface indicate their presence. In Dante's imagery, the Wrathful eternally strike and butt each other—psychologically apt for souls who do not feel themselves unless embattled. When unable to confront an adversary in the slime, one sinner turns "his teeth against himself" (VIII, 63—Argenti was a fierce adversary who opposed Dante's return from exile) as if to underscore the self-destructive torture of chronic anger.

Virgil points explicitly to the way in which the infernal depiction of the Sullen reflects the true condition of the living when he explains to the pilgrim,

> Wedged in the slime, they say: "We had been sullen
> in the sweet air that's gladdened by the sun;
> we bore the mist of sluggishness in us:
> now we are bitter in the blackened mud." (VII, 121–124)

Blake's illustration makes visible the immobilization of the Sullen within the slime, communicating vividly the difference between the acted-out rage of the Wrathful and the contained frustration of the Sullen. Through his art, he emphasizes how sullenness is rage in the guise of withdrawal—one form, we might say, of passive aggression.

29, 30, 31   Phlegyas shuttles Virgil and Dante in his little boat across the swamp of Styx. (He was, in the *Aeneid*, the king of Boeotia who wrathfully burned Apollo's temple when the god ravished his daughter. Apollo killed him and condemned him to Hades.) Eugène Delacroix's mastery communicates the terror of this crossing, the possessed quality of the raging souls who try to climb into the boat, and the awfulness of the destination: the burning towers of the City of Dis.

Whereas Delacroix closes in on the scene, in the Romantic manner, Doré again keeps his distance, reminding us of the vast dark despairing reaches of the journey.

Only Blake focuses on the sharply affective encounter that is the highlight of the ferry crossing, Filippo Argenti's attempted boarding of their boat. This is the first time Virgil and the pilgrim actively reject someone along their path. Dante recognizes him and rejects him as an "accursèd spirit" (VIII, 38), and Virgil shoves the wrathful Argenti away from the boat, saying, "Be off there with the other dogs!" (42). He then embraces, kisses, and praises the pilgrim for being an "indignant soul" (44). With such strong approval, the poet suggests there are people in life, or parts of one's psyche that, once seen, must be brutally refused or pushed away.

Blake wrote of something similar in another context in his *Jerusalem* (41:32–35): "Each man is in his Spectre's power / Until the arrival of that hour / When his Humanity awake / And cast his Spectre into the lake" (Klonsky, 141, citing Albert Roe). Even so, Blake does not convey Virgil's emotional response vividly in his drawing, for Virgil here appears more controlled and firm than passionate. Blake sometimes expresses his feeling that Dante is too mean to the sinners, and the question of un-Christian rejection arises again in more subtle form in the frozen realm of traitors who surround Dis himself (see fig. 99).

29

30

31

32   Like the Pisan master of ca. 1385 (figs. 8, 9, 12, 24), an
illuminator of about fifty years later selects the crucial subject matter for clarity of mes-
sage. A major division occurs between the fifth and sixth circles: a wall, and a gate, the
Gate of Dis, over which the Furies hover. As the Furies threaten to invoke Medusa, Virgil
covers Dante's eyes, the only time he does so during this whole journey of intense look-
ing at everything. At this profound change of level and the realization that there is no
going back, immobilizing despair threatens the pilgrim. (This Venetian manuscript, ca.
1440, is now in Florence. All subsequent Venetian illuminations are from a manuscript
of the same period, now in Venice.)

33   In his imagination of the tower and the gate, Botticelli's style is reminiscent of the Venetian illuminator, but Botticelli indulges an opportunity for fascinating detail and a much broader vision. He includes not only the rescuing angel but some of the thousand Fallen Angels who bar the gate and the Heretics' tombs on the far side. His Phlegyas, at the upper right, is explicitly demonic. Here we see in particular fullness Botticelli's effort to illuminate in loving detail as much as he can of the poem he admired.

34   When Virgil cannot parlay his way in, transpersonal help
in the form of an agent from the realm of the archetypal spirit powers is necessary (see
"The Gate of Dis," below). Those who work with dreams have experiences of this kind
of image, of the intervention that can come when all conscious effort fails.

        In this Lombard manuscript of ca. 1440, by the "Vitae Imperatorum" mas-
ter (see Brieger et al., *Illuminated Manuscripts of the Divine Comedy*, 1:318), we see how
this medieval illuminator has placed his realistic image of the angel at the gate in a scene
that seems to imagine the whole within a kind of underground cave. The background
designs suggest a starry firmament, and the overall effect reminds us that this is an imag-
inary, symbolic world, yet with the everydayness of the angel's human characterization.
In the presence of this angel, the pilgrim and his guide do not seem much afraid.

35   Blake's angel, on the other hand, is gigantic, plainly from the transpersonal realm, and deliberately contrasted with the tiny terrified figures of Dante and Virgil. Blake's Furies have more human faces, and the middle one's somewhat serpentine hair may suggest Medusa, who doesn't actually appear in the *Commedia*. The trumpets are Blake's embellishment. This image is psychologically accurate, for effective help for an ego that is up against a negative archetypal energy requires a positive one of equal power.

and Virgil have come down through upper hell and crossed the marsh of Styx, they stand before the Gate of Dis, the walled city of inner Hell (see figs. 32, 33). Within, the deeper sins are punished and the gate is fiercely guarded by the Fallen Angels and the Furies. The demons resent the presence of a living man not condemned to their domain, and they refuse Dante entrance. It is the one place in their journey together where Virgil cannot gain access on his own authority. Knowing that formidable forces oppose him, Virgil even tries to "speak secretly to them" (VIII, 87), leaving Dante alone while he does so. But he is rebuffed, and he returns to Dante's side, puzzled, uncertain, and nervous when aid does not promptly appear. When the Furies cry out: "Just let Medusa come; then we shall turn / him into stone" (IX, 52–53), Virgil himself becomes fearful in a way that we see nowhere else in the poem. Almost in a panic, he abruptly turns Dante away from the gate and claps his hands over his eyes so that he will not see the Gorgon.

Whereas the poem opened in the Dark Wood of depression, the descent has now brought the pilgrim face to face with the danger of being immobilized by despair. Even the wisest of human guides is helpless here. Virgil realizes that "now we cannot enter without anger" (IX, 33), outright and wrathful assistance from the transpersonal level. For this alone can counter the evil represented by the Fallen Angels and the sinners whose domain they guard. It is that dangerous time in a soul's journey when the encounter with the deeper reaches of the shadow realm may be too much to bear; a personality as yet insufficiently strong must turn away from too direct a confrontation with knowledge of the darker powers that lie beneath the selfish appetites. Dante's acute imagination makes plain why we resist the depressing journey into our personal and collective shadow, for a life may be lost unless there is help from the concerned Other. The danger of psychic paralysis and suicidal despair must be met by a force that is equal and opposite to the more than human destructive powers by which we can be seized.

Entry into the inner city of the damned is not work for the unaided ego, even accompanied by a wise counselor. The way for Dante and Virgil to progress is finally cleared when the angel-messenger arrives, striding across the fetid marsh with high disdain and blasting open the gate without showing any interest in either traveler (see figs. 34, 35). His attitude emphasizes that the realm from which he comes is quite apart from human fears and mortality and one to be regarded from below more with respect than love. At the personal level this may be experienced as an apparently unrelated anger that throws off a despair which may in itself appear quite reasonable. Such anger expresses the transpersonal power of the larger Self, a sacred life-force that thrusts aside those rationalizing demons who urge us to give up the struggle.

It is a part of Dante's extraordinary poise that here in the slime of Styx where the sins of wrath are punished he also provides us with two positive examples of the way justified anger serves us in life's progress: the one personal, when the pilgrim vehemently rejects Filippo Argenti, and the other transpersonal, when the angel intervenes.

36   The imagery of fire begins at the sixth level with the Heretics. Doré is interested only in Farinata, a proud but honorable Ghibelline posthumously declared a heretic, who is full of scorn for his situation. The pilgrim's respect for Farinata, counseled in Virgil's warning, "your words must be appropriate" (X, 39), suggests that Dante's view of certain heresies as sinful may be more ambivalent than that of the Church. (Later we shall meet in Paradise some of those who were condemned for heresy.)

    The Heretics, here the Epicureans, who extoll living in the present moment because they deny the immortality of the soul, are especially ironic examples of the infernal mode-of-being. In Hell, one does not know the present, though one can remember the past and foretell the future as indeed Farinata does when he informs Dante that he will have difficulty returning from exile. The poet's imagination of time for the damned suggests that obsessive preoccupations of every kind (even with the present) shut us off from life so that we cannot experience the here and now that we are in.

    In Doré's rendering of this encounter, Dante and Virgil draw back from the fiery tomb in cautious attention, while Farinata rises from the fires with theatrical illumination. Doré's style here provides a striking example of his ability to create on paper the effect of light that enters and penetrates the pervading darkness of the Inferno. His use of unmarked, or negative, space reveals a talent he exercises brilliantly in illustrating the later cantos of the poem, in which light is of the essence.

    Doré was just twenty-nine when his *Inferno* was published in 1861. He had long had the idea of illustrating many of the West's most famous literary texts but could find no publisher willing to take the financial risk of his Dante project. Already a successful illustrator (though frustrated life-long in his desire to be recognized as a painter in his native France), he undertook the financial risk of the large and costly volume on his own, and it was an instant success. Accordingly, he had no difficulty in publishing his illustrations to the *Purgatorio* and *Paradiso* when they were ready in 1868. But it is important to keep in mind that even then Doré was only thirty-six, not, like Blake or Botticelli, in his full maturity. Doré had an exuberantly playful and theatrically inventive personality, and he was an extremely diligent man. He never married and lived with his mother all his life, dying in 1883 at age fifty-one, only two years after she did. Although his work lacks the depth of the greatest artists, his best work nevertheless has qualities that are remarkably apt not only in the popular engravings for the *Inferno* but also for conveying the atmosphere of Purgatory and Paradise.

37   The work of the Swiss-born British artist Henry Fuseli
has a dramatic Romanticism that often misses the point (as we shall see especially in his
view of Geryon), but in this image of 1774 he gets across the lack of connection between
the two men who share the same tomb. Virgil and Dante are represented oddly, one in a
foppish slouch and the other clutching his guide as if terrified. Although a sentimental
overdramatization goes beyond the text, the impact of the searing heat is striking, as if
we, too, were in the tomb.

37

38, 39   This famous creature, the Minotaur, now threatens the way, but Virgil goads him and, watching for the right moment, tells the pilgrim to run while he is blind with rage. Born of Pasiphaë's passion for Minos's sacred bull, the monster was

> conceived within the counterfeited cow;
> and, catching sight of us, he bit himself
> like one whom fury devastates within. (XII, 13–15)

As guardian of the seventh circle, where the violent are fixed, the Minotaur, like the centaurs at the river of blood, is a fitting man-beast image of unintegrated aggression and sexuality.

Doré, with his nineteenth-century perspective, presents the action from a controlled distance and faithfully suggests the possibility that the monster bites himself in his rage, whereas Guttuso forces us to contemplate the scandalous conjunction of bull and man with the confrontational realism of a television close-up.

38

39

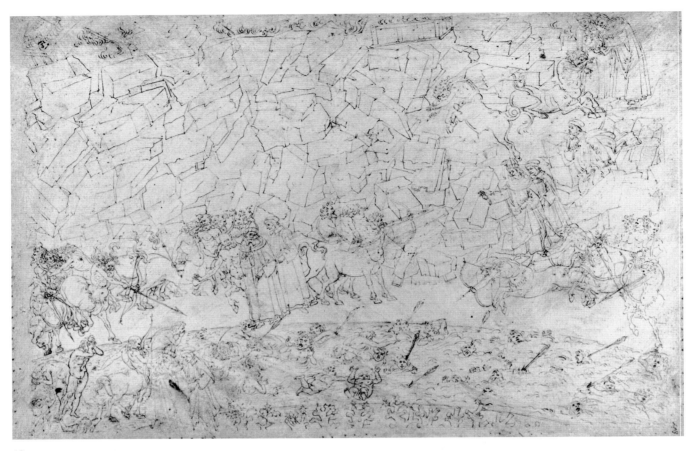

40

40, 41   In the first ring of circle seven, the Violent Against Others—tyrants, military conquerors and mercenaries, murderers and robbers—are immersed in Phlegethon, a river of boiling blood. In the descent to it, Botticelli's tumbled rocks show the effect of the earthquake that by tradition occurred at the time of the Crucifixion. The contrast between Botticelli's vastly detailed vision of the pilgrim and his guide progressively viewing the scene, with powerful centaurs shooting enormous arrows at those souls who dare emerge, and Guttuso's focus only on the faces in pain, horror, and resignation again juxtaposes a cosmic view of Dante's vision with its personal impact. It is as if the older view places everything in an ordered, albeit eternally tormented and awful, world, as against the isolated, even though collective, experience of individual torment.

Guttuso's view seems to include contemporary persons of many kinds. Dante limits immersion in the boiling river to those who are literally guilty of bloodshed, but Guttuso's image suggests a modern social consciousness that perceives violence in many kinds of harassment and aggression.

42, 43   A Florentine illumination of ca. 1400 makes an interesting contrast with one painted a century later by Giraldi, which is much more removed and elegantly allegorical. The different forms of perspective in these two illuminations emphasize different meanings, with the earlier artist giving central importance to the pool of blood in an emphatically foreshortened foreground—that nevertheless has none of the personal emotionality of Romantic and modern illustrators. But Giraldi's rendering is absolutely cool, a stately procession conveying the sense that all is foreordained. He correctly shows the pilgrim, but not his guide, carried by a centaur, stylishly attired. The centaurs have responded with strange courtesy to Virgil's request that one of the centaurs' band "bear this man upon his back, / for he's no spirit who can fly through air" (XII, 95–96).

Giraldi's *Commedia*, made in the 1480s, is the last of the known manuscript copies of Dante's poem.

43

44   The Violent Against Themselves or Their Possessions in
the second ring of circle seven are revealed as Virgil urges the pilgrim to break off a branch
from a tree in this thorny, overgrown, and tangled wood. The tree bleeds and cries out;
it is a man who has rejected the pain of being human and returned to a vegetal level,
rooted in hopelessness. But here the Harpies feed on the leaves, doing perpetual injury,
which at the same time gives the trees a way to vent their pain, creating a cycle of obses-
sive and exaggerated suffering (see "The Wood of the Suicides," below). The hounds that
hunt down and dismember the profligate are depicted as devils in this illumination by
Vecchietta.

45   Botticelli's detailed, precisely outlined entanglement
rewards the necessary scrutiny. Although Botticelli was close in time to the medieval illumi-
nators, working late in the fifteenth century just as printing was taking hold, his Renais-
sance range and attention to specifics, as well as his artistic patience and purpose, provide
us with richly imagined detail—of souls, Harpies, hounds, and trees. As this image shows,
intensely dramatic subjects do not always have to be rendered in large darks and lights.
There is a special horror about this unflinchingly explicit style that through repetition
conveys the monotony of any particular place in Hell.

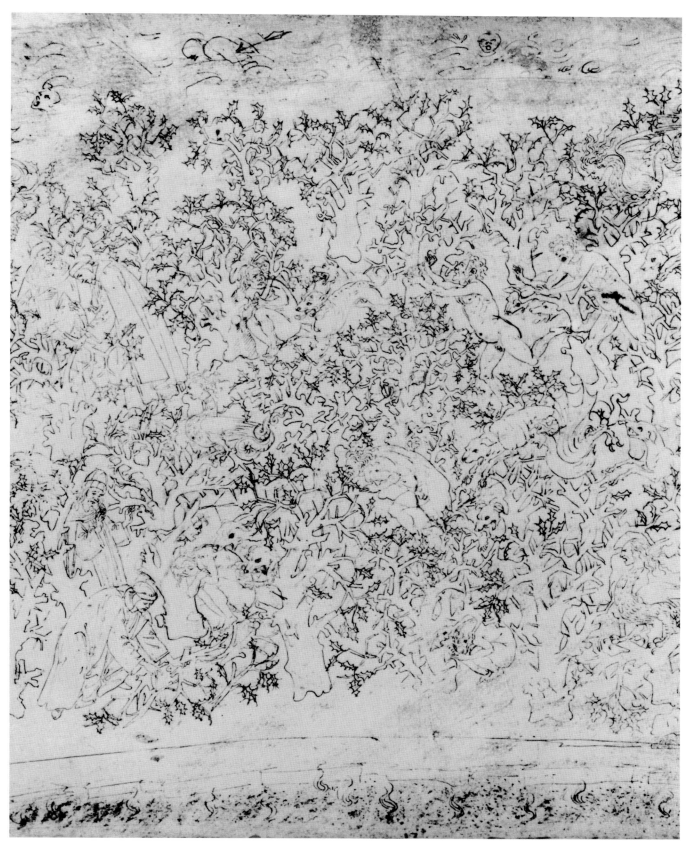

46

46, 47   The bearded man in the tree with his knees drawn up in Blake's rendering is Pier della Vigna, who committed suicide when unjustly convicted of treason to his emperor. The flamboyantly naked bosoms of Blake's Harpies don't seem to belong to the hopeless atmosphere or to follow Dante's description of "the foul Harpies" with "their great bellies feathered" (XIII, 10, 14), though he gets their wide wings, human faces (adding sharp beaks), and taloned feet into his image. By contrast, Doré's Harpies, with their starving ghostlike faces as described in the *Aeneid*, are much larger in scale and altogether more intimidating.

Della Vigna tells the pilgrim: "My mind, because of its disdainful temper, / believing it could flee disdain through death, / made me unjust against my own just self" (XIII, 70–72). More than any other tortured soul in Hell he seems aware of the reason for his presence there.

Doré's Wood of the Suicides recalls in tone and structure the Dark Wood of the beginning (see fig. 1) and supports the connection between depression and despair. Blake's wood is vivid but less horrifying, perhaps because he never takes Hell quite as one-sidedly as the tradition.

The Wood of the Suicides *Surrender to Despair*   Images 44–47

The Wood of the Suicides, who are planted as trees in the second ring of circle seven, picks up themes from both the Dark Wood of the opening canto and the immobilizing despair the pilgrim and his guide faced at the Gate of Dis (see figs. 1, 2, 32–35, 44–47). When the Suicides come before Minos to receive judgment, he wraps his tail about him seven times and they drop chaotically into the second ring of the circle where the violent are punished, sprouting as trees in the gloom wherever they fall. As they disordered nature in life, so they sprout in confusion as weed trees in Hell; as they denied their human mobility and fixated on despair, so they take a vegetative form, planted in place.

The analogy to the wood of depression is clear, but it is here a depression from which the choice of the ego has removed all possibility of change. Life-denying surrender to hopelessness is reflected in the way the Suicides can speak only when branches are broken and they bleed. Hissing and spluttering like steaming logs, they feel sorry for themselves and profess an exaggerated sense of their personal suffering: "Are you without all sentiment of pity?" (XIII, 36). Their ability to express themselves depends on their being wounded, a telling image of the sentimental excess of suicidal desperation.

In their retreat into wooden and irretrievable self-pity, the Suicides reveal the consequences of being unable to bear the tension between the opposites of hope and despair. The image even conveys its potential antidote, the capacity in life to express one's distress and weigh it in the balance with the urge to live. In therapy, the detailed imagined exploration of one's suicidal impulses is often precisely what discloses their one-sidedness and restores a commitment to life with all its suffering.

Caught in almost suicidal immobilization by a depressive complex absorbed from his mother, a young man dreamed that he was encased in a large tree, able only to move about like a robot swaying from side to side. In the dream, his arms protruded like outstretched branches and he could hardly move. Finally, a break came so that he stepped forth elatedly in his normal body. Work on disidentification from the nearly killing complex that had afflicted his mother had freed him at last to reenter the fully living human world.

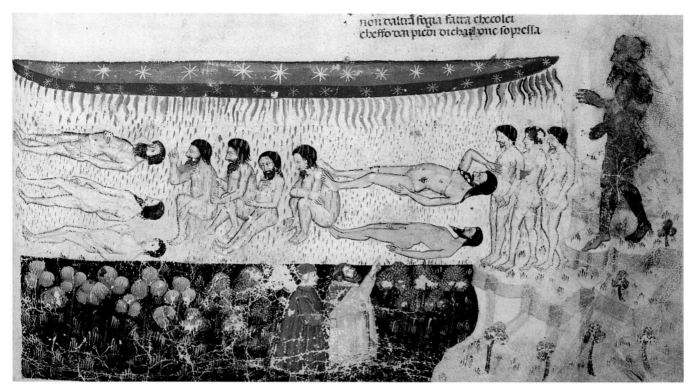

non caltri seqia fatta ebecolei
cheffo dan pidoi dichaduone sopressa

48

48   Here a Venetian illuminator of the late fourteenth century has Virgil point out to the pilgrim a mural-like view of the Blasphemers Against God. Their hot bed of sand beneath a burning rain evokes the fire and brimstone that destroyed Sodom and Gomorrah. Dante, in a more vivid verbal image, describes the "dance of wretched hands" (XIV, 40) as these souls try to beat aside the flames.

          The illuminator's rendering of the scene as an instructive tableau to which Virgil points the pilgrim's attention is his invention. The action is depicted much as part of a vast sacred story might be in the windows of a contemporary cathedral, where it becomes one element in the structure of an architectural vision in service to the divine order.

49   Among the Blasphemers, Guttuso calls attention to Capaneus, who boasted that Jove could not stop his attack on Thebes and was killed by a thunderbolt. He is shown here angrily cursing God and is the very emblem of sin as pathology. Virgil tells him vehemently, "No torture other than your own madness / could offer pain enough to match your wrath" (XIV, 65–66). Virgil's emphasis on the interiority of Capaneus's pain makes him an especially appropriate subject for the modern artist, who isolates the individual in a confused mass of indistinguishable fellow sufferers. The acute anguish of one person is sliced out of its larger context, in contrast to the medieval view, much as a journalist today might record a day in Hell with an individual interview. Although the surrounding structure is not visible in the modern view, the singling out of individuals to make his point is characteristic also of Dante's style.

50 The Old Man of Crete is meant to depict successively degenerating periods of history. This figure has a head of gold, arms and chest of silver, a belly of brass, legs of iron, and one foot of clay. Dante says he is cracked from his throat down, and his constantly dripping tears flow through this crack to form the rivers of Hell. Perhaps these tears express the distress that, though first experienced as simply the pain of our human histories, may later become "the good grief that succors us / and weds us once again to God" (*Purgatorio*, XXIII, 81–82). The Old Man appears remarkably intact in the later Pisan manuscript, seeming to avoid a full confrontation with the fragmentation the poet describes.

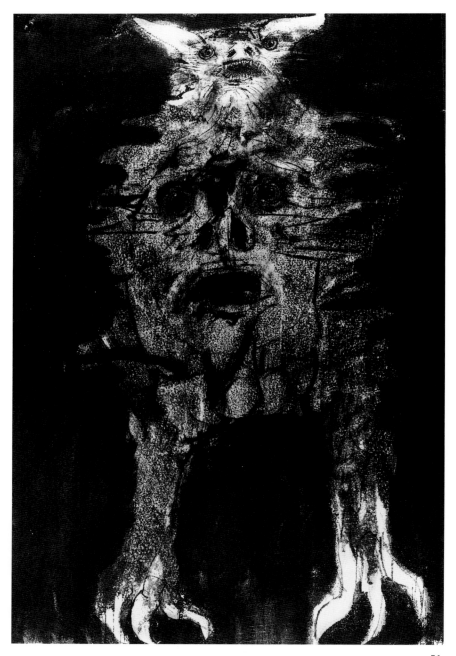

50

51

51 Leonard Baskin—even more than Guttuso, whose illustrations were also published in 1970—depicts the modern psyche's attention to long-repressed or misplaced energies. He calls this creature the Violent Against Nature. Claiming the right to individual response, Baskin's image is a personal reaction to Dante's poem rather than an attempt to illustrate the narrative. Nevertheless, it is a good example of the artist's ability to create an image that transcends personal reaction and conveys a depth of feeling that is true to the spirit of the poem.

52, 53   Two different Pisan manuscripts with similar styles show the incessant movement of the Sodomites in the third section of circle seven. The earlier manuscript, ca. 1345, emphasizes the frenzied rushing figures; the later one, ca. 1385, instead dramatizes the insistent fires of Hell and invokes the pilgrim's compassion for his former teacher, Brunetto Latini. Dante's respect for this brilliant writer makes the traditional judgment of homosexual sterility very poignant. Later, in the *Purgatorio*, Dante will place those atoning for homosexual lust on the same terrace (the highest) as those who atone for heterosexual lust. Here he treats homosexuality as a sin against nature, there as an excess of natural appetite that is dangerous to heterosexual and homosexual lovers alike in its misdirection of the love that is owed to God, or, as we might say, to the inner Other.

52

53

torcendo in su la uenenofa forcha.
cha guifa di fcorpion la punta armaua.
Lo duca diffe or conuien che fi torcha.
la noftra uia un poco in fina quella.
beftia maluagia/che colla fi torcha.
P ero fcendemmo a la deftra mamella.
e diece paffi femmo in fu loftremo.
per ben ceffar la rena ela fiamella.

54

54   The Usurers with their heraldic bibs, who do violence to the bond between money and craft, a sin against "art" as human labor, bring us to the great abyss that separates the travelers from the levels of more intentional evil, here depicted in a Neapolitan manuscript of ca. 1370. This is our first view of the monster Geryon: Virgil summons him as a steed by throwing Dante's belt into the abyss. Geryon has a benign human face, a snakelike trunk, and a scorpion's tail—he is the very image of fraudulence. Yet he can take the travelers where they need to go, deeper into the experience of the dark side of the unconscious.

55   In this version of the scene, from Bologna ca. 1400, the pilgrim's upraised finger and severe look as he sits astride Geryon are projections of the artist. In the poem, the pilgrim is appropriately scared at this point, and Virgil is touching in his care. He says, "I want to be between, / so that the tail can't do you any harm" (XVII, 83–84), and Dante comments,

> I wished to say (and yet my voice did not
> come as I thought): "See that you hold me tight."
>   But he who—other times in other dangers—
> sustained me, just as soon as I had mounted,
> clasped me within his arms and propped me up. (92–96)

The two medieval illuminators, in depicting simultaneously both the usurers in the last segment of circle seven and the departure into the depths of circle eight on Geryon's back, maintain their characteristic sense of the comprehensive movement of the journey as a whole.

55

56 Botticelli maintains a similar breadth of perspective, including not only the usurers and the descent of Geryon but also the flow of the River Phlegethon over the cliff into the circle of fraud. The mythic Geryon appears first in the tenth labor of Hercules, and there he had three heads, six arms, and three bodies joined at the waist. Dante's monster with its human face and scorpion sting derives also from the vision of the locusts after the fifth trumpet in Revelation 9, though the rich conception of the monster of fraud is his own and a powerful magnet for illustration.

Botticelli gives us a good sense of the monster's helicopter motion, which Dante compares with a boat backing off from its mooring, and then he describes the beast as "swimming" in the viscous air.

56

57

57 This image is from an Italian manuscript that dates probably from the fifteenth century. Some illustrators give the creature wings because Dante emphasizes that although Geryon swims down "like an eel" (XVII, 104), he nevertheless gathers the air with his paws and descends so that "I feel only / the wind upon my face and the wind rising" (116–117). Characteristically, the medieval artist strives to make the fabulous readily imaginable.

58, 59 These two versions of Geryon, from the Pisan manuscript of ca. 1385 and from Blake, point up Dante's emphasis on the decorative body of the monster. There is something muted and sad about Blake's monster, and his tail is not dangerous enough. One wonders whether Blake's sympathy with the dark energies affects his rendering.

58

59

60   Doré's Geryon: again, a wonderful sense of the awful spaces but missing the sting in the tail of fraud and the thick atmosphere that needs no wings.

60

61   Giraldi's style recalls his version of the centaurs and the river of blood (see fig. 43). Here the three figures float unperturbed between peaceful hills on a stream that does not exist in the poem. There is no sense of threat, of the poet's soul-wrenching experiences of divine judgment and punishment. The only ominous feature of Geryon is the scorpion's sting, transformed into a tiny dragon's mouth.

62   Fuseli fails entirely to render the benign human face of the monster, making his visage patently evil. He ignores the deceptive countenance that makes Geryon so vivid an emblem of fraud.

61

62

63

63   Botticelli shows the structure of the divisions of the
eighth circle, in this portion where, with poetic justice, the Seducers and Panderers are
forced to move in opposing circles, whipped on by demons, and the Flatterers of the
next pouch flop about in pools of excrement. How the true nature of this sin becomes
its own torment needs no interpretation. Botticelli's use of iterated figures underscores
the nature of both the sin and its punishment. In medieval fashion, his pilgrim and guide
pause at several different vantage points along the way, to view all aspects of the repul-
sive scene. Virgil points out Jason and Thais, who deceived each succeeding lover with
false praise.

        That Botticelli was drawn especially to this action is suggested by his mak-
ing it one of the few illustrations he executed in color.

64   Rico Lebrun, looking through twentieth-century eyes,
reveals the sinner, whose head is almost absorbed by his or her gross body, as carried
rather than whipped on by a demon. This representation emphasizes the inner workings
of the psychological complex and suggests that an obsession with flesh impels seduc-
tive abuses.

        Lebrun died not long after he completed these drawings, printed by
Leonard Baskin's Kanthos Press in 1963, and has been relatively unremembered as the
strong and bold draftsman he was.

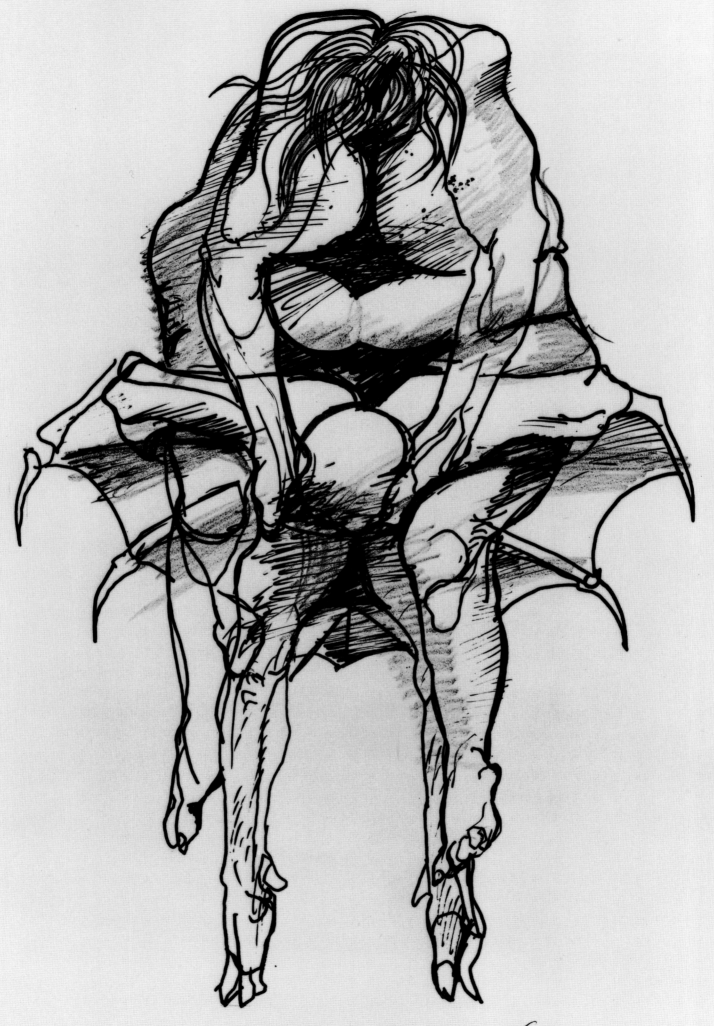

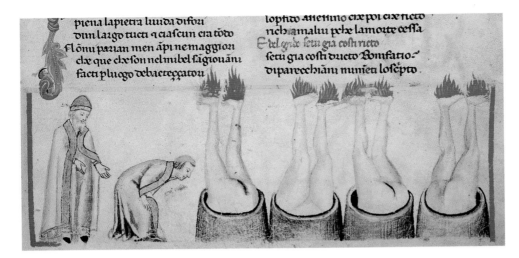

65

66

65   The Simonists (see "Simony and the Separation of Church and State," below), who used their priestly power for personal gain, are crammed upside down in baptismal fonts, waving their legs as their soles burn. The later Pisan illuminator's frankly bare-bottomed exposure of the sinners makes the humiliation of being stuffed into a font whose sacred trust they have violated especially vivid.

66   Blake shows the travelers as Virgil carefully carries the pilgrim into the rough steep pit and up again. This is Pope Nicholas III, who—because in hellish fashion he can foresee the future but is unaware of the present—is expecting Boniface VIII to take his place as the uppermost simoniac in the bottomless font.

This drawing is a good example of Blake's visionary artistry, for again, as with his image of the Sullen beneath the surface of Styx (see fig. 28), he sees through the side of the font to show us with X-ray penetration the whole human form within.

67   Lebrun's simoniac popes press hard upon each other in the claustrophobic space of the font. Like Blake, he uses an X-ray vision to great effect but conveys an even keener imagination of how stifling and oppressive the adhesion of one pope to another, head to butt, might truly feel. The burning feet jut out like twisted torches.

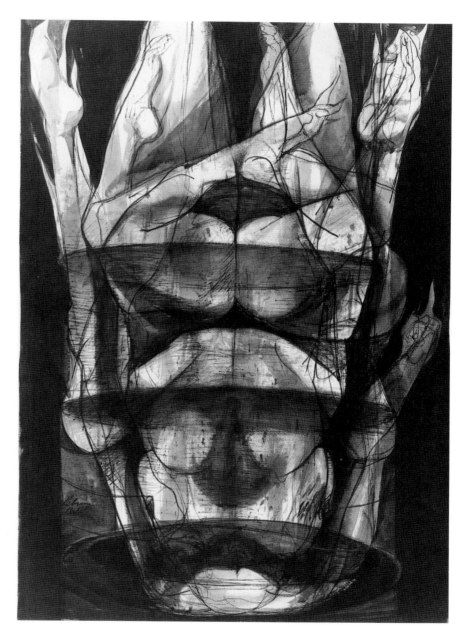

67

Simony and the Separation of Church and State *Betrayal of the Soul by*
Power and Money   **Images 65–67**   Integrity in public life has a sacred signifi-
cance in the grand scheme of salvation. Mortal well-being in the secular world, Dante
asserts in many ways, requires its own kind of devotion, including a well-ordered politi-
cal structure to which attention must be paid. In a way that may at first feel historically
dated, he makes the point that those who would serve the higher powers with integrity
must keep boundaries that limit the temptation to use the allure of their spiritual con-
nection for personal gain. In the corruptions of every kind of ministry, ranging from a
traditional priest's abuse of trust to a New Age guru's greedy way of life, we see modern
examples of what arouses the poet's ire.

Modern readers are sometimes distracted by Dante's obsessive concern
with contemporary politics in the *Commedia*, especially in the *Inferno*, where he dis-
tributes his enemies liberally among the damned. On first impression, lengthy discourses
on the factional conflict between the Guelphs and the Ghibellines and expressed long-
ings for the restoration of the Holy Roman Emperor feel dated and irrelevant to our con-
cerns. But as we look more deeply into the meaning of Dante's passion, we can see the
spiritual thrust of his emphasis and how it applies to modern experience.

In the opening lines of Canto XIX, the poet tells us in an unusual author's
aside that this third pouch of the eighth circle is the place of the "sad disciples" of Simon
Magus, who sought to buy spiritual power from the apostles. Here, the pilgrim comes upon
the Simonists, plunged headfirst into tubes in the rock from which only their naked legs
emerge, the soles of their feet seared by perpetual fire (see figs. 65–67). Having invoked
scriptural authority for the foulness of this crime (Acts 8:18–21, in which Peter rejects Simon's
bribe, rebuking him fiercely "for thinking that money could buy what God has given for
nothing!"), the poet dares to imagine that the flaming feet before which the pilgrim stands
belong to Nicholas III, a pope who reigned in Dante's lifetime. Moreover, we learn that
Nicholas will be pressed yet deeper into his hole (a mock baptismal font) by two other
contemporaries, Boniface VIII and Clement V, when they die and follow him down.

In condemning three contemporary popes, Dante rages against papal cor-
ruption. Driven by worldly avarice, these pontiffs have turned their duty to their flock
on its head—depicted here by stuffing the sinner's head down into fonts that parody the
sacrament of baptism. The poet becomes even more provocative when he explains what
has caused the Church's depravity. The popes' obsession with wealth, he asserts, derives
from the conversion of the Roman emperor Constantine—not from his commitment to
Christianity itself but from "the dower / that you bestowed upon the first rich father"
(116–117). Although the document that supported the so-called Donation of Constan-
tine was already recognized as of doubtful authenticity in Dante's time, the Church's
wealth, which he condemns, was entirely real. Over the centuries, as Christianity was
transformed from a repressed sect to the established religion, Church leaders could and
did indulge their greed. Dante passionately denies the Church's right to rule in the secu-
lar realm, holding that its sole mission is to serve the spiritual well-being of its flock. The
poet finds all about him in thirteenth-century public life evidence of the temptation to
render unto Caesar what belongs to God. His own bitter exile from Florence, from which
he would never return, had been caused by papal intervention in the city's affairs. As a

counterweight to unholy worldliness, Dante repeatedly expresses his longing for the return of an effective Holy Roman Emperor, who would keep order in the secular realm, thereby freeing citizens of all Christian communities from the greed and power of the papacy.

Much in the poet's view foreshadows later historical developments. Fury with avaricious abuses of papal authority subsequently found its expression in the Protestant Reformation and Catholic Counter-Reformation of the sixteenth century. Constitutional separations of church and state in the democratic West today reflect a similar aversion to the alliance of temporal and spiritual power. Although he was not a democrat in the modern sense, Dante insisted that spiritual leaders should not be tempted to greed by direct participation in political life, nor should the fairness of political leaders be warped by religious ideology.

68, 69, 70   In the fourth pouch of circle eight, Rico Lebrun (1963), Bartolomeo di Fruosino (ca. 1420), and Renato Guttuso (1970) depict the Diviners, who presumed to look into the future. Although one of these artists precedes the other two by more than five centuries, their images are similar in their intense focus on the sufferers, making us the direct observers of those who have their heads turned on their bodies so that they must walk backwards if they wish to see where they are going. All three illustrators present the image of inversion clearly. Bartolomeo di Fruosino layers one stiff body before and behind another to create a dense effect, while Lebrun and Guttuso five centuries later depict the contorted anatomical structures with great intensity. The allegory is clearer in the medieval sketch, whereas the feeling of horror is more immediate in the modern renderings. Lebrun places one diviner sitting in another's lap, but each head looks directly away from rather than at the other; thus he reveals that in this condition even tactile intimacy is cold and unrelated.

Dante writes that he weeps,

when I beheld our image so nearby
and so awry that tears, down from the eyes,
bathed the buttocks, running down the cleft (XX, 22–24),

but Virgil rebukes him, calling these souls arrogant and impious for linking "God's judgment to passivity" (30). To foretell the future explicitly or concretely means that one must deny the freedom God provides for active moral choice to change one's destiny.

68

69

70

Credi tu malacoda q̃ uedeini
eſſ uenuto diſſel mi maeſtro
ſicuro gia datuei uoſtri ſcheini

Jo mi uoluerſo la diqſti miei
arrguatoi ſalcun feneſciorina
gire colono elxrio ſaranno rei

71

71   At circle eight, fifth pouch, Virgil tells the pilgrim to hide while the demons rush at him. He convinces their leader, Malacoda, or "Evil-tail," that Dante's journey is willed by God, and ten of them are assigned as escorts. In this pouch, depicted by the Pisan illustrator of ca. 1385, corrupt officials stew in boiling pitch and are torn by the demons' hooks if they dare to come up for air. They are stuck in pitch as graft stuck to their fingers.

72, 73   Blake and Doré illustrate the precarious nature of this part of the journey and the travelers' misgivings. Blake's demons seem to wear masks and convey somewhat the look of a masquerade party; their leader, Malacoda, looks strangely thick in the torso, giving the impression that he was casually drawn. Perhaps Blake had in mind again the deceptive face of fraud, for Malacoda lies to Virgil about the path ahead, but the effect is for the demons to appear altogether less serious than Doré's.

72

73

75

74, 75 A detail from Luca Signorelli's fresco of the Damned in the Orvieto cathedral, ca. 1500, shows the terrible intensity of his flying demons. Signorelli's powerful drawing heightens our sense of Blake's less careful draftsmanship, but Blake's spontaneity often serves the poem well, as in this scene where a clever grafter escapes momentarily by getting the demons to fight among themselves. Blake especially appreciates the comedy inherent in the grafters' capacity to deceive even their deceptive tormenters, depicting the moment before the contending demons fall "into the middle of the boiling pond" so that "their wings were stuck, enmeshed in glue-like pitch" (XXII, 141, 144).

76   When the travelers both with one accord realize they
must not trust the demons further, Virgil picks Dante up again,

> . . . just as
> the mother who is awakened by a roar
> and catches sight of blazing flames beside her
> will lift her son and run without a stop. (XXIII, 37–40)

Virgil's occasional protective interventions remind us that human depravities are some-
times fearful to contemplate even for those who are well prepared and wisely guided.
Blake's illustration balances us on the edge of disbelief, just as Virgil balances on one
foot, but a telling quality of naive fear is communicated by the depiction of extreme haste
and the oval envelope that shields the travelers.

77, 78   In similar views, the Pisan illuminator (ca. 1385) and John Flaxman (1793) depict the Hypocrites, who move heavily in circles, weighed down with gilded lead cloaks. They have pretended falsely to be true believers and do not avoid Caiaphas, the high priest who condemned Christ as a blasphemer, now himself crucified on the ground. In walking leadenly over the horizontal Caiaphas, they emphasize both their and his fixation in matter, never recognizing that divine spirit can be incarnated in human flesh.

Flaxman's more accurate visual perspective communicates through iteration the perpetual burdens of the Hypocrites' cloaks, "of a lead so thick, their heaviness / makes us, the balances beneath them, creak" (XXIII, 101–102). Flaxman expresses more emotional involvement in this scene than is often his style. Because of the varied density of his pencil line, the original drawings reproduced here (from a bound volume in the Houghton Library at Harvard University) are also more lively than the published engravings.

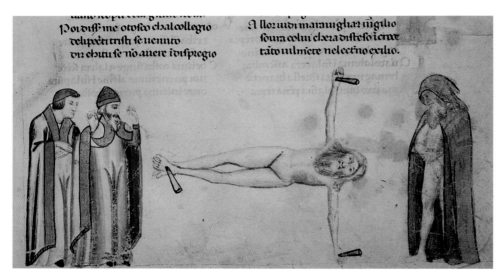

77

78

sum coadunant manum et ipm exerci
tum pl ibiam ducens multos milites
siti labore et spencum morsibz pdidit ue

muit et totus vulcus est effectus. Cur
membra omnia humanum supegressa
modum in saniem et putredinem sunt

79

79, 80   Dante assumes that a person's things are an expression and extension of his being and therefore that to steal them is to brutalize a person's substance. He describes the metamorphoses of men and serpents in the pouch of the Thieves. This Pisan illumination of ca. 1345 depicts one such exchange, in which a winged serpent has pierced a man at his navel, whereupon a closed circle is formed of the smoke that emerges violently from the mouth of one and the wound of the other, and a switch of limbs takes place.

In this arresting image of transformation, Lebrun draws a serpent's head displacing the human one, its coils intimately engirdling and becoming the heavy body.

80

82

81, 82   With horrifying power, Baskin and Blake, working about a hundred and fifty years apart, each render the metamorphosis of one of the Thieves into a hybrid monster, an image of the sneaky reptilian character of the thief. In another sense these images portray the torment of being unable to distinguish what is "mine" from what is "thine."

Baskin's economical drawing has a visceral impact and sculptural strength that reveals the generalized quality of Blake's anatomy, although Blake vividly renders the displacement of the human by the serpentine body. With modern candor, Baskin represents the exchange (and equivalence) of forms as a perverse sexual coupling. The monster grows out of the loins like a self-devouring erection.

Dante exults in his powers of verbal invention in these cantos, declaiming:

> Let Lucan now be silent, where he sings
> of sad Sabellus and Nasidius,
> and wait to hear what flies off from my bow.
> Let Ovid now be silent, where he tells
> of Cadmus, Arethusa; if his verse
> has made of one a serpent, one a fountain,
> I do not envy him; he never did
> transmute two natures, face to face, so that
> both forms were ready to exchange their matter.
> (XXV, 94–102)

The fascination of great artists with the poet's visual images makes it clear that Dante's authorial pride is merited, a not unjustified hubris. Even so, as we see in the *Purgatorio*, the poet presents himself as especially in need of atonement for this vice.

83, 84 In Pisan and Lombard manuscripts, glibness of tongue consumes the Fraudulent Counselors in fire. The Pisan illustrator of ca. 1385 continues to select clear, strong images and to present them with an impressive measured cadence. He chooses to suggest emblematically the human souls contained within each flame. The Lombard illuminator of ca. 1440, in contrast, is both more decorative and more accurate, for, in accord with Dante's description, the human forms are invisible within the heated intensity of each flame, and on the right the Lombard depicts the double flame that "so twinned" (XXVI, 52) the spirits of Ulysses and Diomedes.

83

84

85

85   Ulysses and Diomedes, who persuaded the Trojans to take the Trojan Horse within their walls, share the same tongue of fire in this illustration by Bartolomeo di Fruosino. The pilgrim begs to speak with them, but Virgil suggests he do so in Greek, lest "they'd be disdainful of your speech" (XXVI, 75)—referring to the common Italian in which Dante has boldly elected to write the *Commedia*. In this way the poet again expresses his reverence for the classical tradition he is building on.

         Ulysses tells the travelers a long tale of his last voyage, a boundary-breaking venture to the shores of the Mountain of Purgatory, whose heroic presumption aroused a whirlwind of divine retribution. He falsely advised his companions that they "must not deny / experience of that which lies beyond / the sun" (XXVI, 115–117). Here Dante is asserting the common medieval understanding of the limits to which human intelligence is meant to aspire, even as he writes the poem that stretches those limits beyond the boundaries of what is considered heretical, as we shall see.

86   This soldier-turned-monk, Guido da Montefeltro, was persuaded by Pope Boniface VIII to give evil counsel by offering him absolution in advance. In the final struggle with Saint Francis over his soul at death, a fallen angel referred to as the "black cherub" won and carried him to Minos, who twisted his tail around himself eight times, bit it in anger, and announced Guido's fate (see "A Contention for the Soul," below). Although the Italian illuminator of fig. 85 suggests the human forms within the flames, Flaxman ignores the fiery torment altogether to illustrate Guido's story. Flaxman's fallen angel conveys an energy that does indeed imply that Francis's angelic mission (and posture) will not carry the day.

A Contention for the Soul   Image 86   In the eighth pouch of the eighth circle of the *Inferno* (Canto XXVII), the pilgrim listens as Guido da Montefeltro speaks from within the perpetual flame of a Fraudulent Counselor. Guido wishes to tell the grim tale of the contention for his soul at death between Saint Francis and a fallen angel ("black cherub"), even though he seems ashamed of it (see fig. 86). He says he would not tell his story if he thought his listeners would ever return to the world. He knows that such a return is not allowed under the usual rules of this realm, and the pilgrim remains silent, knowing that he will try to tell all that he has seen when he returns. Most of the souls in Hell do not care about the opinion of others except to bolster their narcissistic self-importance. Perhaps that is what Dante is implying here: that the pilgrim's silent betrayal is justifiable, that Guido is to be viewed as an object lesson because his punishment shows that he always acted with a self-serving expediency, always hiding the truth before others, even though he had once entertained a greater sense of service by leaving the soldier's life to become a Franciscan monk. Guido's behavior is beyond the vacillation between opposites that bind those at the threshold of Hell to their cowardly wavering, but because he was once capable of a choice for good, his choice of evil is all the more reprehensible.

Guido's story makes another crucial point. It shows us the powerful effect of true or false guidance provided in life by those whom society designates as representatives of the highest values. Guido tells the pilgrim that he was led to fraudulence by Pope Boniface himself—"May he be damned!" he exclaims (XXVII, 70)—through a sly deal. Needing to calm Guido's fears, Boniface VIII offered him absolution in advance in exchange for the advice he needed to crush an opponent. Counselors of any kind, but most especially priests and therapists, must be alert to any lurking urge for their own absolution or salvation from those who come to them for guidance.

The tale of Guido and Boniface brings us to an awareness of the human need for divine forgiveness, even though that forgiveness may be sought in half-hearted and mistaken ways. Often the rituals of forgiveness are stand-ins for the archetypal sense of acceptance to which they may connect. Both the pope and the monk enact the rituals of absolution with something like a magical belief in their protective efficacy, like something done to avert the evil eye. But in the end the black cherub stakes his claim and carries Guido to Minos, who will judge his final placement in Hell.

In fact, justice is depicted through the black cherub's claim; the fallen angel yet serves God's larger scheme by insisting on Guido's fraudulence. He rejects the idea that Guido's awareness of the evil he has done is an act of conscience: "No one can repent and will at once!" (119). Guido must finally stand in the midst of his own deeds, regardless of the depravity of his false guide's behavior. The blaming of a person who should have been more responsible (mother, father, analyst) can ultimately stand directly in the way of a true acceptance of one's own blackness and the work of its purgation. Only then, through the experience of self-forgiveness, can one claim one's own life. Thus, with his illustration of this fraudulent counselor, Dante also illuminates the paradox that the black cherub—and the Saint Francis—within each of us function as agents of a structured universe in which one takes one's uniquely responsible place or pays the penalty.

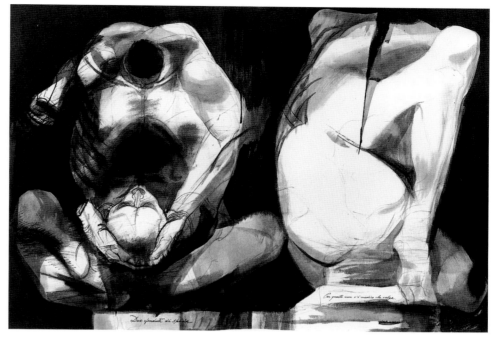

87

87   The Sowers of Discord—religious, social, and political—are repeatedly wounded by a demon warder's sword. They heal only to be split again on each round. Their torment conveys the consequences of a fanatical insistence on distinctions of partisan ideology or theology or creed that fail to recognize the larger need for wholeness. With the perspective of a modern artist (1963), Rico Lebrun's decapitated sinner holds his own head in his lap and looks back at his vacant neck in a moment of self-reflection that is occasionally implied but rarely explicit in the *Inferno*'s text. The artist emphasizes the lonely separateness of the figures here, as at other times he makes us see their cold or hostile entanglements.

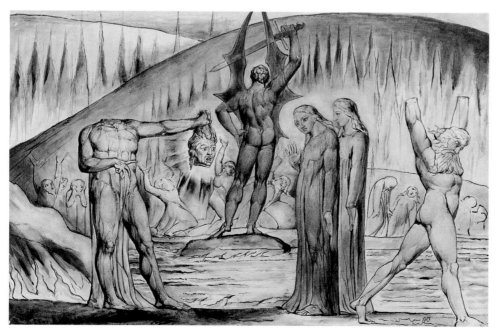

88   In one of Blake's most stunning and effective compositions, Bertrand de Born, who separated Henry II from his son, holds up his own severed head, lanternlike. Those who projected their inner divisions by promoting outer conflicts are now revealed as they truly are: split apart.

89

89, 90   In Dante's time some believed that the prophet Mohammed was a Christian who had defected. Here he holds himself open. "See how I split myself! / See now how maimed Mohammed is!" he calls out to the travelers (XXVIII, 30–31). Once again, the Pisan manuscript of ca. 1385 conveys a settled sense of the larger scheme in which the horrifying torment is located, depicting both the ditch and the travelers on its bridge who witness a stylized vision of Mohammed's punishment. In contrast, Guttuso's zoom-lens plunges us directly into the gory scene and a horrifying confrontation with the gutted sinner. Whereas in the illumination Virgil seems to look away with more interest in the pilgrim's observing attitude than in the scene itself, the modern artist forces us to experience a magnified encounter with this small slice of Hell.

90   H E L L

91　　　　There are four
groups of Falsifiers. The alchemists,
who are called Falsifiers of Metals,
are afflicted with itching scabs.
Those who pretend to be another
person seem berserk, raging and
biting as if trying to incorporate the
desired individual. The money
Counterfeiters are diseased, with
bloated belly and unquenchable
thirst. Falsifiers of Words—liars—
reek of fever. Falsification, the mis-
representation of reality, Dante
asserts, is a form of sickness that
merits the lowest level of the next
to last circle of Hell. In Vecchietta's
scene, individuals of the last two
groups fight accusingly over who
is the more reprehensible. Virgil
rebukes the pilgrim for being fasci-
nated with the altercation—"If you
/ insist on looking more, I'll quarrel
with you!" (XXX, 131–132)—where-
upon Dante feels profound shame.
Although the pilgrim's entire journey
through Hell emphasizes the impor-

92

tance of knowing the darkest poten-
tialities of human nature, voyeuris-
tic dwelling on violence, sex, and
corruption distracts from the larger
goals of the journey.

92, 93 Bartolomeo di
Fruosino and Renato Guttuso focus
on the Counterfeiters of Others'
Persons. The illuminator conveys
with unusually graphic frankness
the suggestion of sexual perversity
in the wild biting and groping of
these sinners. Guttuso is particu-
larly interested in Myrrha, who took
another woman's shape in order to
satisfy her lust for her father and is
able to make her twisted figure
believable.

93

94, 95   The travelers have reached the central abyss or pit of the Inferno. Antaeus, the giant who was born too late to rebel against the Olympian deities, is the one not bound or chained in these Neapolitan and Lombard manuscripts of ca. 1370 and ca. 1440, respectively. Virgil promises Antaeus fame on earth through Dante if he will lift them down to the ninth circle. These elemental figures represent brute force, pride, stupidity, and an innately low level of consciousness. Dante emphasizes how fortunate we are that such power is not in the service (or disservice) of human intelligence:

> Surely when she gave up the art of making
> such creatures, Nature acted well indeed,
> depriving Mars of instruments like these.
>   And if she still produces elephants
> and whales, whoever sees with subtlety
> holds her—for this—to be more just and prudent;
>   for where the mind's acutest reasoning
> is joined to evil will and evil power,
> there human beings can't defend themselves. (XXXI, 49–57)

Modern technology, providing Mars with the power of "instruments like these," exposes us to precisely this risk.

95

96

96, 97   Whereas the medieval illuminators emphasize the
story in their renderings of the giants, Botticelli is preoccupied with imagining the var-
ied appearance of each individual giant, and Doré contrasts powerfully the enormous
size of the giant Antaeus with the tiny figures of the pilgrim and his guide handed into
the cavernous depths of lowest Hell. Doré correctly portrays the gentleness of Antaeus.

98

98   The harsh striated lines of Doré's engraving are particularly apt for depicting the frozen realm of the Lake of Cocytus, which holds Traitors to Their Kin in the icy absence of all human warmth. The feeling of the darkness in deepest Hell is conveyed through the absence of contrast in the dim light.

99   The second section of Cocytus houses Traitors to Homeland or Party. Here Dante inadvertently kicks Bocca degli Abati's head as it sticks up through the ice. Bocca had betrayed the Florentine Guelphs by cutting off their standard-bearer's hand in battle, causing panic and defeat. The sinner so infuriates the pilgrim by having betrayed his party and by refusing to identify himself that Dante threatens to pull out all his hair. Even so, Bocca will not reveal his name, declining in his shame the pilgrim's promise of fame when he returns above, and only another sinner's outburst identifies him. Blake disapproved of Dante's treatment of Bocca and thought that the poet was just as bad as Ugolino (see fig. 101), who gnaws the head of Ruggieri, though the artist seems to have understood Dante's rejection of Argenti (see fig. 31).

Although Blake presents the sinners with part of their bodies out of the ice in order to convey the action more emphatically, Dante stresses that only the heads of the lesser sinners in Cocytus are out of the ice at all, whereas the worst, at the final level, are completely encased beneath the surface.

99

100   Fuseli's Romantic style dramatizes the affect evoked in the encounter with Bocca by giving the pilgrim the appearance of an avenging fury. The giants' feet resting on the ice at the edge of Cocytus can be seen in the top of the drawing.

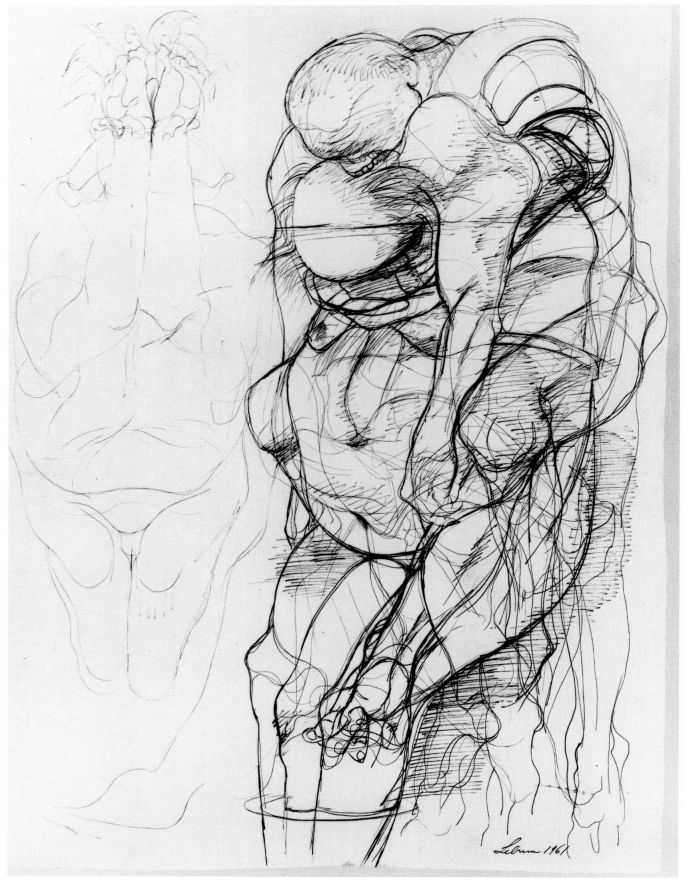

101

102

101   In Lebrun's painful drawing, Ugolino gnaws perpetually at the nape of Archbishop Ruggieri's neck, cannibalizing him as Ruggieri was reputed to have made Ugolino cannibalize his children. The figures almost merge, as if the body of Ugolino has partly digested that of Ruggieri. Although Ugolino and Ruggieri are condemned together to the second round of Cocytus for their joint betrayal of their homeland, the subsequent betrayal of the one by the other is the focus of Dante's narrative. Ugolino tells the pilgrim a pathetic (and now famous) tale of his imprisonment and death with his two sons, when Ruggieri locked them up in a tower and left them to starve.

102   In Vecchietta's typical panorama, we see Ugolino and Ruggieri on the left, Ugolino and his sons in prison in the center, and Fra Alberigo with his frozen tears on the right. Alberigo had murdered two kinsmen at a banquet to which he invited them, thus earning himself a place in the third ring of Cocytus with the Traitors to Guests and Hosts. Dante's deceptive promise to Alberigo, which he does not intend to keep, is another variant of his "unchristian" behavior in the lowest reaches of Hell. This is appropriate to the unequivocal necessity to reject, rather than forgive, the darkest possibilities of human nature—which we have had ample opportunity to perceive in the massively treacherous exterminations of the twentieth century.

103   The Traitors Against Their Benefactors in the fourth section are completely covered by ice but remain "visible as wisps of straws in glass" (XXXIV, 12). The betrayal of one's master or benefactor is the deepest evil of all, like that of Dis (as Dante calls Satan) himself, because the pledge of love and loyalty is the most deliberate, or conscious, of human and sacred commitments. And here is the source of the wind that keeps the lowest circles frozen. Doré's Dis looks more resentful than terrible, but again Doré imagines vast dark spaces and the size of an archetypal power relative to human beings. The tiny human figures in the ice do indeed look like straws in glass.

103

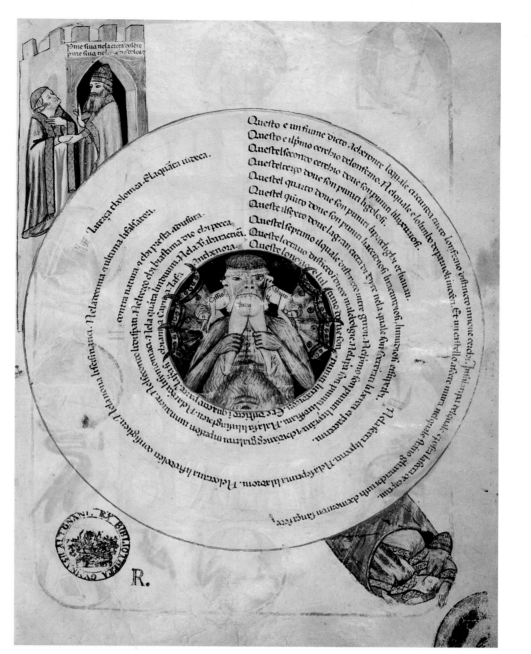

104

104 The Pisan master of ca. 1385 illuminates a manuscript
chart or overview of Hell's center, showing both initial entrance and exit, and placing
the end of the journey of descent in its larger context.

105

105, 106   Flaxman and Botticelli, too, struggle to express the awfulness of Dis, whose three heads are a mockery of the Trinity: " He wept out of six eyes; and down three chins, / tears gushed together with a bloody froth. / Within each mouth—he used it like a grinder— / with gnashing teeth he tore to bits a sinner, / so that he brought much pain to three at once" (XXXIV, 53–57). This creature weeps as he chews Judas, Brutus, and Cassius. In the teeth of Dis, "the divided one" (see "Depths of Despair," below), the artists vividly portray persons "eaten up" by their own pathology. As usual, Botticelli's vision is more sweeping than the later artist's and includes more graphic images of all three heads, Dis's hairy upper body, and the figures of pilgrim and guide as well.

106

107   On double sheets of vellum, Botticelli attempts to capture the majesty of Dis's perverted energy. Dante hides his face and clasps Virgil around the neck. At "the point at which the thigh / revolves" (XXXIV, 76–77)—that is, at the genitals, if they were there—Virgil turns, and the travelers prepare to emerge, guided by the sound of a stream. This is a profound image of the experience that in matters central to the individual psyche, the way out is the way through. The last hairy step cannot be refused, for that is where the enantiodromia, the redirection of a life, takes place.

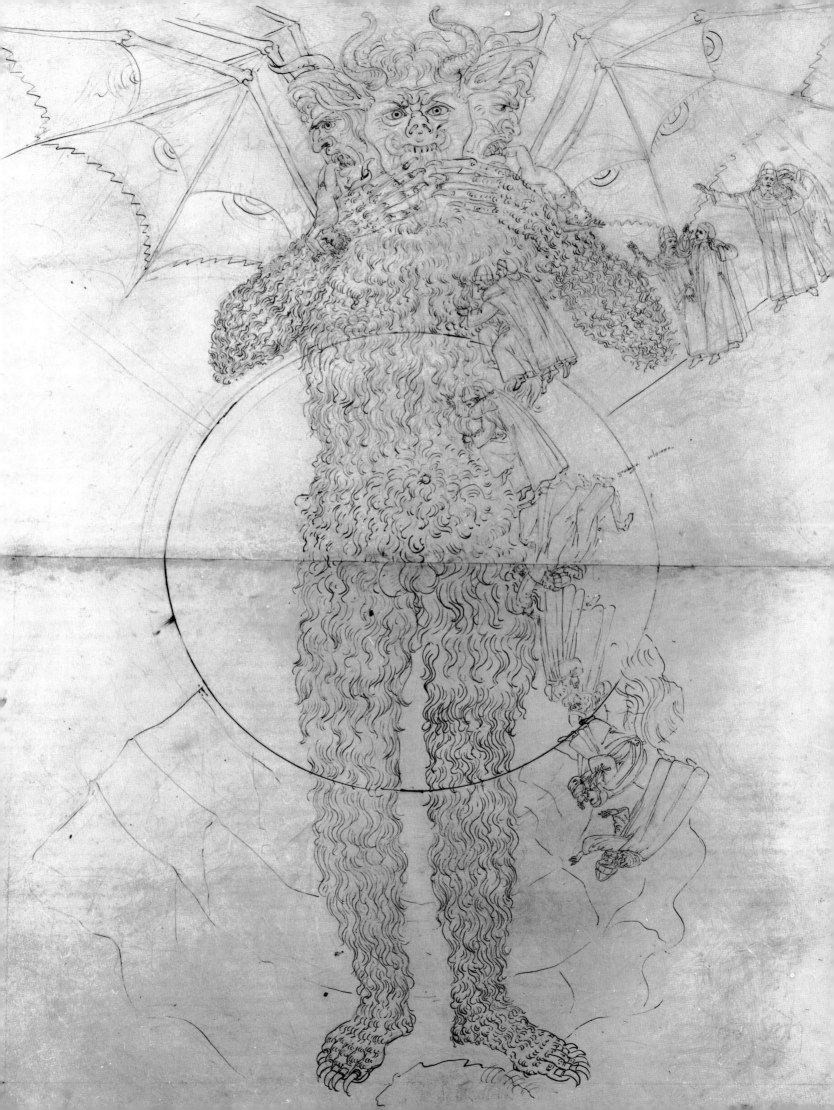

108   Vecchietta as usual adds his own touches to Dante's description, including, on the right, the long amphibian legs and feet appended to the inverted figure of the lower half of Dis.

109, 110   The later Pisan illuminator separates the two parts of the somber and terrifying climb, revealing them with strong, simple shapes. By contrasting the upright figures of the pilgrim clinging to the neck of his guide as he struggles to climb the inverted shaggy legs of Dis, the artist graphically emphasizes the critical change of direction that has taken place at the imagined center of all gravity. "'Hold tight,' my master said—he panted like / a man exhausted—'it is by such stairs / that we must take our leave of so much evil'" (XXXIV, 82–84).

109

110

111

111 In an initial letter of a Lombard manuscript of ca. 1400, the pilgrim and his guide emerge to see the stars. Dis is given the feet of a predatory bird. The stars are connected in an orderly pattern that is typical of medieval decoration and appropriate to the restoration of hope in the new atmosphere.

112 A chart from the Temple Classics edition of the *Commedia* orients us to the relation of various parts of the journey in outline form.

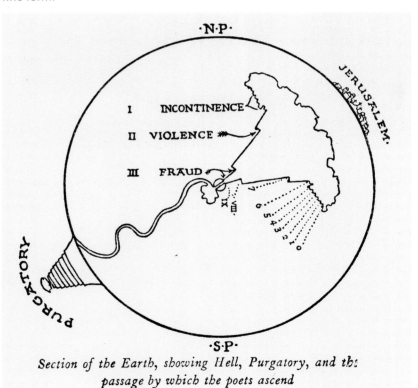

Section of the Earth, showing Hell, Purgatory, and the passage by which the poets ascend

112

Depths of Despair *The Impotent Loins of Dis*   Images 98–111

In the ice of Dis, at the very bottom of Hell, we again find immobilization, this time of those who are frozen at various depths in accord with the denial of warmth, loyalty, and love that their betrayals have represented (see figs. 98–103). Here is the most grievous consequence of despair: violation of the bonds of attachment to those persons and values to which we owe especial loyalty. To breach these attachments is to declare life hopeless at the core, to deny the sacredness of love, which in Dante's view is the motive energy of both the human and the more than human worlds.

Dante calls the figure fixed in the ice at the bottom of Hell "Dis" ("Dite" in Italian) rather than Satan or Lucifer or Hades (see figs. 103–111). Etymologically, mythologically, and psychologically this is a careful choice. The name Satan means the " adversary" with whom we must do battle but also come to terms; Lucifer is the "lightbringer" who accompanies conscious engagement with the shadow; and Hades is simply the "unseen"—the underworld—which we like Dante must come to know. But "Dis" comes from Latin meaning "away from," the root for two, apart, split-off, or separated, as in "divided" or "disease." The figure at the center of the realm of darkness symbolizes what is most split off from consciousness, separated into opposites the ego does not conjoin, giving rise to the psychological splitting and the paranoia that are at the core of destructive pathology.

When we are possessed by the negative projections that see only the mote in the eye of another and never the beam in our own, then we are cut off from the capacity for empathy and caring concern that alone saves us from egocentric isolation. Dis stands frozen in the nadir of Hell as the emblem of lovelessness, the coldheartedness at the core of our deepest failures to be human. Climbing down his hairy flank, Dante and Virgil have to turn downside up, revolving 180 degrees when they reach the level of his loins (see figs. 107–111). There is a Chinese saying that at midnight noon is born. The degenerative center of all darkness becomes the starting point of the travelers' ascent.

Appropriately, neither Dante nor the illustrators provide Dis with genitals, emphasizing the sterility of his being, as opposed to the procreative process of the journey. Here, as throughout the *Commedia*, it is essential to observe experientially the nature of the dark power but never to be arrested in awe of its archetypal authority. Whereas at the Gate of Dis the confrontation with the Furies and the Fallen Angels almost freezes the pilgrim in despair, now he and his guide have passed through a vivid elaboration of the human capacity for fraud and betrayal and they can see clearly the emasculated pathology that is split off from human feeling at the core of evil. Grasping the imagined figure in tangible encounter, they can proceed without delay. The direction of their journey changes, and the pilgrim begins to move toward the illuminated hill whose alluring promise he could not approach when he glimpsed it at the beginning.

two Purgatory

Suffering, Dreams, and Insight (The *Purgatorio*)

113   In Guttuso's painting we stand on the rocky shore of Purgatory, looking into the limpid sky:

> The gentle hue of oriental sapphire
> in which the sky's serenity was steeped—
> its aspect pure as far as the horizon—
>   brought back my joy in seeing just as soon
> as I had left behind the air of death. (I, 13–17)

The artist captures Dante's sense of "joy in seeing" by providing not only the immediacy of a strong foreground but also a splendidly lit landscape of great depth, emphasizing the return to the beauty of the natural world. In the poem's time scheme it is Easter Sunday, the day of Christ's Resurrection, following the descent into the infernal depths on Good Friday, the day of the Crucifixion.

P-g Canto 1

114

114   Blake's unfinished sketch includes a rising sun and carries the feeling of a dawn emergence: the tentativeness of the new place, the blessed relief of delicate light after such thick darkness, the deep pleasure of having "left behind the air of death." Both the wonder and the delicacy of this new feeling after so much distress are psychologically exact. The guide is here about to wash the pilgrim's face with dew, as instructed by Cato: "bathe / his face, to wash away all of Hell's stains" (I, 95–96).

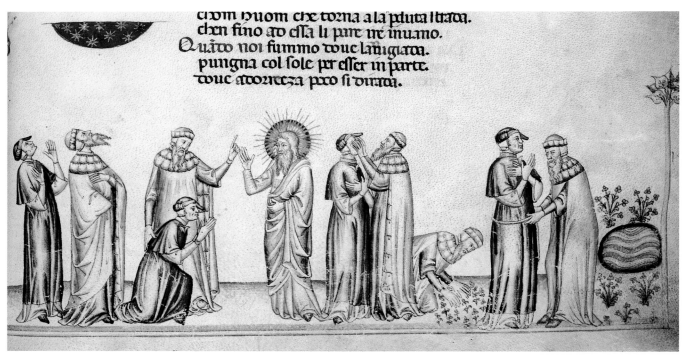

croin huom che toz2na a la pduta lt2aoa.
chen fino ao essa li part me muamo.
Quioo noi fummo ooue latnigiaoa.
pungna col sole per esser in parte.
ooue acoozneeza poro si oua oa.

115

115   Typical of fourteenth-century illuminations, this Neapolitan example depicts a sequence of action in one scene. The travelers look up at the four stars, Virgil urges Dante's reverence toward Cato (who here has a halo—it is interesting to note what elements of the poem are exaggerated or embellished by medieval artists), and Virgil washes Dante's face and helps him tie on a girdle made of rush, signifying humility. At the beginning of the first canto, Virgil's explanation to Cato of the purpose of his journey with Dante gives us another glimpse of the large plan as it is developing and incidentally helps us see why Cato is here rather than in the Wood of the Suicides. Virgil begs Cato's aid for the love of his wife, whom the pilgrims have seen in Limbo, but Cato says it is enough that "a lady . . . from Heaven" (53) sends them. Cato also says that when he was freed to enter Purgatory, he was no longer subject to his wife's power to move him. At the beginning of the *Inferno*, Beatrice similarly observes that "God, in His graciousness, has made me so" (II, 91) that Virgil's present misery does not touch her, even though she is engaged in making an impassioned plea of concern for the pilgrim. Dante holds such paradoxes in the meaning of love—merger and possession versus detachment and care—relentlessly before us throughout the *Commedia* in different contexts and various forms. As the emblem of the man who valued freedom more than his own life, Cato also underscores Dante's espousal of political liberty as essential for the sacred order of life in this world.

116   Vecchietta's illustration of the angel pilot departs from the text considerably but conveys the vivid difference between this boatman and Charon, at the first crossing in Hell. The water may have been made to look like a river in order to sharpen this contrast, or the scene may depict the walls of Rome and the mouth of the Tiber, from which we are told the singing souls are coming. (Note the artist's use of the pointillist style, for instance in Cato's beard.)

The pilgrim meets his friend Casella, and they are diverted for a moment from their larger goal by their mutual love of music when Dante asks Casella to sing one of "the songs / of love that used to quiet all my longings" (II, 107–108). Even Virgil is transfixed with pleasure as the group of souls listens, until Cato chastises them for "negligence" and "lingering" and urges them on their purgatorial way. Here is the first instance of another theme (related to the differentiation of love between persons) that is developed throughout the *Purgatorio*: the poet acknowledges a deep empathy for art and sensuous pleasure while stressing also the arduous lessons in detachment that must be learned from the suffering of maturation.

116

117, 118　　Doré again provides an atmosphere, an experience of the coming of lightness of many kinds, and Baskin puts us in the boat, at the feet of a surprisingly heavy figure in a very light context. Doré's sense of the enormous scale of the space he establishes is characteristic of his cosmic vision and contrasts vividly with Baskin's attention only to the figure of the angel pilot. The modern artist is most interested in his anthropomorphic image of the angelic power, suggesting as it were that the divine comes out of the human rather than the other way around. The majesty of Doré's angel, with "his wings, pointing to Heaven" (II, 34), conveys more of the angel's awesomeness, so bright, the poet says, that "my eyes could not endure his nearness" (II, 39)—whereas Baskin invites us to look the angel directly in the abdomen.

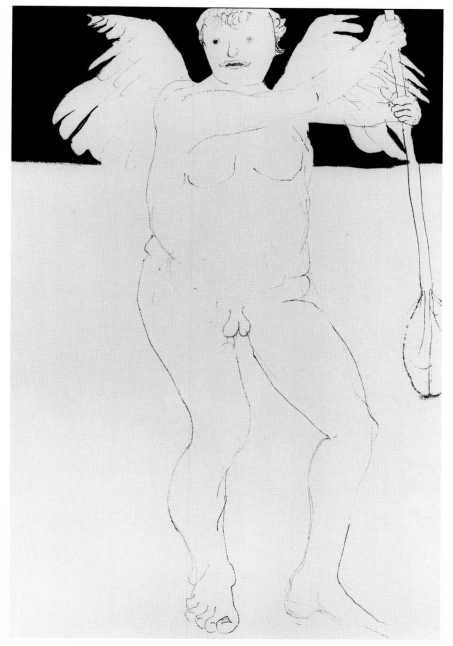

118

119　　　　　　　The angel's boat, as Botticelli clearly shows, is so light that it draws no water, and that is the way Dante specifically describes it. Here are the Excommunicates and some of the Late-Repentant of Ante-Purgatory, who were stubbornly rebellious almost to the last. These souls wait to enter for a period thirty times the length of their delayed repentance. Manfred's conversation with Dante, however, tells us that the prayers of the living can shorten the stay. When looked at in terms of aspects of the individual psyche, this is a very provocative idea. It suggests that those parts of our selves that care most deeply for our development as whole persons can prayerfully seek a measure of mercy, or shorter inner penance, from the transpersonal level of the psyche, and so advance our process of inner transformation (see "Torment and Atonement," below).

119

In another chart from Dorothy Sayers's translation, we see that because the structure of the mountain's terraces (or cornices) is based on the Seven Deadly Sins, the correspondence with Hell's circles is not exact. The three upper terraces (the Lustful, the Gluttonous, and the Covetous) and terrace three (the Wrathful) are the only directly comparable ones. The others (the Slothful, the Envious, and the Proud) can be found scattered in various forms through several of the infernal regions. (For example, there could be said to be excessive pride in Farinata, Capaneus, and the Hypocrites.) The punishments, as in the *Inferno*, are sometimes set forth as images of the sin itself and sometimes as compensatory images. Depending on your angle of vision, both are usually true. The Proud bow in humility under the weight of their heavy stones, but pride itself is also a heavy burden if one sees it objectively. The Envious have their eyes sewed shut, which prevents their obsessive comparisons with others and forces them to look inward, and this blinding also conveys their inability to see any good in others.

Continuing up the mountain, briefly: The Wrathful stumble through blinding smoke, the Slothful run without stopping, the Covetous and Prodigal lie bound with their faces in the dust, the Gluttonous hunger and thirst without satisfaction, and the Lustful burn in the refining fire.

The Dream enters this purgatorial realm of real time, real nights, and real sleep. The pilgrim's three dreams are carefully spaced, the eagle dream just before Saint Peter's Gate, the siren dream between terraces four and five, and the dream of Leah and Rachel just before the entrance to the Earthly Paradise (see "Dream One: The Eagle Is Lucia," "Dream Two: The Siren's Call," and "Dream Three: Leah's Mirror," below).

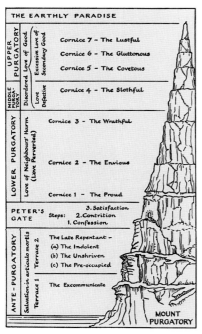

120

121

121   Flaxman's rather cold style depicts the Excommunicates approaching in a way that appears almost playfully anxious, frozen in motion like players in a children's game. This is Flaxman's way of expressing the penitents' reaction to the approach of the travelers, for the poet says,

> As soon as these souls saw, upon my right,
> along the ground, a gap in the sun's light,
> where shadow stretched from me to the rock wall
>   they stopped and then drew back somewhat. (III, 88–91)

Flaxman places the shadow on the ground before the pilgrim and touching the Excommunicates' feet. After Virgil explains that Dante's living body is authorized passage by "a force that Heaven sent him as support" (99), the souls relax and provide helpful counsel concerning the way to proceed.

122, 123   Another group among the Late-Repentant, the Indolent, are depicted by Flaxman and Botticelli. Here, too, Flaxman attends to the action Dante describes, for among the Indolent "one of them, who seemed to me exhausted, / was sitting with his arms around his knees; / between his knees he kept his head bent down" (IV, 106–108). This is Belaqua, who explains that there is no point in his hurrying on—he must wait before he can move up the mountain as many years as he has lived because "I delayed good sighs until the end" (132). Only the prayers of someone who is living in grace can shorten his time outside Purgatory proper.

Botticelli shows the steepness of the "wall of rock so sheer / that even agile legs are useless there" (III, 47–48). As the pilgrim passes the Indolent and begins to climb, he complains that it is too hard, and Virgil tells him, "This mountain's of such sort / that climbing it is hardest at the start; / but as we rise, the slope grows less unkind" (IV, 88–90). Although many illustrators (and chartmakers) represent the Mountain of Purgatory as exceedingly steep all the way up, the poet takes pains to emphasize that although the effort of redemptive psychological work is painfully laborious at first, it becomes lighter as self-knowledge increases.

122

123

conerto ipie maqcouen comuoli
Dico cololale fuelle colepuume
tel gran diso durera quel couducto
clespança mudana afacta lume

crecaumifia uerauam fem
B enfamdel peta chio flana
flupido tucto alcuio delaluce
oue tianoi aaquulon mtrana.

124

124   In the Pisan manuscript of ca. 1385, pilgrim and guide discuss the course of the sun. The illuminator's figures, though simple shapes, communicate a distinct sense of arduous creeping and serious sitting. Each day's hard climb is succeeded by the necessary delay of a night's rest.

    The element of time and its progress through three days and nights is of central importance in Purgatory. In Hell, there is no true awareness of the present. The reality of time in Purgatory is one of many ways in which Dante suggests that the world of purgatorial suffering—suffering that effects change—most closely resembles the mortal realm of everyday life (see "Torment and Atonement," below).

125

125, 126   Blake and
Luca Signorelli both show the steep
ascent and convey an otherworldly
atmosphere, especially Signorelli,
who depicts a barren and rocky
spiral that is set off in space and
appears almost moonlike. Blake's
visionary view is both more relaxed
and more assured. Signorelli's
illustrations of the *Commedia* are
roundels on the wall in the Chapel
of San Brizio in the Orvieto cathe-
dral, ca. 1500.

126

127   Blake's Late-Repentant who died by violence come swirling around the travelers. They are eager for Dante's prayers for them, and Virgil both encourages communication and urges the pilgrim onward.

Blake's rendering of how the souls "wheeled back, like ranks that run without a rein" (V, 42) expresses a lightness of voluntary motion that contrasts vividly with the tightly contained circle of the whirlwind that mercilessly drives the figures of the lustful in the Inferno (see fig. 22).

127

128   This late fourteenth-century Venetian manuscript makes palpable the intense desire of these souls for the pilgrim's prayers, but Virgil walks out of the picture frame at lower right:

> "These people pressing in on us are many;
> they come beseeching you," the poet said;
> "don't stop, but listen as you move ahead." (V, 43–45)

Again Dante emphasizes the urgency of time in this realm, and the manuscript illuminator's desire and ability to tell the story as the poem does is particularly vivid.

Here the pilgrim wants his guide to tell him more about prayers of intercession and is told that it depends upon the "passageway to God" (VI, 42): "But in a quandary so deep" (43), Beatrice will instruct him when the time comes. Virgil is adept at lifting Dante's heart with reminders of the meeting to come.

128

129　　　　　　　Leaving the second section of Ante-Purgatory, the travelers seek directions from Sordello, the famous troubadour, who, though at first suspicious of them, is deeply touched when he discovers that fellow poet and Mantuan Virgil is there. Doré depicts Sordello clasping Virgil's hands as he kneels before him in a darkening scene. In spite of their urgent need to continue on, Sordello explains that "by night / we cannot climb" (VII, 43–44) and adds, "it is / the night itself that implicates your will" (56–57), as if to emphasize the importance of sight for the work of purgation.

130

130, 131, 132   Sordello conducts Virgil and Dante to the Valley of the Rulers, who remain among the Late-Repentant because in life they were preoccupied with their responsibilities. Blake gives this aristocratic group a pleasant grove, rather like his image of Limbo. Preoccupation with service to others, whether in positions of leadership or just at home, despite its benevolence, is a common distraction from attention to one's inner life. It is interesting to consider why the serpent-shadow, "our adversary" (VIII, 95), would appear just here, preening and sleeking itself, and why it takes only the sound of the angels' wings to disperse it. It may simply be a reminder of the fascinating power of all that would betray us, but at this stage of inner development, Dante suggests, even a fleeting image of positive transpersonal energy is sufficient to dismiss the temptation.

        Signorelli's view of the scene again appears to be taking place on the moon or another planet, and the Neapolitan illuminator of ca. 1370 likewise imagines a rather bare landscape. He shows the snake both coming and going, and his angel custodians wear militant garb, rather than the green robes Dante describes. Perhaps the illustrator wished to bring to mind those who guarded the Garden of Eden, for Dante says the serpent was "similar, perhaps, / to that which offered Eve the bitter food" (98–99).

131

132

133, 134   The pilgrim's dream of being picked up by a golden eagle (see "Dream One: The Eagle Is Lucia," below) is the focus of renderings by Botticelli and Doré. Botticelli characteristically shows a sequence of images: the golden eagle, which Dante compares with Zeus' bird in pursuit of Ganymede, carries him to the level of the gate to Purgatory proper. He experiences the action of the dream as entering a realm of fire so scorching and so terrifying that he wakes. Botticelli makes us aware of the severe solidity of the mountain background, whereas Doré presents the terror of seizure and the awesome spaces surrounding the mountain. Neither artist includes Lucia, who actually carries the pilgrim to the gate while the pilgrim dreams. This dream taste of fire foreshadows the flames that one must pass through before entering the Earthly Paradise.

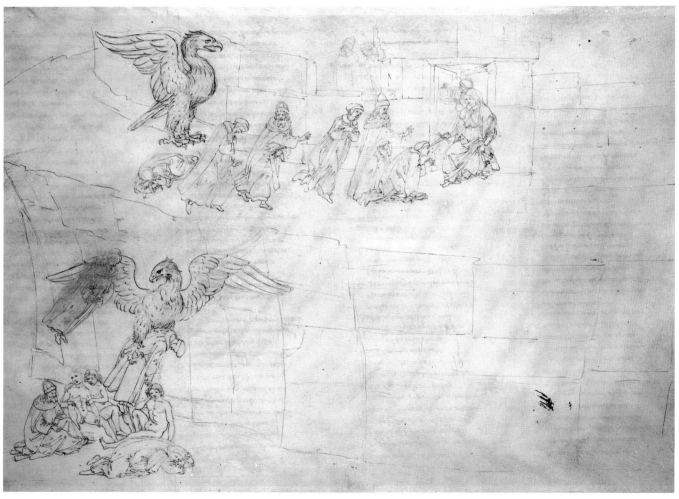

133

135

135 Vecchietta depicts a series of images: Dante dreaming, a homely, more beneficent than terrifying, crowlike eagle carrying the pilgrim up, the angel standing at the gate, and on the other side, the Proud with their rock burdens, but he leaves out Lucia. The angel guardian beckons the pilgrim forward and marks the seven "P's" on his forehead, one for each terrace of the seven deadly sins ("P" stands for "peccata," meaning sin).

136   In contrast with the other illustrators, Blake underscores the inspiring moment with rays of light and shooting stars. Interested in meaning, he portrays Lucia carrying the sleeping pilgrim to the gate, revealing her intervention to be the substantive experience of Grace that the pilgrim perceives as awesomely terrifying in his dream. Medieval bestiaries describe the eagle as a kind of phoenix and tell the story of the eagle who flies to the fiery sphere between earth and moon, burns off his feathers, falls blinded into a fountain, and reemerges as a youth. The pilgrim is now ready to start the work that promises transformation.

136

Dream One *The Eagle Is Lucia*   **Images 133–136**   In the *Com-
media*, Dante the pilgrim has three dreams, and all three come in the *Purgatorio*, in Cantos
IX, XIX, and XXVII—just before, in the middle, and at the end of his ascent up the seven
terraces of Purgatory (see fig. 120). He comes to the seven terraces after traveling through
Ante-Purgatory and later proceeds into the Earthly Paradise. Dante thus restricts his use
of the imagery of dreams to the interior core of the central canticle of his work. Examin-
ation of the dreams, both individually and as a sequence, reveals how deeply they relate
to the development of the soul that is the work of purgation.

At the time near dawn when "our intellect's / envisionings become almost
divine" (IX, 17–18), Dante dreams of being seized by an eagle with golden pinions who
swoops down on him as if he were Ganymede being taken up to Olympus and, "terri-
ble as lightning," snatches him "up to the fire's orbit," where "it seemed that he and I
were burning" (29–31). Scorched in this imagined fire, he awakes in fear and is told by
Virgil that what has actually happened is that Lucia has come and carried him up to the
gate of Purgatory (see figs. 133–136).

A profound point is conveyed by the difference between Dante's inner
experience as it registers in his dream—terrifying and scorching—and the actual event:
helpful assistance from a heavenly intercessor for his upward journey. The pilgrim is
about to begin a difficult climb that will end in passage through purifying flames, at the
top of the seventh terrace, a crossing he later describes as so hot "I'd / have thrown myself
in molten glass to find / coolness" (XXVII, 49–51). At each terrace along the way he will
encounter those souls who are atoning through some form of suffering for each of the
seven deadly sins, and the image of burning with the eagle foreshadows the culminating
suffering of Purgatory proper.

Lucia's intervention is part of the divine plan that permits Dante to observe
and share imaginally in every potential of the soul's condition. What his dream reveals,
however, is that being touched directly by the divine power, by the "light" from which
Lucia takes her name, at this stage of his development is deeply frightening. It is what
we sometimes experience when we encounter the transpersonal level of the psyche,
even though this may ultimately serve us well. The event is too alien to be assimilated
without great preparatory work, the arduous effort required to relate consciously enough
to archetypal numinosity so that one is not carried away by madness or inflation.

The beginning of wisdom, says the ancient text, is fear of the Lord. Recog-
nition of the enormity of transpersonal power, the eaglelike dominion and rapaciousness
conveyed by the analogy to Zeus seizing Ganymede, evokes a fearful respect that alone
makes possible the gradual development of a capacity to survive any interaction with its
creative and destructive energies. If we claim divine power as our own, we fall prey to
the sin of pride, the first and worst of the seven sins for whose atonement Dante will
now witness the punishments. Because he also acknowledges pride as a personal vice,
his terror of the claws of the eagle is the more understandable and is a humbling, indeed
a purgative, reminder that he is little more than a desired morsel in the grip of the living
god. Traditional observations that the eagle is a symbol for Christ suit the connection to
Lucia but do little justice to the poet's emphasis on his nightmarish fear.

The dream also reminds us of how often we experience the events that contribute most to our growth as painful, even excruciating, though from the perspective of our ultimate welfare they are exactly what we require. From the human point of view, the transforming manifestations of divine love (or, in psychological terms, the lifesaving intrusions of the Self) are rarely felt as gentle and nurturing in their immediate impact. So it is here for Dante.

138

137   Blake concentrates on the three steps that lead to the gate of Saint Peter: white marble, polished like a mirror; a dark cracked stone; and red porphyry, leading to the adamantine threshold where sits the guardian angel. The first step is that of contrition, where sinners must become aware and willing to see themselves as they really are; the second is that of the dark and painful upheaval of confession in the face of self-recognition; and the third is that of passionate commitment to atonement, red as blood. These Christian images parallel the need for courageous self-reflection, self-revelation, and commitment to change when entering serious therapy. The threshold is the firm foundation of Peter's Church.

138   An Italian manuscript of ca. 1365 shows a determined angel who marks the seven "P's" and opens the gate with two keys of gold and silver, the one of outer authority and the other of inner "art and skill" (IX, 125). The pilgrim understands that he is the penitent who must cleanse himself through all three stages from each of the seven sins. The angel bids him enter but warns him that "he / who would look back, returns—again—outside" (IX, 131–132). Any sentimental reaching back for the past at this crucial passage is a regression that will break off the forward movement of the inner process.

139   On the first terrace, as shown in this Italian manuscript, the pilgrim and his guide see the Proud, who can barely manage the weight of their heavy boulders. In atonement for imagining themselves to be above others, elevated by the ungrounded inflation of pride, they now willingly bear enormous rocks that bend them to earth. The punishment, as so often, represents the true character of the initial condition, a burdensome impediment to spiritual and psychological development.

140   The travelers come upon images of humility carved in relief. The Pisan illuminator of ca. 1385 portrays David dancing before the Ark of the Covenant as it is carried to Jerusalem, while in the tower window to the right his wife, Michal, scorns his lack of dignity.

141

141   Botticelli shows enormous rocks bringing the penitents to hands and knees, precisely as Dante describes (X, 132). He chooses to illustrate the instructional scenes, here of the Virgin Mary's humility before the angel of the Annunciation and of Trajan's empathic response to the mother's humble plea for her son. On each terrace a scene or story from the life of Mary is used as the leading example of the compensatory virtue.

Although both the medieval illuminators and Botticelli focus on images of the events the poet describes, the earlier renderings have the immediacy of simple sketches, whereas Botticelli's elegant line is both more sophisticated and more inclusive in its scope.

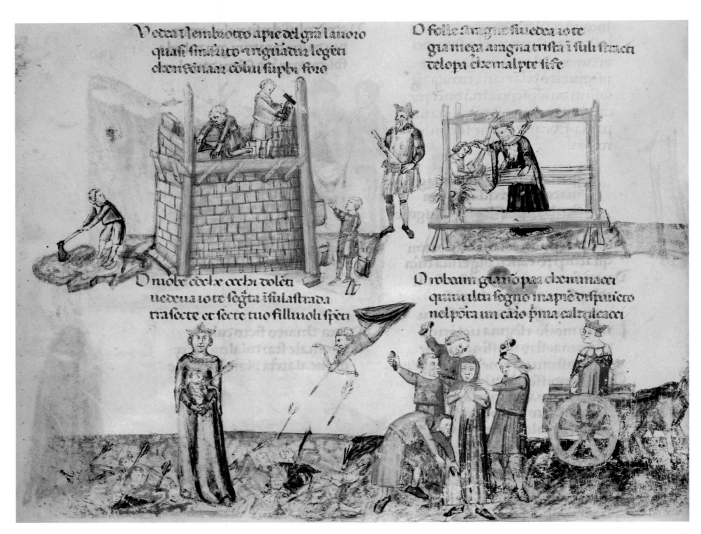

142, 143   Medieval artists were accustomed to teaching with narrative images and often rendered them with detailed relish. Here are two illustrations flowing from Dante's many stories of overweening pride and its horrific consequences. The first, by the Pisan illuminator of ca. 1385, depicts Nimrod, Arachne, Niobe, and Rehoboam. Dante mentions Rehoboam's flight by chariot (XII, 46–48), which was precipitated by the Israelites' rebellious stoning of Adoram, Rehoboam's tax enforcer (1 Kings 12:18). In his enthusiasm, the illuminator includes the stoning of Adoram, not mentioned by the poet, in addition to Rehoboam standing in his chariot. In the second illustration, from a fifteenth-century Italian manuscript, we see Saul pierced by his own sword, Arachne becoming a spider, Queen Tomyris plunging the head of Cyrus (who killed her son) into an urn full of blood, Rehoboam fleeing in his chariot, Sennacherib killed at prayer by his own sons, and the ruins of Troy.

    Teaching by example is a repeated technique in the *Purgatorio,* provided variously on each terrace by carvings, voices, and visions. Always Dante also presents some form of example of the virtue that opposes each sin and of the consequences of indulgence. Explorations in therapy of what it might feel like to do the opposite (thus, to disidentify from a complex) of the "sin" in question, or of what consequences might follow from a magnified indulgence, sometimes open a new level of awareness. Indeed, so can dreams.

144

144, 145, 146   These illustrations of the second terrace show its stony barrenness where the Envious sit, in coarse haircloth cloaks, their eyelids stitched shut with iron wire. All three illustrators—the later Pisan illuminator, Botticelli, and Guttuso—capture the attitude of the blind attending to the sound of a voice. Characteristically, the early illustrators include the pilgrim and his guide as they address the Envious, reminding us of the journey as a whole, whereas the modern artist focuses exclusively on the penitents' suffering. The image of atonement through enduring having one's eyelids wired shut operates at two levels: not only does blindness prevent the sinner from seeing what is enviable, but it also conveys the inability to see objectively that is the condition of the Envious.

145

146

147 In this Italian manuscript of ca. 1365, the voices who tell of examples of generosity are represented by naked figures flying through the air. They may be the artist's attempt to suggest the elevated character of inner voices that offer us a positive alternative.

147

148

148 In the same manuscript, on the next terrace, the third, the pilgrim holds onto Virgil's robe, unable to see in the smoke. The souls that suffer the sin of wrath are chanting a prayer to the Lamb of God. They are grateful that they can still hear. The image of smoke conveys both the implication of emotional fire that accompanies rage and the blinding impact of vicious anger on all those around it.

149

149   Among the
Wrathful, five of whom crouch low
to endure the smoke, Vecchietta
shows the angel of gentleness
appearing over the head of Marco
Lombardo, who stands before Dante
and Virgil to reply to the pilgrim's
question whether the world's cor-
ruption has its cause in Heaven or
on earth. Marco's long speech in
Canto XVI emphasizes the impor-
tance Dante places on personal
responsibility and political inte-
grity—values he also expressed in
making Cato the guardian of the
Mountain of Purgatory (see fig.
115).

150

150   Doré again provides atmospherics. One almost smells and tastes his smoke. The third figure is Marco Lombardo, who says, "I'll follow you as far as I'm allowed" (XVI, 34), while he expounds on the reality of free will. By placing Marco Lombardo's insistence "thus, if the present world has gone astray, / in you is the cause, in you it's to be sought" (XVI, 82–83) directly in the fiftieth canto (of one hundred) of the *Commedia*, the poet stresses that however much we are impressed by the cosmic transpersonal vision of his poem and by God's power over the universe, we must understand that human well-being and cosmic harmony are ultimately ours to win or lose. The conscious and responsible human ego is the determining weight on one side or the other of the scales of meaning, balanced in the purgatorial realm of mortal reality, that ultimately drops us into an infernal or a blessed life experience.

151   Guttuso is concerned with the wrathfulness of intolerance, correctly perceiving our inability to be open to diversity and inclusiveness when we are possessed by angry affect. His modern image renders what is psychologically implied by the sin atoned for in Purgatory, going beyond what the poet represents here to remind us of how the Wrathful submerged in the Stygian marsh kicked and butted each other in the fifth circle of the Inferno.

151

152   On the fourth terrace, the Slothful must run without stopping, as Botticelli shows with vigor. Running is an obvious corrective atonement for the physical inaction of sloth and conveys the commitment of energy that inner work requires. The spiritual sloth atoned for in Purgatory is as common today as in Dante's time, easily overlooked when hidden in the frenetic activity characteristic of modern life.

152

153

153   We have learned that time as we know it prevails on the Mountain of Purgatory, and the two travelers now lie down to sleep for the second night. The pilgrim has another dream. He encounters a sallow woman, "eyes askew, and crooked on her feet" (XIX, 8), with maimed hands. As he gazes, she becomes beautiful in his eyes. She stops stammering and begins to sing. But an "alert and saintly" woman (26) calls Virgil to expose the siren's putrid belly, and the stench awakens the pilgrim. To the right of the sleeping pilgrim Vecchietta shows both the siren (in her contorted form) and the haloed woman who reveals her. These contrasting figures suggest the fine distinctions to be drawn among the feminine elements competing for attention within the masculine psyche (see "Dream Two: The Siren's Call," below).

154   An angel of zeal appears. The pilgrim admits to his guide that the transformed woman in his dream has so beguiled him that he "cannot relinquish thoughts of it" (57), and Virgil assures him he can indeed now leave off thinking of "that ancient witch" (58) (who offers a fantasy of slothful pleasure that will cut short every quest) and redirect his sight upon the heavenly spheres. The Pisan illuminator of ca. 1385 uses the image of a ladder to depict the ascent to the next circle. As usual, his fine sense of dramatic shape informs each pictorial element.

155   Dante often uses the image of the falcon: here, in another illumination from the same manuscript, he compares the pilgrim—as he responds to Virgil's urgings—to the falcon, which "when the falconer has called, bends forward, / craving the food that's ready for him there" (65–66). You may remember that Dante also uses this image in a negative sense: in reference to Geryon, who descends and sets himself "embittered and enraged, far from his master" (*Inferno* XVII, 132).

Dream Two *The Siren's Call*   **Image 153**   The pilgrim dreams for the second time when he sleeps between the terraces of the Slothful and of the Avaricious and the Prodigal, midway up the mountain. It is a dream full of psychological acumen, revealing how the processes of projection, self-deception, and self-awareness operate in everyday life. Initially, Dante reports, "a stammering woman came to me in dream: / her eyes askew, and crooked on her feet, / her hands were crippled, her complexion sallow" (XIX, 7–9). At first sight, he sees her clearly enough, an unappetizing figure at best, but then:

> I looked at her; and just as sun revives
> cold limbs that night made numb, so did my gaze
> loosen her tongue and then, in little time,
>   set her contorted limbs in perfect order;
> and, with the coloring that love prefers,
> my eyes transformed the wanness of her features.
>   And when her speech had been set free, then she
> began to sing so, that it would have been
> most difficult for me to turn aside. (XIX, 10–18)

She tells him she is the pleasing siren who so satisfies her listeners that they break off their journey. The workings of projection are exactly rendered, for it is the pilgrim's gaze through rose-colored glasses, "with the coloring that love prefers," that makes the siren appear alluring, even though he has already observed her ugliness. She takes on an appearance derived from seeing in her something that comes not from her but from a hidden place in himself. She becomes, as we say, the hook on which he projects a part of his own soul, as we do when we fall in love.

But then in the dream another woman appears, "alert and saintly, / to cast the siren into much confusion" (26–27), and she calls upon Virgil for help. Virgil rips the seducer's clothes off, "showing me her belly; / the stench that came from there awakened me" (32–33). The truth-telling woman (who, the dream makes clear, now exists within the pilgrim's psyche) calls on the carrier of reason, experience, and understanding—also internalized—to expose the siren tendency. As if to be certain that we get the point, Virgil addresses the pilgrim's befuddlement when he wakes by telling him,

> "The one you saw . . . that ancient witch—
> for her alone one must atone above;
> you saw how man can free himself from her.
>   Let that suffice, and hurry on your way." (58–61)

By understanding what in ourselves is represented by the figures in our dreams, we can acknowledge our vulnerability to the siren-witch power, disrobing and exposing the shadow element for which "one must atone above," and thereby making it more amenable to our control.

The tasks assigned to the terraces of upper Purgatory include seeing a fantasy-laden obsession with sexuality for what it is, a kind of witch-possession. This is another of Dante's acknowledged sins. The dream occurs between the terrace of sloth, which lends itself to escapist fantasy, and the terraces of appetite, where the distractions of greed and lust are atoned. In the imagery of Purgatory, we learn from the conscious suffering of our vices what we need to free us from a blind or self-deceiving personal complex. Jung remarks that neurosis is a fraudulent or dishonest suffering (see, e.g., *CW* 17: para. 154), and here we see that we must suffer naked self-exposure if we are to deal honestly with our inner reality. The dream of the siren presents an example of how this works in the world of the "living," through a kind of self-analysis by the poet, just as it is done through the use of images by the atoning souls in Purgatory.

In *Dante's Poetry of Dreams*, Dino S. Cervigni astutely remarks on the pilgrim's moral backsliding in this dream, in the middle of the poem, and notes the emphasis placed here on his need for divine assistance from the "holy woman" (135). But Cervigni does not extend his commentary to the psychological significance of the pilgrim's dreams as inner experiences. A vivid regression such as this often marks the point just before a transition to a higher level of development. It is as if the complex, in this case Dante's acknowledged vulnerability to sexual fascination, counterattacks forcefully in a final struggle for supremacy. Paradoxically, when an individual's development has progressed this far, the violence of the wounded complex may then release a non-ego healing energy, "alert and saintly," that calls up from parallel depths the specific antidote required.

Whereas the first dream conveys the impersonal quality of positive archetypal energy through the nonhuman image of eagle power, the second dream presents a negative archetypal element in human guise, as witch or siren. The unconscious level the pilgrim encounters here is closer to human nature but still has a magical core that transcends human limitations. Her siren song is less fearful to the pilgrim than the eagle's power, yet it leaves him dangerously "beguiled" and preoccupied until the clear-eyed woman and Virgil make the interpretation clear.

aun fen leo tia men che lialtri eretto

156

156, 157   This late fourteenth-century Venetian illuminator calls attention to the angels who appear on every terrace; the first had reassured the pilgrim that from this point on the climb would be easier. Unlike a real mountain peak, the curve of the Mountain of Purgatory becomes gentler toward the summit. Inner travelers often find that after a certain degree of struggle, the more accustomed they become to attending to the depth level where dream and fantasy contribute, the easier it is to go forward. On one of the higher terraces an angel encourages the pilgrims, affirming that these stairs are less steep than those before, and another angel shows them a way between the rocks. With the brush of a wing, the angels remove a "P" at the end of each purgative experience. Besides providing much-needed encouragement, these interventions from the realm of the spirit help the ego to clarify the beginning and end of important stages in the inner work, to help it hold onto the knowledge gained.

157

158   On the fifth terrace, Doré shows the pilgrim's empathy for the Avaricious and the Prodigal, who lie face downward weeping. The souls here "cleave to the dust" (XIX, 73) as a corrective for—and emblem of—their excessive attachment to material things. Doré does not take literally the sufferer's statement to the pilgrim: "justice here / fetters our hands and feet and holds us captive" (123–124).

159 Hugh Capet talks to Dante openly and sadly of the avariciousness of his sons. This is a thoughtful exploration of inheritance and how children can betray the hard-won ethical development of their parents (rather than having to struggle out of and beyond a parental lack of awareness). Inwardly, it could be put that a gifted individual can be betrayed by the underdeveloped parts of the personality that may become dominant in a later time. In the Venetian manuscript the purgatorial figures, usually portrayed naked, are fashionably dressed, and the three youthful figures behind Hugh Capet may represent his sons.

160 On this terrace, the travelers meet Statius. The ancient poet who modeled his major poem after the *Aeneid* embraces Virgil with great emotion when he discovers who he is. It is poignant that Statius, whose secret Christianity is, so far as is known, an invention of Dante, pays tribute to Virgil's Fourth Eclogue for having instigated his conversion. He says to his mentor, "You did as he who goes by night and carries / the lamp behind him—he is of no help / to his own self but teaches those who follow—/ . . . . Through you I was a poet and, through you, / a Christian" (XXII, 67–69, 73–74). Botticelli shows the penitents bound hand and foot, as Dante describes them, making the suffering seem more arduous.

159

160

162 Botticelli's tree, "tapered downward" and fully inverted, is laden with the fruit of grace (which cannot be grasped). The tree is both a reproach and a goad to their longing for grace. The souls here pray for their mouths to be opened to give praise. We recall in contrast the infernal circle of the Gluttonous, guarded by Cerberus, lashed with freezing and filthy rain.

162

161

161 The strange trees of the sixth terrace, where the Gluttonous atone, inspired this imaginative Italian illuminator of the late fourteenth-century. This is his way of depicting the tree that blocked the way and demanded attention: "that tree there tapered downward, / so as—I think—to ward off any climber" who would seek access to its sweet fruit (XXII, 134–135). The artist cuts off the lower branches to create the forbidding taper but leaves the tree rooted in the ground. A voice from within the branches—here given an open-mouthed face—makes the denial of food explicit and names examples of moderation and temperance: Mary at Cana, the matrons of Republican Rome, and Daniel, who refused Nebuchadnezzar's food and drink. Virgil and Statius do a convincing and humorous double-take beneath the tree from which the voice descends and over which "bright running water fell from the high rock" (137).

163

163, 164 Vecchietta and Guttuso emphasize the starved bodies of the penitent souls, Guttuso in an exaggerated way that brings concentration camp survivors to mind, as well as the horror of pathological sacrifice. Those who are starved involuntarily are the victims either of others' pathology, as in the camps, or of their own false penance, like the victims of anorexia. Both pathologies are hellish, but on the purgatorial mountain the penitents suffer conscious knowledge of their greedy self-indulgence and cheerfully, though painfully, accept atonement (see "Torment and Atonement," below). Guttuso's image attends the suffering vividly but seems to miss its redemptive character, neglecting here the balanced metaphor of this part of the poem.

164

Torment and Atonement *Two Kinds of Suffering in the* Commedia

Images 24–25, 161–164   Hell is full of suffering. Each of the torments of the damned reflects with some precision the nature of the sin that is punished: the uncommitted, stung relentlessly by pursuing wasps, run after ever-wavering banners just as they had no goals of their own in life; the lustful are swept away in a whirlwind, as they were swept away by uncontrollable passion; the murderers are immersed in boiling blood as they immersed themselves in bloody violence; and the most heartless traitors of all are fixed in an ice that reveals the frozen and loveless condition of their souls in this world. The many-layered images of each torment illuminate graphically the psychological and moral depravity, the injuries to self and others, that comprise human evil.

The souls gradually ascending the Mountain of Purgatory also suffer, often extremely, but in the ways the poet images their suffering he makes moral and spiritual distinctions of great psychological subtlety. Some of these are stated in the twenty- third canto of the *Purgatorio*. There, on the sixth terrace of the mountain, the pilgrim encounters his old friend Forese Donati among those atoning for the sin of gluttony (see figs. 161–164), and their exchange underscores the difference between the meaningful suffering of the saved, in Purgatory, and the punitive suffering of the damned, in Hell.

Gluttony is punished in the third circle of the Inferno. There, those who were mired in gluttony in life and died unrepentant continue thus in Hell, gobbling up the filthy, frozen slush that perpetually falls on them. Their unbounded greed for more nourishment than life requires is mirrored by their torment, which expresses the cold, life-denying sterility of their obsession with oral pleasures. The hunger of their hearts and souls has been displaced on gratifications that cannot truly nourish. More deeply understood, they get in death what they sought in life. In modern life, gluttonous eating is perhaps less common than compulsive buying, but sterile displacement of the soul's hunger lies at the core of both.

For the gluttons who suffer on the terrace with Forese Donati, appetite is equally keen. All endure sharp pangs of hunger and thirst for the scented fruits of the purgatorial tree. Forese reports to his friend:

> The fragrance of the fruit and of the water
> that's sprayed through that green tree kindles in us
> craving for food and drink; and not once only,
>   as we go round this space, our pain's renewed (XXIII, 67–70),

for intense longing makes the sinners aware ever and again of the depth of their desire. But here the yearning is not indulged; rather, it is completely unfulfilled. Starved, these souls appear "so emaciated that / their taut skin took its shape from bones beneath" (XXIII, 23–24) and the "orbits of / their eyes seemed like a ring that's lost its gems" (30–31). So wasted away is Forese that only when he speaks does the pilgrim recognize him.

As he continues his address, Forese makes the distinction that decisively separates the damned from those in Purgatory:

> as we go round this space, our pain's renewed—
> I speak of pain but I should speak of solace,

> for we are guided to those trees by that
>
>   same longing that had guided Christ when He
>
> had come to free us through the blood He shed
>
> and, in His joyousness, called out: "Eli." (70–75)

The reference is to Christ's final words, "My God, my God, why have you forsaken me?" (Matt. 27:46), his extreme moment of both suffering and commitment. The pain of purgation is similar to Jesus' acceptance of the call to sacrifice his life in order to free humanity from sin. Like his suffering, and unlike the torments of the damned, the pain of those being purged is willingly accepted and endured in full awareness of its meaning. They have come to understand in time the significance of their hunger, whose true object is the sacred goal of their ascent. As Christ's yearning was to make possible the salvation of humankind, so each soul who rises from terrace to terrace, bearing his or her own cross, carries forward one individual's part of that great work. The atoners suffer acutely from keen desire for imagined fruits they will never taste, but they bear it as "solace" in confident knowledge that their starved yearning will find its true object when their atonement is fulfilled.

A few lines later, the poet has the pilgrim emphasize again the purpose of purgatorial suffering, affirming "the good grief that succors us / and weds us once again to God" (81–82). This is the point. In Purgatory, the sinners are not blind to their sin; they feel it intensely. But their suffering is known to be a blessed grief that will unite them in oneness with God when sufficient time has passed.

There is profound psychological meaning in the sometimes excruciating pain of purgatorial suffering: the crushing stones borne by the proud, the choking smoke enveloping the wrathful, the fire hotter than molten glass searing the lustful. Those who are saved are not sinless—far from it. Rather, they are those who have come in time to know and take responsibility for the shadow qualities that split their personalities and cause them to act destructively toward themselves and others.

The secret of salvation in Dante's world is neither repression nor perfect obedience to the commandments. It is insight into the nature of who one is, how one injures, what it feels like to be oneself the victim and to make others the targets of one's desirousness, rage, pride, and deceits. Those who make it to Purgatory are not less shadow-driven, narcissistic, obsessed, or pathological than others, but they have not refused to make conscious what they are, to bear the burden of themselves, and to come in time to take full responsibility for their own natures. By coming to know what operates in us behind appearances, whether driven by unconscious instinct and aggression or by more deliberate betrayal, we can choose to take a stand against whatever in our personal character moves us to wound others and our larger selves.

Atonement, the poet says in many ways, takes time; the passage of time is central to the work of purgation. Because the pilgrim knows that Forese had come to consciousness of his deformed appetite only at the end of his life, he wonders how his friend has moved so quickly to this terrace near the top of the Mountain of Purgatory: "I thought to find / you down below, [among the late-repentant] where time must pay for time" (XXIII, 83–84). In response, Forese explains that this is the work of his wife, "my

Nella who / with her abundant tears, has guided me / to drink the sweet wormwood of torments" (85–87). In his imagined afterworld, the poet makes it clear, only one effective exchange is possible between the living and the dead: the prayers of the living can substantially shorten the time required for those in Purgatory to complete their ascent.

It is psychologically true that a new level of self-awareness can be achieved only with sustained effort over an extended time, but how much time depends in part, Dante asserts, on the attitude of those who are central in our lives. Taken objectively, this expresses the reality that the caring concern of those who love us can accelerate our growth and act as a catalyst for inner healing. Taken subjectively—in terms of what we can do for ourselves—prayerful engagement by the ego with the inner figures of parent, beloved, or child, as a means of reaching out to the larger powers that seek our development, often moves the process more swiftly.

For those in Hell, however, time has a markedly different aspect. Tormented forever by punishments that reflect the inner realities of their passions, violence, and betrayals, the damned have no awareness of time present. They may see into the future, but as it approaches they lose all cognizance of its reality. Just as they lacked empathy and a feeling connection to others in real time, so those stuck in Hell are enveloped in a narcissism that shuts out knowledge of the contemporaneous world. Instead, as is often the case with persons driven by pathology, they may have an uncanny sense of what possibilities lurk ahead but lack a sound relation to life and persons as they are. How well we know this from the perceptions of those who are paranoid!

This is what Dante conveys by presenting those in Hell as unable to know the present. They can see into the future, but in their bitter refusal to grow and develop they are denied access to what they see, frozen out of time forever. In Purgatory, on the other hand, time present becomes time future, and night and day, stillness and movement, sleeping and waking flow into each other as they do in life. The cyclicality of organic life is fully reflected in the *Purgatorio*.

Indeed, although the *Commedia* overtly sets all its images in afterlife, the psychological world of Purgatory reflects lived experience, especially as we strive to make it conscious. Not only is purgation governed by the natural rhythms of time, but it is also the realm of every kind of awareness. In its action, the poet includes thought and reflection, vision and reverie, dream and fantasy, focused attention and even wandering distraction. But when he becomes distracted, Virgil or, later, Beatrice chides the pilgrim for his inattention, for the poet repeatedly stresses that consciousness in the largest sense is the primary requirement for spiritual development.

165   The lustful souls move in a kind of dance within the fire giving each other brief kisses as they pass. They chant and sing the names and stories of the chaste, in strong contrast to Francesca (*Inferno*, Canto V), who dwells on the pitiful tale of her mutual seduction with Paolo and their murder by her husband.

       As usual, but especially in this case, this masterful Botticelli drawing bears careful scrutiny, each tiny line a part of the beautifully conceived whole. Botticelli, like Blake, was deeply involved with the *Commedia* in the maturity of a long, creative life. A particular tenderness seems to have gone into his encounter with Dante, most affectingly in the way he develops the subtle relationship between Dante and Beatrice in the *Paradiso*.

165

166 Blake's angel shows the way as Dante wrings his hands while Virgil and Statius urge him on with raised arms. The "happy" angel tells them: "Holy souls, you cannot move ahead / unless the fire has stung you first: enter / the flames, and don't be deaf to song you'll hear / beyond" (XXVII, 10–13). Feeling "laid within the grave," the pilgrim says, "I joined my hands and stretched them out to fend / the flames, watching the fire, imagining / clearly the human bodies I'd once seen / burning" (15–19). Virgil reassures him by noting that "though there may be / suffering here, there is no death" (20–21). Even so, Dante stubbornly refuses to pass through the fire until Virgil reminds him that Beatrice is beyond these flames.

166

167 And here is Blake's splendid rendering of Virgil beckoning to Dante from the flames. The pilgrim observes that the flames were so intense that he'd have thrown himself "in molten glass to find / coolness" (XXVII, 50–51). Blake apparently used the Four Muses, the "daughters of inspiration," as guides, representing the demands of the "divine imagination" that he felt Dante feared. The text actually speaks of one guiding voice, as Dante, Virgil, and Statius emerge from the flames, that sings, "*Venite, benedicti Patris mei*" (58), in allusion to the invitation Christ will issue to the blessed (Matt. 25:34) at the Last Judgment. The voice comes from within a light so intense that Dante cannot bear to look at it, a characteristic of divine numinosity that persists for the pilgrim until he has ascended through most of the celestial spheres.

Although progression up the Mountain of Purgatory generally becomes easier as the ascent proceeds, the precarious pathway around the terrace of the Lustful underscores its difficulty:

> There, from the wall, the mountain hurls its flames;
> but, from the terrace side, there whirls a wind
> that pushes back the fire and limits it;
>   thus, on the open side, proceeding one
> by one, we went; I feared the fire on
> the left and, on the right, the precipice.
>   My guide said: "On this terrace, it is best
> to curb your eyes: the least distraction—left
> or right—can mean a step you will regret." (XXV, 112–120)

This is that rare place in the pilgrim's all-seeing journey where Virgil urges him to "curb your eyes," and we recall perhaps the terrifying prospect of seeing Medusa at the Gate of Dis, another great transition point.

Now all attention must be concentrated within, for there is a fearsome risk of losing one's balance. What is suggested symbolically is not only that the fire is fierce but also that the risk of falling is profound. As Dante has recently experienced the seductive power of the fascinating dream-siren, the image conveys the knife-edge risks of falling again into the unconscious,

167

on one hand, and of being scorched terribly by lurching prematurely into the fire, on the other. The way must be carefully prepared and the ego focused on the task at hand with intense inner concentration—indeed, it is yet two more cantos before the passage is achieved.

168   Having traversed the refining fire, Dante and Statius sleep while Virgil watches, and Dante dreams of Leah and Rachel (images of the active and contemplative religious life), depicted by Blake within the full moon (see "Leah's Mirror," below).

168

169   The strength of Botticelli's simple lines delineating the figures of Statius, Virgil, and the pilgrim celebrates the transitional event he depicts. Here Virgil places a laurel wreath on Dante's head, having told him: "you have reached / the place past which my powers cannot see" (XXVII, 128–129),

> Await no further word or sign from me:
> your will is free, erect, and whole—to act
> against that will would be to err: therefore
> I crown and miter you over yourself. (139–142)

The poet makes very clear here that in order to bear the dialogue with representatives of the illumination that is to come, the ego must be strongly developed in everything Virgil represents.

Dream Three *Leah's Mirror*   **Images 168–169**   In the third dream, the central figure is no longer threatening at all and has instead an emphatically appealing human character (see fig. 168). At the end of his climb up the Mountain of Purgatory, having passed through the fires that convey the fiercely cleansing power of love at its most intense (the pain that accompanies the task of learning detachment for the sake of truly objective caring, the opposite of narcissistic lust), Dante is overcome by sleep: "sleep, which often sees, / before it happens, what is yet to be" (XXVII, 92–93).

> . . . in my dream, I seemed to see a woman
> both young and fair; along a plain she gathered
> flowers, and even as she sang, she said:
> "Whoever asks my name, know that I'm Leah,
> and I apply my lovely hands to fashion
> a garland of the flowers I have gathered.
> To find delight within this mirror I
> adorn myself; whereas my sister Rachel
> never deserts her mirror; there she sits
> all day; she longs to see her fair eyes gazing,
> as I, to see my hands adorning, long:
> she is content with seeing, I with labor." (97–108)

Here is a beguiling figure with no terrifying power or deceitful allure. She reveals, as dreams also do, not the risky or dangerous potential that lies hidden from daylit awareness but the potential for greater completeness that is yet to be claimed but is now at the threshold of the pilgrim's development. The Leah figure foreshadows Matilda, whom Dante will soon encounter, who in turn precedes the longed-for meeting with Beatrice. It is significant that Dante has chosen Leah for this role, not her sister, Rachel, who was preferred by Jacob. Leah, the plainer yet prolific mother of most of Jacob's sons, is every inch a human woman, not the object of alluring fantasy. It is she who represents Dante's human soul as he approaches psychological maturity and readiness to enter the Earthly Paradise.

Leah, her words make clear, has a preference for the active life, gathering, fashioning, and adorning, whereas Rachel spends her day in contemplation: "she is content with seeing, I with labor" (108). Yet they are both accompanied by mirrors and both engage in reflection (as Helen Luke points out), Leah appreciating the incarnate product of her labors, Rachel gazing into her own eyes. They are concerned with meaning—with reflection in its deeper senses, not in narcissistic self-absorption—but for Leah, delight in the decorative work of her "lovely hands" is its own reward. This is the stage that the pilgrim has achieved, ready now to move into the realms where he will require a spiritually centered, more inward guide.

Virgil now gives Dante his parting blessing, acknowledging that his role as guide "through intellect and art" (130) has come to an end. He stresses that, having learned from observation of "the temporary fire / and the eternal fire" (127–128) in Purgatory and Hell, the pilgrim has achieved a degree of self-sufficiency that makes his will "free, erect, and whole" (140; see fig. 169). From Virgil's point of view, he is ready to "let your pleasure be your guide" (131), reminding us of Saint Augustine's advice to the faithful: "Choose, and do what thou wilt." (Augustine is commenting on 2 John 6, that the commandment to "follow love" means "Dilige"—choose lovingly—"et quod vis fac.") Put psychologically, it is as if he has worked through to an appreciation of both his personal and the broadly human shadow worlds and has undertaken conscious responsibility for his own dark places.

From observing the many modes in which we may become stuck determinedly in desirousness, hostility, aggression, deceit, and betrayal, unwilling to suffer the lash of self-awareness, the pilgrim has moved through the terraces of penitence where he, among the others being purged and in his own way one of them, witnesses the conscious and voluntary suffering that recognition brings. He is no longer at risk of being carried away or seduced by archetypal energies. He is capable of enactment in reality, as the choice of Leah as a soul figure makes clear, and also of contemplating the meanings of what he does and what he sees.

Passage through the refining fire of the final terrace of the Mountain of Purgatory is a great transition, a kind of baptism by fire that releases the pilgrim to approach a higher level. Virgil as guide may also pass the fire into which the angel calls the travelers, yet he can go no further than the lower bank of Lethe. Nor can Dante make the next crossing until in great sorrow he earns his baptism in Lethe's waters. To Virgil, he is quite complete—"therefore / I crown and miter you over yourself" (141–142)—but Beatrice will not yet be nearly so pleased with him.

170   Now the travelers approach the Earthly Paradise. The Sacred Wood is described as dense, although the poet notes that the newly flowered branches move easily in the breeze. Botticelli draws an inviting open appearance of straight young saplings. Dante takes the lead for the first time and entreats the solitary woman he sees across the stream to approach and speak to him. She does, graciously describing in rich detail the plants and waters and breezes there. She sets the tone of the Earthly Paradise when the pilgrim first enters it in Canto XXVIII, but it is only in Canto XXXIII that we learn her name is Matilda (see "The Wood of the Earthly Paradise," below). Botticelli's ability to convey the graceful power of spiritual feminine energy begins to be visible here.

171   Blake reveals the whole splendid procession in which the chariot containing Beatrice appears (adding two angels at the head of the retinue). Dante, with Virgil and Statius behind him, speaks with Matilda across the River Lethe. The Heavenly Pageant is led by a seven-branched golden candelabrum (looking like trees, from a distance) that paints a seven-striped rainbow on the sky. Behind it come twenty-four elders (the books of the Old Testament), four beasts (the four Gospels) who guard a chariot (the Church) drawn by a griffin (the two natures of Christ) in which Beatrice sits, veiled. The griffin's wings rise so high that they are lost to sight. At the right wheel dance the three Theological Virtues (Faith, Hope, and Charity), at the left the four Cardinal Virtues (Prudence, Temperance, Justice, and Fortitude). Next come two elders (Luke and Paul) then four more elders (James, Peter, John, and Jude), then a single elder (John of Revelation). When the chariot draws opposite Dante, there is a thunder clap and every-thing halts. Dante describes the ringing shouts of "Hosanna!" and the singing, to Beatrice, as with one voice: "You, among the daughters / of Adam, *benedicta* are; and may / your beauties blessed be eternally" (XXIX, 85–87). "Benedicta" here echoes the words of the angel to Mary (in the Vulgate, Luke 1:28), much as *"Benedictus qui venis"* (XXX, 19) echoes the greeting to Christ when he entered Jerusalem (see "The Wood of the Earthly Paradise," below).

171

172

172   The twenty-four elders walk two by two (says the poet—the illuminator has them almost four by four), crowned with lilies and singing, in an Italian manuscript of the late fourteenth century. John sleeps, at lower right, in front of the four epistle-writers, and behind them are balanced Luke and Paul. The ritually emblematic style of the medieval artist is much in evidence here, including the stained-glass look of the seven figures in the right-hand quadrant.

173 In an Emilian (or Paduan; Peter Brieger et al. are unsure) manuscript of the second quarter of the fourteenth century, the two-wheeled chariot becomes a decorated farmer's wagon, but the griffin accurately shows its golden eagle foreparts (Christ's divinity) and its red and white lion hindparts (his humanity). Carefully depicted are the seven Virtues and the seven Elders, including John of Revelation, who appears to be nodding off. What Dante says is that "when all the rest had passed, a lone old man, / his features keen, advanced, as if in sleep" (XXIX, 143–144), to suggest the inwardness of his vision. Both illuminators include John with the others and emphasize his drowsiness with a markedly different posture rather than the separateness that would be harder to fit within the frame. The homely simplicity of the Emilian and the emblematic directness of the late fourteenth-century Italian illuminator both contrast in their two-dimensional focus with the more visionary depth and scope of Botticelli and Blake.

173

174   Blake adds several touches of his own in this grand image. Milton Klonsky (often following Albert Roe) discusses the symbolic meaning to Blake of many of these (*Blake's Dante*, 158–159). One of the three Theological Virtues has five babies (emblematic of the vegetative senses) that seem generated by a vortex, like that in Ezekiel, a wheel in the middle of a wheel, full of eyes. Blake gives a nimbus to each of the four creatures of Ezekiel that traditionally came to represent the Evangelists. (In his *Four Zoas*, Blake equates the Man with creative imagination, the Lion with reason, the Ox with love, and the Eagle with the physical body.) Beatrice is shown here as an unveiled, sensuous natural woman, and she is given a gold crown for good measure. Note how the pilgrim hangs his head in distress as he receives Beatrice's rebuke. Apparently he is already across the river, in direct contradiction to Dante's narrative, in which the pilgrim's remorseful response to her censure is a precondition of the crossing.

174

Chossi centro una nuuola di fiori.
che dele mam angeliche saluia
en chatoeua in gui centro e di fuori.
Socto cinoroeo uel cintra d uliua.
donna ma parue socto uerde manto.
uestita di color di fiamma uiua.

e lo spirito

175

175   The Neapolitan illuminator of the late fourteenth century presents Beatrice supported by angels in a mandorla. By association with the frequently used image of the figure of Christ within a mandorla frame, the illustrator emphasizes Dante's allusions to Beatrice's Christlike power. Standing before Beatrice, the pilgrim reveals his astonished dismay in the face of her censure. The reader feels Dante's extraordinary power to express both joyous heights and poignant depths of emotion throughout this canto.

176   As Beatrice launches into a full-scale reprimand of Dante for the improper use of his gifts, the angel choir overhead breaks into a song of compassion. He weeps and swoons, and wakes in Matilda's arms, as she pulls him through Lethe and makes him drink, to wipe away all memory of his sins. The four Cardinal Virtues take him to Beatrice—all this action is displayed at once by Botticelli. He suggests the infinite height of the griffin's wings by having them break through the lines of the sky, an unusual device that underscores the numinosity of the great pageant.

176

Uaa ou abi diltanti e monenti
oun moto pria ll monia di fame
che libero homo lun rechaffe ardenti
Si ll llarebbe un agno itra oue brame
oi fan lupi igualmente temendo
ll ll llarebbe un cane intra oue oame.
Perche llo mi taca me non riprendo
oa li mei oubii oun moto ll ll pinto

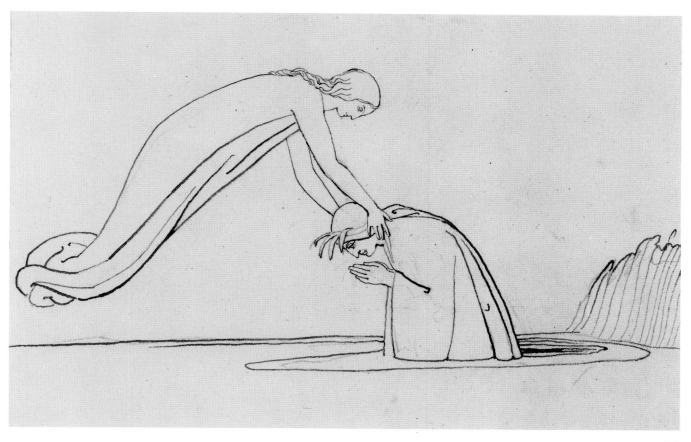

177   An early fifteenth-century Paduan illuminator's almost comic artistry, with darts from Beatrice's eyes tipping over the pilgrim, emphasizes the power of her gaze. This illumination actually illustrates her glance of love, in the first Heaven of the Moon in Paradise, but it might equally well represent the sting in the look that causes the pilgrim to swoon here. It will be many cantos into the *Paradiso* before the pilgrim can bear the full attention of her eyes without being overcome.

178   Flaxman gives us a spare view of the Lethe scene with Matilda, whom he shows floating more like a spirit than the earthly woman Dante presents. Flaxman's economy of style is easy to read but sometimes points up the rich complexity of Dante's, which Botticelli especially captures.

179   Botticelli shows the next events: the griffin binds the chariot to the tree of good and evil, which bursts into leaf and flower. Then Dante witnesses an enactment of the corruption of the Church. An eagle, a fox, and a dragon attack the chariot, which then turns into a seven-headed beast carrying a giant and a harlot. Dante's distress with the corruption of the Church is imaginatively rendered with great emphasis here in the Earthly Paradise and underscores the latent evil that is always present in utopian or edenic fantasies.

It is noteworthy that this allegory of collective evil follows not long after the pilgrim's regression in his dream of the siren. We are constantly reminded of Dante's deep concern for collective as well as individual welfare and of his powerful conviction that spiritual leadership should not be joined to worldly power. A modern pilgrim's equivalent might be the regression that can come at the most developed stages of inner work, or the kind of exaggerated image a dream throws out in warning when temptation is particularly strong. These convey the need for a morally alert as well as a strong ego in the pursuit of true self-knowledge: a developed ego, especially in a position of leadership, is also capable of more destructive abuse if there is a regression to shadow-driven greed or violence.

180 Blake's chariot puts forth heads—three oxen-horned, four uni-horned. The giant is about to beat the roving-eyed harlot in jealousy and rage. Dante's imagery comes from Revelation 13:1 and 17:3ff. Blake shows the harlot "holding a gold winecup filled with the disgusting filth of her fornication" and suggests that "she was drunk, drunk with the blood of the saints" (Rev. 17:4, 6). Dante's allegory of the corrupt popes' adulterous dalliance with worldly power is abundantly clear, though readings of the specific details are varied.

180

181 Flaxman's version is rather dry when compared with Blake's, and the harlot looks childishly innocent. His power to render emotions is limited, and here he leaves out one of the seven heads.

181

182

182 An Italian manuscript of the late fourteenth century depicts a fountain that is the self-renewing source not only of Lethe and Eunoe but also of the four rivers of Paradise. The double river is Dante's invention. The pilgrim says he sees the source where the seven Virtues halt, "at the edge / of a dense shadow" (XXXIII, 109–110) as of a mountain. There Beatrice chides him again and even teases him a bit, and then she instructs Matilda to lead him to drink of Eunoe. (*Eu*, "good, with *nous*, "mind," means "memory of the good": in psychological terms, one has examined the texture of one's developmental history, discarding the threads that are not truly one's own, so that one grasps and "remembers" the unique pattern of an individual life.)

183 The pilgrim is dunked in Eunoe; Botticelli returns to the forest of slenderly graceful trees with which his vision of the Earthly Paradise began (see fig. 170).

> If, reader, I had ampler space in which
> to write, I'd sing—though incompletely—that
> sweet draught for which my thirst was limitless;
>   but since all of the pages predisposed
> for this, the second canticle, are full,
> the curb of art will not let me continue.
>   From that most holy wave I now returned
> to Beatrice; remade, as new trees are
> renewed when they bring forth new boughs, I was
>   pure and prepared to climb unto the stars. (XXXIII, 136–145)

Matilda

The pilgrim now approaches the third wood of the *Commedia*, the Wood of the Earthly Paradise. It is, mythologically, the wood of unfallen Man, the Eden of the age of innocence at the time of creation. For Dante, however, it is not a prior condition but an experience that follows the journey through the Inferno and Purgatory. He has suffered the Woods of Depression and Despair and now earned access to the pleasing wood that forms the summit of the Mountain of Purgatory (see fig. 170).

Here the atmosphere is subject no longer to mundane weather, only to the gentle breezes generated by the motion of the heavenly spheres. The emotional atmosphere is one of joy, to which a singing woman gathering flowers gives chastely erotic voice. Matilda, as we later learn her name to be, echoes and enlarges the image of Leah in Dante's dream and volunteers to help him understand: "I have come ready / for all your questions till you're satisfied" (XXVIII, 83–84; see fig. 171).

What is striking in view of Dante's yearning devotion to Beatrice, whom he knows from Virgil he is soon to meet, is the profound allure Matilda has for him. He addresses her as "lovely lady, you who warm / yourself with rays of love" (43–44); tells her she reminds him of Persephone as she tempted Hades; sees in her eyes the light of Venus smitten with love for Adonis; compares his desire to reach her with Leander's urge to cross the Hellespont; and tells us that she sings "like an enamored woman" (XXIX, 2, in language that echoes the contemporary love poetry of his friend Guido Cavalcanti). Thus Dante makes it plain that the energy that reaches out to Matilda is unabashedly erotic—but it is eros in the service of transformation, for what Matilda sings is "*Beati quorum tecta sunt peccata!*" (3), "Blessed are they whose sins are forgiven."

Matilda represents the lure of a soulmate who calls us inwardly to the Quest, the promise of loving connection to soul and spirit that encourages the depth of humiliating confession and self-acceptance required before the deepest transformation can take place. In the image of Matilda, the joyful magnetism of Paradise, both earthly and heavenly, is evoked; we feel it bodily even as we are continuously aware that all Matilda stands for is sacred, not profane. As one student of the poem put it, "Matilda, in love with God, in her infectious joy lures the soul back to the fullness of divine unity." Thus we feel not that Dante has surprisingly betrayed his loyalty to Beatrice (as he is tempted to do in dreaming of the siren) but that Matilda is part of the higher world of love the pilgrim is about to enter. She evokes in him (and the reader) a passionate aspiration that he will sorely need when at last he does stand before Beatrice.

Beatrice

Beatrice appears to the pilgrim in a guise so laden with scriptural associations that she takes on divine authority—in images that suggested heresy to some guardians of sound theology in Dante's time. She is borne in a chariot drawn by a griffin and preceded by a procession that overtly alludes both to the procession in the Christian book of Revelation and to its source in the Old Testament description of the "throne" bearing "something that looked like the glory of Yahweh" in Ezekiel (1:28; see figs. 171–176).

Before this point in the poem, we are aware of Dante's passionate desire to see his long-lost love; we know of the heavenly compassion that has led Mary to urge Lucia to press Beatrice to seek out Virgil to lead Dante on his journey; and we have every reason to trust in Beatrice's goodwill as the driving energy of the pilgrim's salvation. But we are not prepared for the spirit in which she first encounters the object of her care. Beginning to recognize her veiled presence, the poet feels "the mighty power of old love" (XXX, 39) and turns to share his tremulous joy with Virgil, only to discover that Virgil, his task completed, has quietly departed. Grief dispels his joy and brings tears to his eyes. To this Beatrice responds—as her initial greeting—with unexpected fierceness:

> Dante, though Virgil's leaving you, do not
> yet weep, do not weep yet; you'll need your tears
> for what another sword must yet inflict. (55–57)

"Regal and disdainful" (70), she chides him mercilessly for having failed to live up to the potential inherent in his devotion to her, a magnet that might have drawn him on more swiftly to his goal if he had allowed himself to "know that man is happy here" (75). She accuses him of betraying her and of following "counterfeits of goodness" (131) in the secular world instead. She tells the angels, who would be more compassionate, of her exasperation and says that

> . . . I'm more concerned that my reply
> be understood by him who weeps beyond,
> so that his sorrow's measure match his sin. (106–108)

The "sin" to which she refers is not so much the specific moral failures observed and expiated to Virgil's satisfaction before this transition but rather, from Beatrice's transpersonal perspective, "the refusal of the responsibility of joy and freedom on the threshold of a new awareness," as Helen Luke puts it (105). The contrast between Virgil's parting encomium (XXVII, 127–142) and Beatrice's accusatory greeting throws into sharp relief the difference between a classical view of personal responsibility, in essentially ethical terms, and a sacred concern for psychological and spiritual transformation. Approaching such a joy is difficult for the developed ego to "deign" to do (Beatrice asks, in the Italian, "*come degnasti d'accedere al monte?*" XXX, 74), and it is only fully valuing all that Beatrice stands for that makes it possible.

When the pilgrim bursts into tears and Beatrice wrings from him confession that "Mere appearances / turned me aside with their false loveliness, / as soon as I had lost your countenance" (XXXI, 34–36), it softens her fierceness momentarily, for

> . . . when the charge of sinfulness has burst
> from one's own cheek, then in our court the whet-
> stone turns and blunts our blade's own cutting edge. (40–42)

But soon she returns to the attack. With a very human sense of her own worth, Beatrice reminds him that her beauty and appeal should have been sufficient so that "No green young girl or other novelty— / such brief delight—should have weighed down your wings" (58–59). Overwhelmed with remorse, Dante can only look down in silence, while Beatrice tells him to "lift up / your beard, and sight will bring you greater tears" (68–69). He observes, "I knew quite well—when she said 'beard' but meant / my face—the poison in her argument" (74–75); looking up, he sees that now

> Beneath her veil, beyond the stream, she seemed
> so to surpass her former self in beauty
> as, here on earth, she had surpassed all others. (82–84)

In response, remorse and "self-indictment" so overwhelm the pilgrim that he faints. Beatrice has achieved her intention that he discharge the debt of penitence in full.

In trying to suggest something of the subtle intertwining of transpersonal and personal levels of psychic experience in this great and long-awaited encounter between the poet and his beloved, one can only skim the surface of what is conveyed in Cantos XXIX–XXXI of the *Purgatorio*. On one hand, Beatrice is forcefully presented as the symbolic equivalent of deity: not only does she appear in the chariot of Ezekiel and Revelation, but Dante compares her explicitly to Christ, for the elders of the procession introduce Beatrice's appearance by crying, "*Benedictus qui venis*" (XXX, 19), almost precisely the language (in the Vulgate) with which the multitude welcomes Christ's entry into Jerusalem (Matt. 21:9). Although Dante has changed "venit" to "venis," so that the phrase reads "Blessed are you who come" rather than "he who comes," he has left the masculine form of "Benedictus" unchanged; the allusion to the Gospel is unequivocal.

Unlike Christ, however, the divine figure here is human in both her parents. Not only is she a human person with divine stature, she is quintessentially a woman as well—more than enough to evoke a charge of heresy from a traditional point of view. In fact, as Dante here becomes fully a participant, not just a witness, in the moral and psychological action of his poem, all of those who speak and do for him in the Earthly Paradise are women. The poet's insight into how a deep approach to psychic wholeness takes place for a man is psychologically both acute and modern. The Self, as Jung remarked, cares not for our comfort but only for our wholeness; it often requires us to undergo a suffering, which its feminine element here forces upon Dante, that is most unwelcome to the ego.

In her likeness to godhead, Beatrice is an awesome figure, a "mysterium tremendum" whose numinosity makes her a personage of archetypal, sacred scale. In this guise, it is the less surprising that she comes to Dante sternly, like the image of Din or Geburah, the manifestation of divine judgment on the Kabbalistic tree. She knows his moral faults and holds him accountable until he can fully and in the most acute suffering acknowledge them for himself. The meaning of the whole action of redemption that is the theme of the *Purgatorio* is condensed in these scenes.

On the other hand, it is one of Dante's great achievements that Beatrice is so personal. She is genuinely offended that after her death he has betrayed her memory for an interest in many distractions, including philosophy and other women, as if she is unable to allow him to live a fully mortal life just because she cannot. Or again, the idea that a "green young girl or other novelty" should appeal to him when she is so much the more beautiful conveys a bit of vanity that is strikingly human.

Thus Beatrice combines in extraordinary measure both the larger-than-life qualities of the Other who calls him to his vocation ("when you have returned beyond, transcribe / what you have seen" XXXII, 105–106) and the intimate companion who addresses him as "tu" and "Frate" (XXXIII, 21, 23, in the Italian) like a well-loved sibling. This mixture of qualities is sensitively rendered in Botticelli's many drawings of Dante and Beatrice together, for she is always a little larger than he, with an elegant grace that conveys her archetypal dimension, even as she is rendered in familiar companionship within the circle of their togetherness (see, for example, figs. 188, 201). The power of achieved *coniunctio* with the anima who is at once sacred mediatrix and personal soulmate has rarely been rendered so effectively.

At the deepest psychological and religious levels there is a profoundly modern meaning to the way Beatrice incarnates in her symbolic person the conjunction of divine and human. It is as if in his image of her Dante expresses his view of the meaning of Christ's life and death: not only is it a unique event in the history of human development, to be worshiped as the exclusive truth of sacred being, but it is the forebear of the profound truth that God is capable of continuous incarnation in every man and woman. This the mystics of every great religion have always known, but dogmatists say otherwise. In the modern world where fanaticism endangers human survival, Dante's vision is wise and timely.

Lethe and Eunoe

After his swoon at the edge of Lethe, the pilgrim wakes to find himself plunged up to the throat in the river by Matilda, who is calling out to him to hold on to her (see figs. 176, 178). Now at last he is ready to be purged of the memory of his sins in the first of the two rivers of the Earthly Paradise. There is precise psychological meaning in the pilgrim's immersion in Lethe just when his awareness of his failure to be loyal to his deepest commitment reaches its peak and remorse overcomes him. He is at the fine line between a necessary acceptance of responsibility, with the suffering that accompanies it, and a paralyzing remorse that would lead to despair. We recall the other woods where the pilgrim has experienced or observed the effects of immobilizing gloom, but we also know that he would not be in this verdant forest if he were not to be reborn.

In his swoon of distress with himself we feel how deeply affected the pilgrim is by regret for his past behavior. But in accepting full responsibility, he shows that he is no longer the man he was then and so is prepared for release from a fixation on his guiltiness. Matilda, as the agent of divine forgiveness, plunges him into Lethe to free him from morbid preoccupation with his sins and his despairing shame. He is ready now to forget the sins he would no longer commit, and so he can die to his former self in this second baptism.

Dante uses the Edenlike image of the Earthly Paradise to convey the possibility of renewal through return to a kind of innocence: not the innocence of ignorance, of humanity before the Fall, but innocence earned by conscious awareness of and atonement for the greedy, hurtful, and treacherous elements in each of us. With the growth of ego strength that enables us to examine and bear the bad news about ourselves comes the equally necessary capacity to let go of the resentments, bitternesses, and guilts of the past, so that we may move forward into a new and more conscious association with the transpersonal powers. As the commentary on Hexagram 25 of the *I Ching* puts it, when "movement follows the law of heaven, man is innocent and without guile. . . . Man has received from heaven a nature innately good, to guide him in all his movements. By devotion to this divine spirit within himself, he attains an unsullied innocence that leads him to do right with instinctive sureness and without any ulterior thought of reward and personal advantage" (trans. Richard Wilhelm, 100–101).

This is the meaning of immersion in the second river, Eunoe, the river of "good mind" (see fig. 183). From here, the pilgrim may be born into a gradually deepening ability to perceive and relate to the divine power directly—or, as we might say, may move along the Chinese Way toward increasing wholeness and a more conscious connection to the larger Tao. This is the river of transformation where one is forgiven and forgives oneself. After immersion in Eunoe, one remembers—literally, re-members the personality dismembered by life's sufferings, or in reductive analysis—rather than forgetting. One remembers but doesn't dwell upon the failures of nurture, the woundings and the betrayals, given or received, in an earlier time. One remembers who one is.

When the personal past has been sufficiently worked through, one can go on to another level with a "good mind." We recall here the attitude of Oedipus at the end of his life, when in Sophocles' *Oedipus at Colonnus* he makes it clear he no longer feels guilty that he killed his father, married his mother, and abused his power. After many years of suffering atonement and growing self-knowledge, he accepts who he was as his destiny and is glad to have reached the place where his remains will bless the soil of those who receive him in death.

three Paradise

The glory of the One who moves all things
permeates the universe and glows
in one part more and in another less.
I was within the heaven that receives
more of His light; and I saw things that he
who from that height descends, forgets or can
not speak. . . . (I, 1–7)

The Interiority of Divine Reality (The *Paradiso*)

184   As Beatrice and Dante ascend into the overarching
space beyond the Earthly Paradise, the increased light is presented by Giovanni di Paolo
as an image of Love superimposed on the concentric rings of the nine heavenly spheres
that they will traverse. Giovanni di Paolo makes his first appearance as an illustrator
here, for he shared the illumination of this Sienese manuscript with Vecchietta and was
responsible for the *Paradiso* only (see "On the Illustrations" and Pope-Hennessey, *Para-
diso*). He also includes Glaucus and several small gods on the left because Dante says
that, watching Beatrice, "within me I was changed / as Glaucus changed, tasting the
herb that made / him a companion of the other sea gods" (67–69). Presumably the ani-
mals walking the sea with the ocean creatures are additional symbols of the possibility
of supernatural transformation here.

185   In the Venetian manuscript of the late fourteenth century, Dante prays to Apollo, god of music and poetry, who sits on the second crest of Parnassus (the muses to whom he addressed himself in Purgatory were on the first crest). He says that in the test ahead he needs both crests. He humbly hopes that his small spark may inspire "better voices after me" (I, 35). (He doesn't want to risk the fate of Marsyas, who dared to compete with Apollo and was flayed for his effrontery.) It is important to note Dante's capacity to include the numinous energies of earlier mythologies where they clearly still have meaning for him, with no apologies to his Christian faith.

186   In the same Venetian manuscript, by a different artist, as Beatrice and Dante arrive in the first heaven of the Moon, Dante says that "her gladness matched her loveliness" (II, 28). Gone now is any hint of Beatrice's anger with his lapses, though she continues to teach him, sometimes as a mother might a child. She tells him to direct his mind to God in gratefulness for bringing them there. As he enters the paradisal realm, he expresses his experience of its magnetic energy, remarking: "I reached a place where I could see / that something wonderful drew me" (25–26)—that is, something more than is known to the ego on its own.

        In this illumination and most of the others that follow from the same manuscript, the paradisal background becomes a deep, vivid blue. Here it sets off the loveliness to which Dante refers.

187   Giovanni di Paolo (ca. 1445) details some of the lessons Beatrice begins to give to Dante about the conditions and qualities he is encountering. Looking forward to the journey, the poet observes that

> What we hold here by faith, shall there be seen,
> not demonstrated but directly known,
> even as the first truth that man believes. (43–45)

In the *Paradiso*, while Beatrice continues both as guide and teacher, much of the pilgrim's learning will now be by direct experience, through such inner spiritual encounters as the mystics claim. This increasingly becomes the case as his gradual maturation leads him to become more and more identical with the poet who is conceiving the whole. By the end of the poem, the pilgrim's visionary experience is presented as a wondrous confrontation with deity that the poet's artistry has prepared him to know "directly," in all its mystery.

But here Beatrice is very much in her instructional mode, correcting the pilgrim's misunderstandings of the nature of the moon and its reflected light. Her elaborations cannot be represented fully by the visual artist, though he depicts a lunar eclipse and the experiment with three moons and a light that she describes.

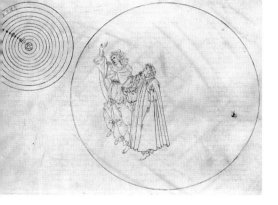

188

188   Botticelli concentrates on the relationship between Beatrice and Dante throughout the ascent through the heavens. We shall see how subtle and varied and focused their relationship becomes by means of a particular device: they are usually enclosed in a simple circle. Although some commentators are disappointed that Botticelli doesn't include many of the other forms in these heavens, others feel that he has identified the essence of the *Paradiso.*

189   When Dante glimpses his first faint vision of the Blessed,
keen to talk to him, Beatrice urges him to speak and listen, trusting what they will say.
Piccarda Donati tells her story and opens the subject of commitment to vows, of absolute
and relative will, on which Beatrice discourses later. Piccarda had been taken forcibly
from her convent by her brother Corso Donati and required to marry against her will,
which raises the question of her responsibility to her vows. Dante also asks her whether
she has no yearning to be higher, "in order to / see more and to be still more close to
Him" (III, 65–66), and she answers, "we only long for what we have" (71). She goes on
to explain that "to live in love [carità]" (77) is to be attuned to God's will for us, or, as
we might say from a psychological point of view, to accept the boundaries of our per-
sonalities set by the inner demands of our true Self, which is "God's will." We therefore
do not want more for ourselves than is in accord with our deepest nature, and that is as
close to the ultimate reality as we can wish to be. Within the limits of our own natures,
we are fully proximate to the divine essence. And Beatrice adds in the following canto
that Dante is being shown the blessed souls in a hierarchy of an anthropomorphic kind
because this is all finite human intelligence can comprehend.

Flaxman abstracts his rendering of this encounter by the use of a circle
also, though his is incomplete and about the blessed souls rather than the central pair.

189

190   Piccarda again. This Venetian illuminator always brings the delicate sparks and bits of flame encountered in each of the heavens into solid fleshly form. This artist is a choreographer of hands, and his interest in various personal inter-actions makes up for his unrefined style compared with the illustrations of the prior can-ticles in the same manuscript. His paradisal souls wear strongly colored robes.

191

191, 192   After Piccarda sinks into space, "as / a weighty
thing will vanish in deep water" (III, 122–123), Beatrice speaks further to the pilgrim's
questions. She talks of unfulfilled vows, absolute and relative will, and the source of her
radiance. Here Botticelli includes several other figures representing the souls the pilgrim
and Beatrice encounter, but they are smaller than the dominant couple. As mentioned
earlier, Botticelli always makes Beatrice larger than Dante, numinously authoritative,
often floating a bit above, yet at the same time tenderly reveals her elegant feet so that
we do not forget her graceful humanity.

192

193

193   Doré represents the many "splendors," the glowing lights in the second Heaven of Mercury, who draw near and want to speak with the human visitor. He gives them bodies that the poet carefully avoids describing. Here, as often in Doré's *Paradiso* engravings, his representation of the light of Heaven is as convincingly imagined through the use of negative, undrawn, white space as his use of line is effective in conveying the dark oppressiveness of Hell's vast spaces. Given that the engravings for publication in 1868 were made by several artisans working from Doré's drawings and printed on paper that is now very brittle and acidified, his artistic vision communicates with remarkable effectiveness.

194   Giovanni di Paolo shows us Justinian and illustrates his narrative (VI, 1ff.) with Aeneas and Constantine holding the Roman standard and Justinian kneeling before Agepetus, the sixth-century pope who convinced the emperor of the dual nature of Christ, thus saving him from heresy. Here, as often in his poem, Dante pays homage to the importance of worldly order that Rome represents. Just before this encounter, the poet breaks in and aims to heighten the reader's engagement by exclaiming: "Consider, reader, what your misery / and need to know still more would be if, at / this point, what I began did not go on" (V, 109–111).

194

The Necessity of Incarnation   In Canto VII, Beatrice explains why God had to be embodied in human flesh for humankind to be redeemed. Incarnation was necessary both for humanity to pay the price for original sin —for having presumed to be like God, knowing good and evil—and for humankind to become worthy of restoration to a state of grace in communion with God. As she observes,

> either through nothing other than His mercy,
> God had to pardon man, or of himself
> man had to proffer payment for his folly. (VII, 91–93)

Because humans lacked the value to offer adequate compensation for the hugeness of their presumption, and yet God did not wish to pardon from mercy alone, he chose to ennoble humankind by entering human flesh so that an adequate sacrifice could be offered. Through the Incarnation, Christ became the God-man whose Crucifixion was an adequate payment for human sin. Moreover, the deification of humankind through the birth of God in human form makes humanity also more worthy of forgiveness: God's mercy in these actions is, at once, greater and more justified.

Beatrice explains these theological points with proper scholastic clarity, but hidden within her meaning is an even deeper paradox. In order for God to forgive man and woman for the offense of desiring to become like him, God must give human beings the status, the likeness to deity, they originally wanted. But this time, instead of being stolen by a greedy ego, the divine element passes to humanity by the grace of God. Through the figure of Christ, man and woman become God.

Hints of the Incarnation and the godlikeness of human beings have been perceived at multiple points in the Old Testament in such images as the suffering servant in Isaiah and the "being that looked like a man" borne (like Beatrice) in the chariot of Ezekiel's vision (1:26). In *Answer to Job*, Jung writes at length of the divine confrontation with Job as revealing Yahweh's need for incarnation and reflection in human nature. Beatrice's explanation emphasizes God's need to raise humanity to a more godlike status in order to forgive, and she affirms God's beneficence in raising humans to divine status in the figure of Christ. To what extent this deification is potentially inherent in all humankind or is limited only to the historical figure of Christ is a question that is raised repeatedly as the *Paradiso* moves forward.

195 Flaxman shows us Justinian, who discourses on the Roman Empire. Once again Dante expresses his desire for an effective secular order and its separation from the papacy. Flaxman attempts to convey the luminosity of Paradise by sprinkling about the Blessed many variants of stars or sunbursts as naively as any earlier artist.

195

196

196 "I did not notice my ascent to it, / yet I was sure I was in Venus when / I saw my lady grow more beautiful" (VIII, 13–15). In each heaven, Dante describes wheeling lights, hosannas, gladness added to gladness, as he meets particular glowing lights.

Now in the third heaven, as depicted in the Venetian manuscript, this light, whom he realizes wants to please him, introduces herself as Cunizza, sister of the violent tyrant Ezzelino, who is forced to boil in the River of Blood. The pilgrim stands before the fully dressed and embodied "light" and points to himself:

"Pray, blessed spirit, may you remedy—
quickly—my wish to know," I said. "Give me
proof that you can reflect the thoughts I think." (IX, 19–21)

197   Here is Flaxman's rendering of the same encounter. Cunizza is a particularly vivid example of how Dante used historical persons to make a symbolic point. Cunizza's passionate nature involved her with many men through all the phases of her life (scandalously so to some observers), but she looks back on her loves, no matter how unwise, as meaningful steps in her approach to the Higher Love: "in myself I pardon happily / the reason for my fate" (IX, 34–35). Again we see Dante's discrimination concerning motive and degree of awareness. One might say that she is to the whore in the dragon chariot as Cato is to Pier della Vigna in the Wood of the Suicides. Conscious devotion to the larger goals of life puts in perspective the relative seriousness of violating specific commandments by those who truly come to know themselves.

         Cunizza is a joyful instance of Dante's presentation of person after person in Paradise who brings there his or her whole set of weaknesses and strengths, having sought growing awareness and whatever transformation was possible throughout a life's journey. Some of Cunizza's loving had undoubtedly been caught in merging and projection (like Paolo and Francesca), and she had to have lived willingly through the painful smelting out of the essence of unpossessive love described on the terrace of the Lustful. Her lifelong focus on relationships has become her fulfillment rather than her torment. The energy of eros, Dante makes plain, is the energy of sacred devotion, and work on relationship is a step along the higher road.

198 Giovanni di Paolo shows Cunizza with Folco, a love poet turned monk and bishop. Folco holds forth on the corrupt church and its temporal dominion, illustrated at the right, with a Fallen Angel (see fig. 240) atop a steeple in communion with lords of the Church.

This artist characteristically depicts a spacious sky in which the spheres of Paradise exist and a distant local landscape pertinent to the subject of the narrative. His paired floating figures of Beatrice and Dante show Beatrice touching the pilgrim's back (as, at other times, his shoulder or head) in an affectionate gesture rarely used by other illustrators.

198

199   The Venetian manuscript places the pilgrim under the sign of Aries, the ram, at the spring equinox, as he and Beatrice enter the fourth Heaven of the Sun. In Canto X, Dante discusses the zodiac and the seasons. In the next section of the painting, Saint Thomas introduces some of the other eleven lights in his circle of venerable wise men. (Again, here are quite solid bodies, as is usual in manuscript illuminations.) Solomon and the Roman philosopher-statesman Boethius are included among the wise Christian spirits. Solomon will speak to Dante of the Resurrection (see fig. 206).

200 The twelve lights in an Italian manuscript of the fif-
teenth century. The medieval illuminators had no difficulty assuming that their embod-
ied images of what the poet describes as lights were symbolic representations not to be
taken literally—any more than the pilgrim's whole journey was—and therefore no vio-
lation of the spirit of the poem.

200

201   Botticelli's Bea-
trice may be saying, "Give thanks,
give thanks / to Him, the angel's
Sun, who, through His grace / has
lifted you to this embodied sun"
(X, 52–54). Dante says he forgot
Beatrice momentarily in his wor-
shipful attention and seemed sur-
prised that "she was not displeased,
but smiled at this" (61). Whatever
traces of human vanity Beatrice
displayed on meeting the poet
have now vanished behind the
priority of transpersonal values.

202   The poetry of the
beginning of Canto XII itself dances
as it describes the circling dance
of two rings of souls, depicted here
in the Lombard manuscript of ca.
1400. The images range from "the
millstone of holy lights" (2) to gar-
lands of "those everlasting roses"
(19) and reach back to recall the
rainbow of Yahweh's covenant with
Noah and its assurance that divine
rage would not again flood the
entire world.

201

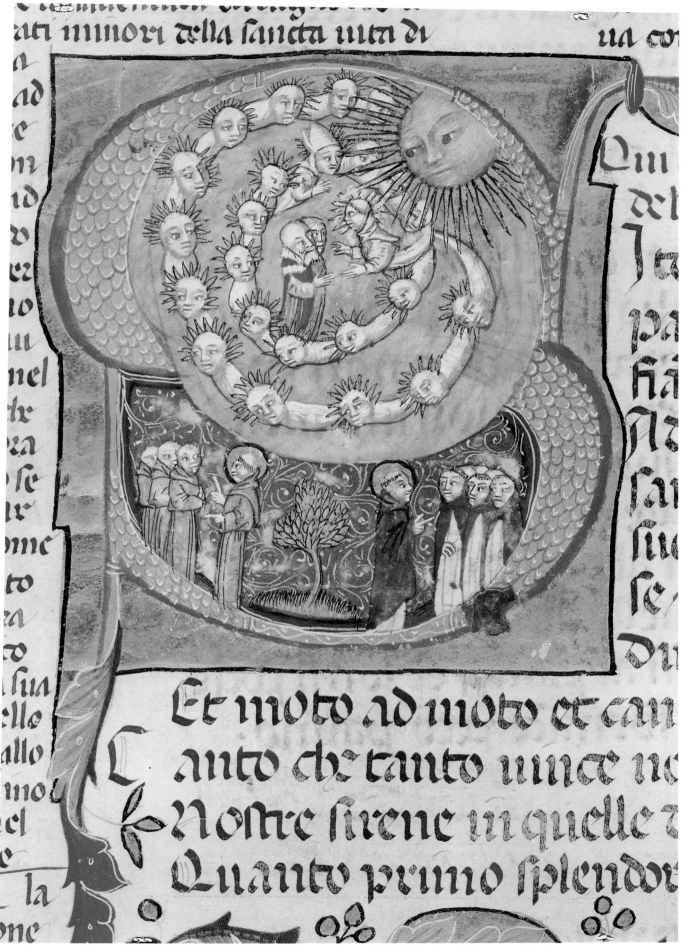

Et moto ad moto et can
anto che tanto vince no
Nostre sirene in quelle
Quanto primo splendo

matre psone idiuina natura /
cinuna psona ella elimana.

dal suo hicente rechено si distina /
diluí nedal amoz chenlui sintrea.

203

203, 204 A late fourteenth-century Italian illuminator and Doré are worlds apart in their visions of rings of souls in concentric circles. The illuminator imagines them as three circles, within each other, whereas Doré correctly has two circles but puts the pilgrim and his guide between them. The manuscript uses crudely ordinary solid figures that are nevertheless full of the joy of the passage. For his part, Doré emphasizes the numinous splendor of the paradisal level. It is a tribute to the breadth of Dante's imagination that both dancing joy and overwhelming awe are combined in the poetry of the *Paradiso*.

204

205   Saint Bonaventure speaks in response to Saint Thomas's praise of the way he did not take. Dante connects the loving way of Saint Francis and the intellectual way of Saint Dominic and promotes a unity of feeling and thought through this caring exchange. Bonaventure introduces the other eleven souls in his ring, including "at my side" (XII, 139) the heretical Joachim of Floris (see "Joachim of Floris," below). Giovanni di Paolo characteristically elevates the figures of Beatrice and the pilgrim, as well as Bonaventure, the figure who addresses them.

206   Still in the Heaven of the Sun, the pilgrim and his guide stand firmly before the figure of a bearded Solomon and other souls. The Venetian illuminator has no difficulty presenting the blessed spirits in human form and in highly fashionable attire. Beatrice asks the souls to describe their radiance at the Resurrection and how it will be possible for them, reunited with their bodies, even to bear the brightness, "to see such light and not be harmed" (XIV, 18). Solomon's modest voice replies that at last the extraordinary brightness that now envelops them will be

> . . . surpassed in visibility
> by reborn flesh, which earth now covers up.
>   Nor will we tire when faced with such bright light,
> for then the body's organs will have force
> enough for all in which we can delight. (56–60)

Dante uses the theologically correct doctrine of the resurrection of the fleshly body at the Last Judgment to underscore the significance of incarnation. Human reality in its most ultimate form combines the union of paradisal spirit and human flesh, "glorified and sanctified" and "being all complete" (43, 45), so that it is then able to endure the divinely increased luminosity of the human essence that is most like God. This implication that God's own essence is also human is posed imponderably in the poet's final vision.

206

Joachim of Floris   Image 205   Throughout the *Commedia*, Dante locates historical as well as legendary and mythological figures to make a salient point either explicitly or implicitly. Some of these invite reflection, for the placements occasionally seem to violate his structure. Such a one is the Abbot Joachim of Floris, who is introduced by Saint Bonaventure—"and at my side / shines the Calabrian Abbot Joachim, / who had the gift of the prophetic spirit" (XII, 139–141).

From a medieval theological perspective, Joachim is a questionable candidate for Paradise. What he prophesied, about one hundred years before Dante's time, was that after a first historical period of the Father, described in the Old Testament, and a second of the Son, reported in the New Testament and carried by the Church into his own time, there would come a new era of the Holy Spirit—a time of individual spiritual knowledge, led by contemplatives who would receive divine inspiration directly. Joachim was charismatic and devout, but his ideas were condemned by Church councils with increasing ferocity as the thirteenth century unfolded, and Bonaventure was one of his sharpest critics. By the time Dante wrote, Joachim had been judged a heretic; his ambivalent standing as both saint and heretic continues to this day.

Direct access to spiritual knowledge through the Holy Spirit, claimed especially by Franciscan and other revolutionary movements in the religious ferment of Dante's time, has long been a source of unease for the Church. The Holy Ghost movement can be seen as a forerunner of Protestantism and its claims to an unmediated relationship with God. Joachim himself even foresaw a coming union of Christians with infidels in direct communion with God, a daringly symbolic attitude that, as we know, has yet to be realized in the world.

In spite of all the controversy that Joachim aroused, Dante places him in the fourth heaven with Bonaventure and other great Church thinkers. In doing so, the poet not only emphasizes his inclusive and conciliatory image of Paradise but also implies agreement with a more mystical than institutional view of God's accessibility to every person through the indwelling of the Holy Spirit.

207

207, 208　　　　　　　These two manuscripts show the cross-
become-circle in the fifth heaven. In the depth of Mars, the pilgrim sees the
image of painful sacrifice that has found its meaning, fiery illuminations surround-
ing the mortal suffering at the center of the cross. He attempts to describe "Christ's
flaming from that cross" but "can find no fit similitude for it" (XIV, 104–105).
This mid-fourteenth-century Italian illuminator presents an embodied Christ sur-
rounded by little suns; the Venetian artist avoids the central image and embodies
the lights.

209   For Doré the lights become figures that look like angels. The spiritual significance of Christ's suffering humanity is emphasized in Doré's control of line and light, though his drawing of a greatly elongated cross fails to honor the balance of the opposites implicit in Dante's image of "a circle's quadrants" (102) forming the cross.

209

210   Cacciaguida in Mars. The light that now addresses Dante as "blood of mine" (XV, 28) urges him to speak up, to let his voice—"bold, / assured, and glad" (67–68)—proclaim his will and longing, even though it is true that everything is known here already. There follow three cantos exploring Dante's individual heritage back to Cacciaguida, his great-great grandfather. By laying out the history of Florence when he lived, Cacciaguida roots the poet's origins in the honorable days of an earlier time. He also tells him not only how it has been in his family but how it will be for Dante in his exile. (Dante dares to ask this question.) Then Cacciaguida presses him to fulfill his poetic vocation, to tell of his experience of Truth, harsh as it might seem to some who are unready for it. From the voice of his heroic ancestor comes the call to bear witness courageously to the ultimate realities that are revealed to him in his personal isolation. The Paduan illustrator gives Cacciaguida a youthful and radiant appearance.

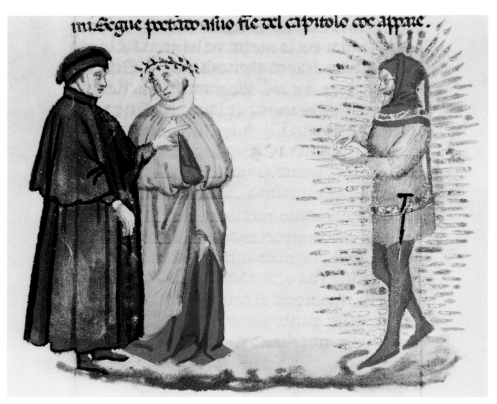

210

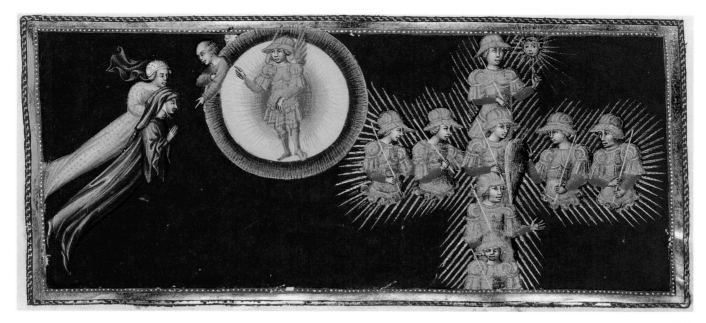

212

211 Giovanni di Paolo, in contrast with the Paduan, presents Cacciaguida as a balding older man emerging from an illuminated circle displaying the winged figure of Mars. To its right, the artist presents eight of the warriors on the cross, including, as Pope-Hennessey points out (126), the figure of Joshua at the top with an image of the sun in his hand that he made stand still in the battle of Jericho. In Canto XVIII (35ff.), where Cacciaguida names the souls who appear in the cross, Dante is at pains to explain that with each name he sees "a splendor thrust along the cross" (38), not a visible body. In addition to Joshua, Maccabeus, Charlemagne, and Roland (among others) wheel their flames about with gladness as they are pointed out. Through his emphasis on personal family history and on fellow warriors of the past, the pilgrim's ancestor affirms with force the poet's use of personal examples in his poem. The reader is helped to understand that it is necessary to experience even the vast cosmic vistas in personal terms.

From this sphere on, Giovanni di Paolo's illuminations are increasingly symbolic and dramatically patterned, with powerful use of strong color and gold leaf.

212 Beatrice becomes still more brilliant; the pilgrim sees

> . . . such purity within her eyes,
> such joy, that her appearance now surpassed
> its guise at other times, even the last. (XVIII, 55–57)

Botticelli's capacity to render Beatrice both familiar and glorious is beautifully effected here.

213

213, 214   We leave the red passion of Mars, entering the sixth heaven, the temperate white sphere of Jupiter. Dante watches as souls spell out the shapes of letters. (He invokes the aid of Pegasus in this attempt to describe what he sees.) The deep spaces and vast sweep of Doré's souls contrasts with the linear, relief-like style of Flaxman's drawing. They give two versions of Dante's description that the souls initially flock like birds: whereas Doré's move in great sweeping circles, characteristically ordered, Flaxman's mass together in a triumphal column. Gradually, they spell out in Latin, "Love Justice you who judge the earth" (XVIII, 91–93).

215   The souls now form into an eagle shape, rendered here by Giovanni di Paolo. "O gentle star" says Dante to Jupiter itself, "what—and how many—gems / made plain to me that justice here on earth / depends upon the heaven you engem!" (XVIII, 115–117). As above, so below.

Dante emphasizes the degree to which human justice depends upon the imprint of transpersonal order. Our need to confront collective murder with justice from a higher realm is as sharply felt today as in Dante's time.

214

215

217   Dante speaks of his amazement at finding Trajan and the Trojan Ripheus (a character in the *Aeneid*) among these lights in the eagle's brow. He ponders this further inscrutability of the Largest Plan (see "The Trojan Ripheus," below).

        Whereas Doré shows the figures of Dante and Beatrice as observers overwhelmed in scale by the heavenly vastness and forms the eagle by drawing a flock of souls with wings like angels, the late fourteenth-century Italian illuminator gives priority to the delighted appreciation of the poet and his companion, standing near an eagle outlined by stars and filled in with sketchy bodies. It is as if this medieval perspective is so familiar with archetypal awesomeness that it can be presented with far more joy than fear. In contrast, Giovanni di Paolo (see fig. 215) also depicts the journeyers' pleasure but gives the eagle a proud visage and sharp claws worthy of attentive respect.

216   As the eagle's wings open, Dante describes each soul: like a ruby that reflects the sun's rays so that each seems the total sun. And then the beak begins to speak, as if there were one voice "from a multitude of loves" (XIX, 20). Dante tells the reader that not only is this indescribable but nobody has ever even *imagined* such a thing before. With the image, he evokes the power of transpersonal illumination to unify multiplicity or to make multiples of its own unity. Characteristically, Doré catches the wonder of the scene.

The Trojan Ripheus   Image 217   If Dante's placement of Joachim of Floris in the fourth heaven is unorthodox, what are we to make of the presence of Ripheus—an obscure Trojan who died long before the birth of Christ—in the cluster of stars that form the eyebrow of the great eagle of Divine Justice in the sixth heaven of Jupiter? Here, on his own authority, Dante puts a minor figure from the *Aeneid*, one who was praised by Aeneas for his justice and uprightness. Among the souls nearby are David (whose star makes up the pupil of the eagle's eye), the converted Roman emperor Constantine, and even the Emperor Trajan, who is known to have died a pagan in A.D. 117. Trajan's presence is puzzling to the pilgrim, too, but as the eagle explains (consistent with medieval legend), Pope Gregory's prayers had brought Trajan briefly back to life so that his conversion could be effected. Trajan

> was kindled to such fire of true love
> that, when he died a second death, he was
> worthy to join in this festivity. (XX, 115–117)

Trajan's salvation is brought—barely—into accord with doctrine through a second chance, but for Ripheus there is no evading the stunning incongruity of his redemption.

Nor does the poet tread lightly around the apparent difficulty. Rather, he uses it deliberately to emphasize again the crucial importance of the inner condition of the soul. Unable to contain his question after the eagle's enumeration of the souls who make up his eye, the pilgrim bursts out, "Can such things be?" (XX, 83; see fig. 217), to the delighted amusement of the assembled souls, whose "lights flash" in a "vast festivity" (84). Patiently, the eagle recounts to him the meaning of the paradox:

> The other [Ripheus], through the grace that surges from
> a well so deep that no created one
> has ever thrust his eye to its first source,
>   below, set all his love on righteousness,
> so that, through grace on grace, God granted him
> the sight of our redemption in the future;
>   thus he, believing that, no longer suffered
> the stench of paganism and rebuked
> those who persisted in that perverse way.
>   More than a thousand years before baptizing,
> to baptize him there were the same three women
> you saw along the chariot's right hand side. (XX, 118–129)

Ripheus's anachronistic baptism by Faith, Hope, and Charity is understood to have been wholly nonmaterial, a spiritual event that takes place within the soul of the one redeemed. The poet uses this image to stress the inscrutability of divine election but also to show that any soul may know the true God inwardly, before and without scriptural revelation or ritual baptism. Whereas virtuous pagans who lacked this vision (including Virgil) are confined to Limbo, untormented but out of God's light, exceptional persons like Ripheus, who had an inner perception "of our redemption in the future"

(123), are redeemable. Here the poet reaches out once more beyond the literalism of institutional practice to assert—late in his poem and in his lifetime—the centrality of psychological or symbolic truth. Salvation ultimately depends upon the inner condition of the soul, not upon the instruments of the Church.

218   As they enter the seventh heaven, the sphere of Saturn, Beatrice stops smiling, telling Dante: "Were I to smile, then you would be / like Semele when she was turned to ashes" (XXI, 5–6). Semele burns at the lower left, because she insisted on looking at her divine lover Zeus.

       Many flames descend the golden ladder of Saturn, as if "poured out" (33), says Dante, and he compares them to common jackdaws that rise wheeling in flocks, some flying off, others turning back. Giovanni di Paolo shows the flames as angels on the ladder and Saturn as a wise old man with the sickle of mortal limitation, whom Dante calls "that dear king whose rule undid all evil" (27) in the legendary golden age of the ancients.

219   Doré also makes the flames or "splendors" angelic but gives them steps rather than the ladder Dante describes. His choice enables him to suggest the enormity of heavenly distances by means of an uncountable number of steps.

Jalalta canta che ali feruc
pront al configlio chel mondo govina
forzeggia qui fi come tu oblerue.

Fra due lin dicalia furgon fali
e no molto dultana ala tua pi
tanto che từom allất fonam pi

S. Picrro damiano :.

220

220, 221   Another characteristic of the Heaven of Saturn is
its silence, because the singing would overwhelm mortal ears. Appropriately, this silence
surrounds Saint Benedict, founder of the contemplative order. Benedict introduces some
of his brothers with affection and mourns the corruption of his order. Dante asks to see
his face, but Benedict says that will happen in the Empyrean: "There, each desire is perfect,
ripe, intact; / and only there, within that final sphere, / is every part where it has always
been" (XXII, 64–66). He tells Dante that the ladder reaches to that sphere, which is why
he cannot see the top of it. The Italian (ca. 1365) and Venetian illuminators as usual
depict not only Benedict's face but also his body.

221

223 In the eighth heaven, Dante prays to the image of his birth sign, Gemini, the Twins of the zodiac: "O stars of glory . . . all of my genius— / whatever be its worth—has you as source. . . . To you my soul now sighs devotedly, / that it may gain the force for this attempt" (XXII, 112–114, 121–122). The zodiac reflects the influences that govern one's innate character, and the pilgrim's prayer parallels today's desire to "become what we are meant to be." The Venetian illuminator presents the Twins in highly visible form.

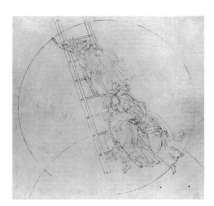

222

222 The action depicted by the lower pair of figures in Botticelli's drawing shows the pilgrim at the bottom of the ladder turning bodily to Beatrice, who appears to clutch him tightly as they begin the ascent from the Heaven of Saturn to the Heaven of the Fixed Stars. The travelers follow the Benedictine flames that have swept upward. Contrary to Botticelli's image, Dante says that "the gentle lady—simply with a sign— / impelled me after them and up that ladder, / so did her power overcome my nature" (XXII, 100–102).

223

224   Giovanni di Paolo gives us a graphic interpre-
tation of the orbits of the seven planets as they can be seen from the overarching
distance of the Fixed Stars. In addition to noting Leda at the center with her twins,
Castor and Pollux, representing Gemini, John Pope-Hennessey points out that
the Sun, in his flaming chariot on the left, precedes the figures of the Moon,
Mars, Mercury, Jupiter, Venus, and Saturn on the right in the order of the days
of the week, not of the heavenly spheres.

Beatrice encourages the pilgrim to look back through the spheres
to earth and, from his new perspective and new sense of his identity, he notes,

> My eyes returned through all the seven spheres
> and saw this globe in such a way that I
> smiled at its scrawny image; I approve
>   that judgment as the best, which holds this earth
> to be the least; and he whose thoughts are set
> elsewhere can truly be called virtuous. (XXII, 133–138)

In this sphere, Dante can again look on the brilliance of Beatrice's
smile, after he has been strengthened by the radiance he sees here.

225   On the left, the Venetian illuminator illustrates Dante's awareness of Beatrice's intense expectancy of what is to come as she points to the "sun above a thousand lamps" (XXIII, 28), the light of Christ. With her left hand, in the conflation of the artist, Beatrice also points to her face, as she urges the pilgrim, unable yet to look continuously upon Christ's "glowing Substance" (31), to

> Open your eyes and see what I now am;
> the things you witnessed will have made you strong
> enough to bear the power of my smile. (46–48)

The depth of the pilgrim's encounter with divine numinosity begins to be assimilated sufficiently for him to bear its manifestation in the smile of his beloved guide.

The scene of Christ and Mary in triumph, on the right, was not unusual for a medieval artist. The image of Mary here foreshadows her place in the poet's ultimate vision of the Rose. His description of his awakening to what he is offered through her mediation evokes echoes of the experiences of mystics everywhere.

225

226

226   Botticelli's realm of the Fixed Stars depicts the flame
that has Christ's face. The poet's lines are less literal. Christ's "glowing Substance" Beatrice
describes as "the Wisdom and the Potency / that opened roads between the earth and
Heaven, / the paths for which desire had long since waited" (XXIII, 37–39). There is a
faint image of the twins of Gemini next to the bull of Taurus at the bottom of the drawing.

Here Botticelli has expanded his heavenly scene with images of many
flames. Beatrice is urging the pilgrim to look on "that / fair garden blossoming beneath
Christ's rays" (XXIII, 71–72), where the flame of Mary is surrounded by the apostles in
the smaller circle immediately above the journeyers. Dante holds his hand before his
eyes because—though he can now look directly on Beatrice—he cannot yet sustain
the vision of Christ's flame. He and his guide are again the circled focus of the artist's
presentation.

227   Giovanni di Paolo paints Saint Peter, robed and haloed, welcoming the pilgrim by including him in a circle of naked souls. As "keeper of the keys of glory" (XXIII, 139), Peter plays a crucial role both in the poet's individual salvation and in his passionate concern for the troubled Church.

227

228

228   Flaxman's Peter appears like a shooting star with some of his companion splendors. Although his cool draftsmanship lacks the depth and scale of the greater artists, Flaxman's starburst outline has dramatic immediacy, and his emotional involvement with the poem feels stronger than usual.

229 At the request of Beatrice, Peter examines the pilgrim on the subject of faith, here depicted in the Venetian manuscript. We are told that the saint is so gratified at what he hears that he blesses him joyously in the manner of this realm: the singing apostolic light encircles Dante three times because "the speech I spoke had brought him such delight" (XXIV, 154). In his response, the pilgrim has emphasized that "faith is the substance of the things we hope for / and is the evidence of things not seen" (XXIV, 63–64). The essence of faith, its "quiddity" (65), rests in inner, not sensory, experience. Inner experience, as we sometimes need to be reminded today, is in itself "substantial."

229

230 Next, in this image by Giovanni di Paolo, Saints James and John examine the pilgrim on the subjects of hope and charity. One of the most poignant passages of the poem expresses the poet's passionate hope to return to Florence with dignity in his lifetime, which the reader knows he never will (see "Prayer Denied and Prayer Affirmed," below).

230

highly personal way, the poet contrasts his external with his spiritual life in two passionate prayers on his own behalf late in the poem. One we know from history will be denied; the other we have every reason to believe is granted.

At the beginning of Canto XXV, the pilgrim has just been examined by Saint Peter on his understanding of Faith and is about to be questioned by Saint James concerning the nature of Hope. The poet chooses this moment to break into the poem in person so that he can share his own most poignant earthly hope, his desire to return from exile to a place of honor in his native Florence:

> If it should happen . . . If this sacred poem—
> this work so shared by heaven and by earth
> that it has made me lean through these long years—
> can ever overcome the cruelty
> that bars me from the fair fold where I slept,
> a lamb opposed to wolves that war on it,
> by then with other voice, with other fleece,
> I shall return as poet and put on,
> at my baptismal font, the laurel crown;
> for there I first found entry to that faith
> which makes souls welcome unto God, and then,
> for that faith, Peter garlanded my brow. (XXV, 1–12)

The tentative opening of this prayer conveys to us how tender the subject is for the poet, how deeply wounded he is by the exile that the vengefulness of his political enemies at home has forced on him. As readers, we know only too well that this prayer was not answered, that even the power of his "sacred poem" was insufficient to overcome the obstacles to his return. We feel the tragic archetypal meaning of exile: it is the alien yet fertile ground that nurtured the poet's great achievement, and it required a sacrifice that was not mitigated in this life. What seems little enough for Dante to seek, at the human level, in recompense for his enormous contribution to human culture, wrenches our hearts with its denial.

The prayer is doubly poignant because most prophecies in the poem are written at a time when the author knows that the anticipated events actually took place. They carry the weight of historic fact for the reader. Here, however, the poet dares to express his uncertain hope for the future, and we are painfully aware that his creative gift will not soften his worldly fate.

Dante, this time as pilgrim, makes a second highly personal prayer, in his final address to Beatrice. This prayer conveys the certainty of a hope that will be realized. In Canto XXXI, the protagonist stands transfixed before the wonder of the Rose, like a barbarian struck dumb by his first sight of Rome:

> . . . then what amazement
> must have filled me when I to the divine
> came from the human, to eternity

from time, and to a people just and sane
from Florence came! (XXXI, 36–40)

The world of Paradise is a world of justice, free of the political paranoia
that bars him from his homeland. In thanking Beatrice for having interceded to make
possible his saving journey through the psychic otherworld, he asks one special blessing
so that he may be worthy of a place among the heavens of the stars:

"Do, in me, preserve
    your generosity, so that my soul,
which you have healed, when it is set loose from
my body, be a soul that you will welcome."
    So did I pray. And she, however far
away she seemed, smiled, and she looked at me.
Then she turned back to the eternal fountain. (XXXI, 87–93)

Knowing as we do the power of Beatrice's smiles, so great in the *Paradiso*
that the pilgrim cannot at times be exposed to them lest they consume him like divine
fire, we, with the poet, are confident this prayer will be received. Once again, the prayer
itself reminds us that what ultimately matters is the soul's inner condition. The poet
does not ask that Beatrice intercede outwardly that he may ultimately merit salvation,
but that she keep herself alive *in him* so that he may not again lapse into forgetfulness. If
she preserves her generosity in his soul, then his prayer will be answered. In the world,
the poet must relinquish his desire, but in eternity we know he is assured his place.

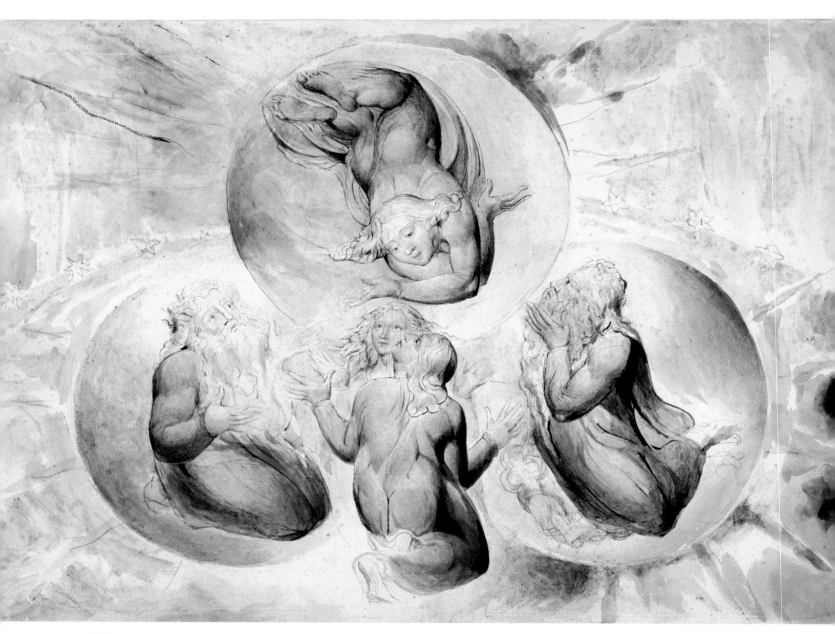

231

231, 232   Blake and Doré reveal the vast differences in their imaginations of the same scene. Blake's strong fourfold pattern of cuplike shapes seems to foreshadow the final Rose image, and each figure conveys movement or vital energy. Doré's rendering is more upright and stiff, his Beatrice very understated.

John, flanked by Peter and James, becomes the examiner here, on the subject of charity or love. Before the examination begins, the pilgrim is blinded by staring at John's light, expecting to see his resurrected body (John tells him that the prevailing belief in his bodily assumption into Heaven is false). It is as if the poet wishes to emphasize that we are blind if we imagine symbolic truth too literally. His sight is restored, after the examination, by Beatrice's glance, perhaps suggesting that staying connected to one's personal god-bearing image can protect us from the excesses of identification with transpersonal authority.

In response to John's request that he "voice aloud / all of the teeth by which this love [of God] grips you," (XXVI, 50–51), the pilgrim declares:

> My charity
> results from all those things whose bite can bring
> the heart to turn to God (55–57)

and goes on to cite the pain of existence in the world, the death of Christ, and all those things that "drew me from the sea of twisted love / and set me on the shore of the right love" (62–63). The sufferings of love, its "teeth" and "bite," help us to separate from the distortions of temporal attachments and to seek love's truest object at the transpersonal level. (See "Love and Vision," below.)

232

233   Botticelli depicts the blinded pilgrim and includes the circling flames that are now in the image of his relationship with Beatrice. The flames named between them are the three evangelists who have just tested the pilgrim's mind and heart, and now also the flame of Adam.

233

234   Giovanni di Paolo shows us the figure of the pilgrim kneeling before a youthful Adam in reverence. Behind Adam, he depicts the forest of the Earthly Paradise atop the Mountain of Purgatory and the four rivers flowing from the edenic world. Knowing Dante's mind without having to be told, Adam answers his question about the length of time he lived in Eden by telling him:

> On that peak rising highest from the sea,
> my life—first pure, then tainted—lasted from
> the first hour to the hour that follows on
>   the sixth, when the sun shifts to a new quadrant. (XXVI, 139–142)

Here Dante chooses the shortest of the possible times, one morning only, for Adam's life in Eden and seems even to emphasize the human inclination to sin by pointing out that this brief time before expulsion was divided between being "pure" and "tainted." But Adam also stresses that his exile was caused not by "the act of tasting of the tree" but rather by "my trespass of the boundary" (116–117). Thus he underscores the human drive to go beyond the limits, especially in the knowledge of good and evil, which is the particular potential in human awareness.

234

235

235 Before they leave the heaven of the Fixed Stars, Dante and Beatrice pale before a dramatic change in Peter's light. First his flame and then all the Heaven of the Fixed Stars become blood-red with anger as he delivers a condemnation of those who have corrupted his church, and he urges the poet to speak plainly of what he has heard when he returns to earth. Peter serves as model for the indignation that gross abuses must evoke even if we have achieved mature detachment. The Venetian illuminator cools the scene with blue, though the lights above the figures are agitated and Peter's angry color appears in his gown.

236

236   After Beatrice again urges Dante to look earthward at all the spheres he has traversed, they enter the ninth Heaven of the Primum Mobile. "The powers that her gaze now granted me / . . . thrust me into heaven's swiftest sphere" (XXVII, 97–99). Beatrice tells him that

> The nature of the universe, which holds
> the center still and moves all else around it,
> begins here as if from its turning-post.
>   This heaven has no other where than this:
> the mind of God, in which are kindled both
> the love that turns it and the force it rains. (106–111)

This Venetian artist imagines a splendid Christ at the center of the pure spark or fixed point of "acute" light (XXVIII, 16) around which all revolves. He surrounds the face of Christ with an unusual red-pink background, instead of the customary blue, perhaps to suggest the intensity both of this light and of Christ's passion. In imagining the Primum Mobile, the swiftest of the spheres, Dante emphasizes the stillness of "that fixed Point" (95) at its center. Its intense interiority is required to hold together "the circle that loves most and knows the most" (72).

237 Giovanni di Paolo presents a luminous and more symbolic image of the divine point of light surrounded by the angelic circles, but the face within it, which Dante does not describe, does not look specifically Christlike. John Pope-Hennessey attributes it to Boreas, with whose gentle breeze from the northeast the poet makes a simile here (XXVIII, 81) as Beatrice's explanation clears the pilgrim's mind and "truth was seen" (87). Since nothing in the poem describes any face in this point of light, the Venetian's choice of a Christlike center seems more appropriate, and Giovanni di Paolo's rendering appears rather mysterious. Boreas was normally represented with three winds flowing from his mouth and cheeks, so that this does not seem as likely a reading as the simple suggestion that for Giovanni di Paolo the divine light has a singular human face, much as its Trinitarian nature is explicitly represented in his following illustrations.

237

238

238   At the center of the upper edge of this drawing by Botticelli, we see a lightly sketched circle representing the Trinity. This circle is the focus of nine hierarchies of angels, together with the pilgrim and his guide. Botticelli gives angelic forms to the nine rings of fire as they are revealed to the pilgrim through Beatrice's words in Canto XXVIII.

239

239   Doré presents a different perspective on the same scene, suggesting the nine rings of angelic fire—around the fixed point—where

> . . . all delight to the degree
> to which their vision sees—more or less deeply—
> that truth in which all intellects find rest. (XXVIII, 106–108)

Beatrice speaks movingly to the pilgrim in Cantos XXVIII and XXIX of profound matters having to do with the interweaving of love, vision, grace, and will. She makes the point that "blessedness depends / upon the act of vision, not upon / the act of love—which is a consequence" (XXVIII, 109–111). The profoundest love, the objectivity of *caritas*, requires first an overarching consciousness or vision, for it is more encompassing than instinctive attachment or desire. Doré captures the cosmic scope of the poet's vision, suggesting in its enormous breadth of view the detachment and objectivity of love based in vision but diminishing the figures of Beatrice and the pilgrim so severely that human warmth is eclipsed by awe and wonder.

Love and Vision   **Images 236–239**   The subtle relation between love and vision, as Beatrice explores it for the pilgrim's enlightenment, is touched on in several ways as the poem develops. Because love is the motive energy of all life, both bodily and spiritual, and includes among its objects all those for which our excessive or warped desires lead us into sin and pathological behavior, it is crucial for us to understand its place in the sacred order. Notably, love is such a central feature of the divine essence that both punishment for the excesses of erotic love in Hell (see figs. 21–23) and atonement for these sins in Purgatory (see fig. 167) are located at the uppermost level of each condition. Yet neither the torment of the whirlwind that punishes nor the suffering of the fire that purifies these "least of sins" is to be taken lightly. Indeed, moving through the fire on the terrace of the Lustful is presented as the pilgrim's most difficult passage, greatly feared and almost more than he can do. In part, the poet uses this presentation of the difficulty to acknowledge his own indulgence of erotic fascinations. Even so, there is more to the symbolic power of this truly terrifying fire (molten glass is enticingly cool by comparison) than this acknowledgment explains.

The poet makes passage into the realm of transformed passion and the objective caritas of paradisal love more than a simple matter of conscious determination. Outer vision on the terrace of the Lustful is dangerous: "On this terrace, it is best / to curb your eyes: the least distraction—left / or right—can mean a step you will regret" (XXV, 118–120). Only undistracted inwardness will serve. The twin risks of fire or precipice convey specific meanings, fire as the experience and awareness of the pain caused by erotic projection, obsession, and betrayal, on one hand, and, on the other, the terrifying drop into the unconscious caused by being unable to bear this pain.

Deliberate movement into the flame must be chosen, with full awareness of its meaning, by the one who will grow from the experience. This is what is missing in Dante's going forward only because he is impelled by Virgil's reminder that he will see his beloved. Beatrice knows, as Virgil does not, that this is not enough. He must come to contrition for the hurt he has caused her (and himself)—fully realized, accepted, and atoned for—before he can be truly ready to enter the Earthly Paradise and then to undertake the paradisal journey with his spiritual guide.

As we saw in the presentation of Cunizza in the Heaven of Venus (*Paradiso* IX), the sequence of passionate loves for which she cheerfully forgives herself was for her a stairway to Paradise. But the poet makes it clear in the difficulty of the final terrace of Purgatory that it is not enough to follow one's heart—more is involved. What more this is has been suggested in part by the angel's call though the fire in *Purgatorio* XXVII when he says, "you cannot move ahead / unless the fire has stung you first" (XXVII, 10–11). Beatrice then illuminates the incompleteness of the pilgrim's atonement, In spite of the symbolic passage through the fire that is good enough for Virgil, when she greets the traveler for the first time with so fierce a dressing down that he faints (XXX, 55ff.; XXXI, 85–90). Even the angels present at this scene have compassion for the target of her rage: "Lady, why shame him so?" (XXX, 96) they say, but it softens her not at all, and before he finally swoons in true contrition and repentance, she has indicated what the deeper problem is. After she died, she explains to the angels with just a touch of the vanity that makes her humanness so convincing, "I was less dear to him," and "he followed counterfeits of goodness" (129, 131) rather than the true vision that loving her had originally inspired. He has had to go through the visitation of Hell and the viewing and partial experience of Purgatory to recover his awareness of the "deep design of God" (142) and so be allowed to pass through Lethe and ascend with his companion to the spheres of Paradise.

The fullest explanation of what has been at stake is not explicit until Beatrice teaches Dante the relation between love and vision. In the next to highest sphere of heaven, the Primum Mobile, she tells her (now fully worthy) companion, "blessedness depends / upon the act of vision, not upon / the act of love—which is a consequence" (XXVIII, 109–111) and that "affection follows / the act of knowledge" (XXIX, 139–140). By this she does *not* mean that every form of love derives from a high vision or true knowledge—as we have seen, she has chastised the pilgrim thoroughly for his self-betrayals, in the name of love, by the seductions of "green girls" or fascinated projections onto the sirens of philosophy or politics. What she means is that truly objective caring, *agape*, or caritas, the highest form of love, is possible only within the container of a higher, wider-knowing consciousness, one that relativizes all attachments and gives them rightly ordered priority in a transpersonally centered vision of our place in the universe. It is only through this vision, this gnosis, that conflicts of loyalties can be resolved, that each affection, attachment, and love can be kept in the right relationship to all the others of one's life. And for this to be so, sacrifices must be made, sometimes very painful ones, as the passage through the fire shows. Contrition for all the hurts one has caused in the name of love must become fully conscious if one is to achieve the detachment that makes objective loving truly possible.

It is striking how lucidly Dante makes it clear that the souls in Paradise are no longer wrenchingly touched by the sufferings of the good in earthly life, not to mention the torments of the damned. Even Beatrice, whose heart is large, is unmoved by the thoroughly ethical Virgil's being deprived of the divine light in Limbo, when she descends to ask him to guide her friend, who requires a specially sanctioned experience for his salvation, on the first part of his journey. The point is made explicitly by Cato, guardian of Purgatory, when he emphasizes that even his loyal and worthy wife, Marcia, sharing a place in Limbo with Virgil (who calls on Cato for help in the name of her enduring love), "has no power to move me any longer" (I, 89). And the priority of objective vision over the avoidance of suffering is most obvious in the brutal integrity of Beatrice's deeply caring concern for the pilgrim, in which there is not an ounce of pity to dilute the larger truth.

This is the understanding that puts the power of Amor in the poet's early dream—"Ego dominus tuus" (see the Introduction, above)—into perspective. Blake worried about Dante's struggle to claim his poetic genius in the face of Beatrice's power over him, and he distrusted it, but to address the question, the poet has himself provided first Beatrice's impassioned judgment upon him and then the larger vision she presents here in the *Paradiso*. Beatrice underscores, against her vanity, that it is insufficient for the poet's soul to be drawn to salvation only by personal eros for her. It is not enough, as Virgil supposed, for that to be the motive power for his travel beyond the flames. That, too, has been foreshadowed in the early dream by Beatrice's reluctance to eat the flaming heart. She has no interest in desirously devouring him but rather wants him, as he himself perceives by the end of the *Vita Nuova,* to set her in a context that honors her call to present her within a higher vision. This Dante does so well that he even takes care to make it clear he will *not* be by her side or share the same level of Paradise with her, if he himself is called into the divine light.

Only when one's relationship to the overarching vision (in which each claim on us has its place) is known within may we hope for access to the power of love that opens what the alchemists call the *multiplicatio,* that final stage of the process where a few loaves and fishes mysteriously multiply, when there is truly enough love to go around without narcissistic neediness and self-centered manipulation. This is not the common human condition, and we get only miraculous intimations of its reality from time to time, but it is at the heart of sacred vision; it is when one ventures to hope that God is Love. Not the love that springs from undifferentiated benevolence, nor the love that makes Amor present himself in Dante's early dream as his Master, but "the Love that moves the sun and the other stars" (XXXIII, 145).

240

240   Beatrice reminds the pilgrim in Canto XXIX that "The fall had its beginning in the cursed / pride of the one you saw, held in constraint / by all of the world's weights" (55–57), and then goes on to contrast with this brief reference to the chief of the Fallen Angels, the modesty, exalted vision, and other virtues of the loyal angels, "those whom you see / in Heaven here" (57–58). Prodded by this allusion, Giovanni di Paolo chooses to show us Michael and Raphael casting the blackened angels, now devils with tails and webbed reptilian feet, into a pit beneath the emblazoned figures of the Trinity. It is as if he wants to underscore Beatrice's passing suggestion that though Dis—or Satan or Lucifer—is out of sight in Paradise, he is never out of mind. Indeed, Giovanni di Paolo provides the visual image that Dante might have offered verbally but elected not to do at this point in the poem.

241

241   In the Empyrean, the tenth and highest sphere, Dante and Beatrice have reached

> . . . the heaven of pure light,
>   light of the intellect, light filled with love,
> love of true good, love filled with happiness,
> a happiness surpassing every sweetness. (XXX, 39–42)

A radiance envelops the pilgrim that makes him able to bear the visions of this realm, and he sees light that takes a river's form, "light flashing, reddish gold, between two banks / painted with wonderful spring flowerings" (62–63). Botticelli helps us enjoy the flowerings, and the "living sparks" (64) that Dante says are cavorting in the stream. Here we can particularly feel the relation between this flowering paradise and the earthly one atop the Mountain of Purgatory. Botticelli provides a wide context for the central figures of his unfinished drawing. Their size and elegance, especially again of Beatrice with her lovely feet, insists on the centrality—even in the wonder of this sphere—of the feminine mediatrix and her beloved human pupil.

242   Giovanni di Paolo's "living sparks" leap and dive in fully realized naked flesh and are even more lively than Botticelli's. His illustration retains the Trinitarian figures of the previous sphere.

242

243, 244   The Emilian (or Paduan) artist of ca. 1340 and
Blake realize the scene very differently. The Italian imagines gold and red circles glowing
in darkness, the stream banks sheathed in gold. Blake brings in elements of his own vision
of a columnlike river of light, described in a letter to a friend, which occurred some twenty-
five years earlier on a beach in West Sussex. Dante kneels to drink, as commanded by
Beatrice, but in Blake's imagination of the scene she holds a mirror, perhaps to give form
to the poet's assertion, as the river of light transforms into the Celestial Rose, that it mirrors
"all of us who have won return above" (XXX, 114).

PAR. Canto 30

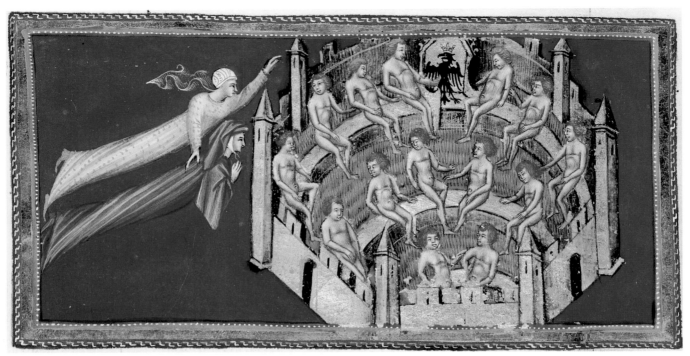

245

246

245, 246   Beatrice points out to the pilgrim selected sections of the Rose, which in Giovanni di Paolo's first image becomes a kind of amphitheater, an arena that focuses all attention on a political action of sacred import. A throne (above) awaits Henry VII, who was to Dante the symbol of rightful leadership on earth. The saints in his second image (below), surrounded by angels, are all comfortably cupped in the petals of a lovingly rendered naturalistic rose.

Just as the poet stresses throughout the *Paradiso* that equality in the presence of the sacred mysteries can be communicated to human perception only in familiar hierarchical terms, so the medieval illuminator most often uses very literal human images to convey what he knows—and the poet insists—are symbolic representations.

248

247, 248   Beatrice draws the pilgrim into the Celestial Rose; from different standpoints, Doré and Blake both suggest the vastness and glory of the atmosphere. Blake's Rose is more substantial, and his quarrels with Dante's image-meanings become acute. Most centrally, he was outspoken against what he called the pernicious dogmas of the Immaculate Conception and the Virgin Birth, which he felt blighted sexual love. Here Mary wields the lily of chastity as a scepter to command obedience, but both Mary and Beatrice (below her) are sensually rendered and hold looking glasses, which Milton Klonsky points out reflect, for Blake, the permanent realities of the vegetative realm.

              Characteristically, Doré emphasizes the immensity of the Celestial Rose, a numinous largeness that makes the human figures very modest in its presence. The difference of scale between the human (including Beatrice) and the divine expresses the traditional perception of God's great Otherness. Blake, on the other hand, presents us with a vision of the Rose as it might be seen within the psyche of a viewer who is at one with it rather than objectively separated from it. The joy of the blessed is palpable.

249   Another Italian illuminator of the fourteenth century attempts to come closer to the placement of the blessed described in the poem and marks initials beside the figures where they sit gazing at Mary in glory. Adam and Peter are called "the two roots of this Rose" (XXXII, 120).

249

250

250   Mary increasingly becomes the focus of the poem in the last three cantos (see "Beatrice, Lucia, Mary," below). Saint Bernard appears to tell Dante that Beatrice sent him to mediate a further connection to the Lady, who is likened to the sunrise and surrounded by more than a thousand festive angels, through whom he may penetrate the radiance of the Primal Love. Bernard also indicates that Beatrice has taken her place in the Rose, and Dante, now filled with both uncomplicated gratitude and inner awareness, offers her a prayer that ends:

> Do, in me, preserve
>   your generosity, so that my soul,
> which you have healed, when it is set loose from
> my body, be a soul that you will welcome. (XXXI, 87–90)

Beatrice's smiling response to this prayer indicates that the poet's quest for inner completion is nearing fulfillment (see "Prayer Denied and Prayer Affirmed," above).

The Venetian illuminator concentrates on the first rank of souls and some of the angels around Mary as, at lower right, Bernard begins to direct the pilgrim's gaze upward.

Beatrice, Lucia, Mary   Image 9   Having seen Mary in her place
at the top of the ranks of human women who dwell conjoint with God, we return to open
out a fundamental theme. Despondent in the Dark Wood, the pilgrim takes heart when
Virgil appears as a guide serving three extraordinary women who intend to help him.
He has been singled out as worthy of their care. Throughout his arduous journey, against
a background of inexorable judgment, the motif of empathic love and individual signifi-
cance builds from this threefold feminine chord of the beginning: Beatrice, Lucia, Mary.

In Canto II, Virgil describes how a lady called to him in Limbo, a lady so
lovely that he begged to serve her. The courtesy of the exchange between them sets the
tone for Dante's ensuing development of a distinct kind of feminine energy. Beatrice
makes clear to Virgil that she has chosen him as guide because he is honest and courteous
and because he is persuasive. The fame of his golden tongue "is still a presence in the
world / and shall endure as long as the world lasts," she says (59–60). She tells Virgil
that the original source of her request for his aid is a "gentle lady" in Heaven (Mary)
who weeps for the pilgrim's distress "so that stern judgment up above is shattered" (96).
Mary then calls on Lucia, "enemy of every cruelty" (100), to whom Dante has apparently
been devoted, saying, "Now your faithful one / has need of you, and I commend him to
you" (98–99). Lucia delivers the message to Beatrice, taking her to task (somewhat as
Beatrice later does Dante): "why have you not helped him who loves you so / that—for
your sake—he's left the vulgar crowd?" (104–105). It becomes clear that this trilevel
compassion, in varying degrees of accessibility, is not offered gratuitously. Dante the
pilgrim has lived his life and used his art in such a way as to merit concern, even though
in the Dark Wood he loses all trust in the meaning of his struggles and longings and must
finally address the canker of self-doubt and isolation at his core.

Virgil ends, "And, just as she [Beatrice] had wished, I came to you: / I
snatched you from the path of the fierce beast" (118–119). Having told all this and seeing
that the pilgrim is still immobilized by fear, he exclaims in exasperation:

> What is it then? Why, why do you resist?
> Why does your heart host so much cowardice?
> Where are your daring and your openness
> as long as there are three such blessed women
> concerned for you within the court of Heaven
> and my words promise you so great a good? (121–126)

With this, the pilgrim's "exhausted force" returns, and he tells his guide to lead on.

This triple endorsement of the pilgrim in his search spans vast realms
of space and time, reaching in its imagery from the eternal Empyrean Rose down to the
daily life of Florence. In our modern disenchantment with the traditional Judeo-Christian
relegation of Goddess powers to a place of exile, or to pallid handmaidenship, we are
moved to look carefully at Dante's fourteenth-century description of a feminine power
that directs the course of his pilgrim's journey from beginning to end.

Beatrice

Commencing with her role in this initial triumvirate of feminine energy and concern, the figure of Beatrice develops throughout the poem. The poet creates a specifically feminine analogue of Godhead, a feminine mode of the passion that moved the judging masculine God to suffer mortally in order to bring a new level of significance to humankind. The new dispensation of numinous power intentionally reaching down to experience the human world has been imaged in feminine form in the Gnostic Sophia, the Hebrew Shekinah, and the Buddhist Kuan-yin. She is potentially incarnate in every person, because she is the spirit of specific embodiment in earthly form. Dante has dared to approach this mystery and to distinguish three levels of it; even on the most accessible level he still describes Beatrice as a mixture of human and divine, as parallel to Jesus. As noted earlier, when Beatrice first appears in the Earthly Paradise, all voices in the great pageant shout, "Blessed art thou that comest" retaining the masculine ending, "*Benedictus qui venis*," that refers to Christ (XXX, 19). (In some manuscripts, the text has Beatrice assert royally, "ben sem, ben sem" ["we are, we are Beatrice" (73), as if to emphasize her more-than-personal nature, but the more widely accepted reading is "ben son, ben son" ["I am, I am"], which Allen Mandelbaum, Charles Singleton, and John Ciardi—but not Dorothy Sayers—all prefer. Either way, the poet's iteration stresses her authority, as if the pilgrim might carelessly have underestimated it.)

Although we know little of Beatrice's earthly story, we do know from Dante's writing the living power she held in his youthful soul, a power first envisioned by his unconscious as the devouring of his heart at the behest of Love. As the *Commedia* unfolds, we see how in the mature poet this power (which today we might call an obsessive, dangerously consuming anima possession) is transformed into the feminine guide-companion of a highly developed male psyche. Women reading the *Commedia* today might want to imagine what such a story would be like from their perspectives, paying attention to whatever images have presented themselves during their journeys thus far. What would remain the same is the attitude of respect Dante brings to his images, no matter what kind of energy they present. The passion he brings to his experience of the inner feminine elements is compelling in part because it retains a personal dimension to the end. It is heartfelt throughout, but not sentimental, because Dante lets himself be guided by and submits to the kind of inner feminine wisdom that is not all-accepting but demands a responsible attitude toward life and one's own creative wellspring. He has moved beyond the state in which many men assume life-long they must either struggle against the feminine power or be devoured by it.

The first word we hear of Beatrice in the *Commedia* is spoken by Virgil to the pilgrim in Canto I. He explains that he will guide Dante first through an eternal place where they "shall hear the howls of desperation" (115) and then through a realm where the souls "are content within the fire" (118–119); after that, "a soul more worthy than I am will guide you" (122). Beatrice will take the pilgrim where Virgil cannot go. She has lived the passion and the joy of the "good news" offered by a transpersonal energy that no longer keeps itself in a separate realm. She stands for the potential in the individual imagination to comprehend and live under the leadership of the Self.

The pilgrim will not see Beatrice until he has struggled up the Mountain of Purgatory to the Earthly Paradise, but Virgil uses her image to hearten him often, especially when he quails confronting the final refining fire of the seventh terrace. "Now see, son: this / wall stands between you and your Beatrice" (XXVII, 35–36). After they enter the flames, Virgil continues talking of Beatrice: "I seem to see her eyes already" (54). With this image, emphasizing the significance of Beatrice's eyes, the poet implies that seeing with the aid of her vision will soon be his reward for having consciously endured the purification of his desire. From the perspective of Dante's early dream, we might say that the inflamed youthful heart Beatrice had eaten is now nearly transformed by the fiery processes of many years of inner work. The poet has brought his inner pilgrim to the place where he is ready to enter into conscious dialogue with the internalized reality of the figure who has carried for decades the projection of his soul.

Throughout their subsequent travels from one heaven to another of the *Paradiso* (so touchingly depicted by Botticelli), Beatrice teaches the pilgrim when and where and how to look. Through her eyes he learns to see, and also to ask, that he may understand. Beatrice constantly affirms and anticipates Dante's need to question, echoing the importance of asking "the question" in the stories of the Holy Grail. But whereas in the grail story the emphasis is on the one deep question that needs to be asked, in Dante's compendium of medieval knowledge all questions that go to the heart of sacred feeling (as distinguished from the barren abstractions of philosophy) are of legitimate concern to his soul's intimate guide.

Lucia

Whereas Beatrice is first the inner magnet drawing the pilgrim into his arduous journey and then the guiding companion for his ascent through Paradise, Lucia's role is limited to two important mediations between levels. In the first, she serves as messenger from Mary to Beatrice as the divine goodwill descends in compassionate determination to lighten human darkness, and in the second, she intervenes to hasten the pilgrim's ascent to the gate marking the atoning terraces of Purgatory proper. While the pilgrim dreams of the fearsome eagle sweeping him suddenly up into a searing fire, Lucia is actually carrying him in her arms up the steep climb below the entrance to the terraces of Purgatory. Beyond the gate to which he is borne, he will discover that the souls on each terrace know, accept, and work on their own neurotic dividedness, with the help of examples given by voices and visions.

In his dream, the pilgrim speculates about the uniqueness of the eagle's location: "This eagle," he thinks, "may / be used to hunting only here; its claws / refuse to carry upward any prey / found elsewhere" (IX, 25–28). The same may be said of Lucia, whose intervention in the journey parallels the eagle's in the dream, making a unique transition point. When Dante wakes in fear, Virgil reassures him, telling him that at dawn a lady came who said: "I am Lucia; / let me take hold of him who is asleep, / that I may help to speed him on his way" (IX, 55–57). He continues, "here she set you down, but first her lovely / eyes showed that open entryway to me; / then she and sleep together took their leave" (61–63). Pilgrim and guide go on, then, to discover the three steps, the gate, and its custodian, whose face is too radiant to look upon. He challenges their presence:

"Where is your escort? / Take care lest you be harmed by climbing here" (86–87). But this angel becomes graciously welcoming when he hears from Virgil that Lucia has indeed brought them there. As Virgil puts it, "a lady came from Heaven and, familiar / with these things, told us: 'That's the gate; go there'" (89–90). This exchange with the guardian underscores Lucia's special standing in the *Commedia*.

In Christian tradition, Lucia was a fourth-century martyr who became patron saint of those who suffer defects of sight; she presumably originated as the early Christian version of Juno Lucina, a Sabine goddess of light whose temple was built in the eighth century B.C. At this place in the poem, she marks the entry of an elevating grace that is portrayed as being equivalent to the eagle's flight. If we think about Dante's faithfulness to her, she appears to represent the light of the conscious awareness he sought throughout his life.

Lucia's benevolent transport conveys the loving care that we intuit is the intent of deeper illumination, whereas the eagle's rapacious grasp evokes the fearfulness we actually experience in moving from the familiar to a new level. A developing ego may even know that surrender to the agent of the Self will be enlightening, but the loss of control is terrifying all the same. When we are fearful at this point in analytic work, beyond the time when caution is required, our dreams may reveal a readiness in the unconscious through a Lucia-like image.

Such an image is always arresting, whether it comes with fierceness or benevolence, and it is important to resist the alluring temptation to dwell on its numinous wonder; rather, it is instead our responsibility to find ways to go where it points. The image gives us a glimpse of a higher level which is easy to lose, especially when the resistance of a personal complex makes us fearful. We may be at one of those transitional moments when the ego is ready to follow the promptings of the larger self, but resistances that were once conscious have now dropped into the shadow and hold us back. It is time then to ally ourselves with the urge to conscious incarnation that illumination from the Lucia level promotes.

Mary

Mary has been present throughout the *Purgatorio* as first and best of the various corrective examples offered on each terrace to the souls who seek to transform those qualities that have kept them isolated and divided in themselves. Events in her life are shown or told to illustrate humility, generosity, gentleness, and the other opposites of the Seven Deadly Sins. As the image of earthliness herself, she stands for the fact that it is necessary to *experience* alternatives in mortal flesh before a sustained transformation of self-destructive patterns can occur.

When they reach the sphere of the Fixed Stars, Beatrice tells Dante that he can look upon her now: "the things you witnessed will have made you strong / enough to bear the power of my smile" (XXIII, 47–48). But then she presses him to look for Mary:

> Why are you so enraptured by my face
> as to deny your eyes the sight of that
> fair garden blossoming beneath Christ's rays?

The Rose in which the Word of God became
flesh grows within that garden. (70–74)

The verses that follow sing and circulate like the splendid images they describe and reverberate with "the deep affection" shown for Mary there. She is urged to enter the Empyrean with her son, where she is crowned and takes the central place in this Rose of sacred flowering.

The unconscious itself, as the matrix that is the ultimate ground of everything that comes to consciousness, is generally perceived as having a feminine character. From this feminine ground, as Jung and his followers put it, it is necessary for men and women alike to separate a "masculine" kind of ego, the stage of development that is portrayed worldwide in multifold myths of the hero's task or journey.

A developmental perspective of this kind deepens our understanding of the role of the three women. Writing of the unfolding progression of consciousness, Erich Neumann speaks of the ultimate experience, for the mature ego, of reconnection to a special kind of feminine wisdom, a wisdom that is far more encompassing than any individual's waking awareness. This wisdom is experienced by the creative individual as the fountainhead of imagination and vision, as source of symbol, ritual, poetry, and law. Neumann says that this wisdom "intervenes, summoned or unsummoned, to save man and give direction to his life" (*The Great Mother*, 330). Dante's description of the entrance of Beatrice, Lucia, and Mary into the middle of his life provides an example of just this phenomenon.

Neumann writes more specifically, in "Stages of Religious Experience and the Path of Depth Psychology" about the development of the kind of feminine power, related to and on an equal footing with a masculine power, which is described by Dante. "In the world of the Great Mother, nature is experienced as an independently revolving wheel [as in fig. 27] which, in the coexistence of black and white, day and night, good and evil, is unaware of justice or grace as the law of the world. Its most characteristic quality is the equilibrium of construction and destruction, life and death. It is indifferent and unrelated to the ego and to man. Therein lies its greatness, but also its inhumanity. With the experience of being 'intended' and taken seriously, the ego overcomes this stage of anonymous existence and acquires a new dignity, expressed in the realization of a grace and justice inherent in the structure of the world" (23). Mary, for Dante, expresses this realizing, form-giving energy.

Women today are struggling with the realization of a specifically feminine aspect of that ego which Neumann has called masculine in relation to the unconscious. It involves claiming a feminine birthright, to be a true daughter of the Sophia mother rather than of the Elemental mother. These women make the discovery, for instance, that although they are unconsciously still a container for father's ideas and attitudes, they have also been identified with the elemental feminine in holding onto father (and husband) as *child*. They have feared the unknown good of a separated independent life and the chance of a real partnership with a grown man. Mary's role can symbolize the sacrifice of the son so that the man may live, as Esther Harding puts it in *Women's Mysteries* (chap. 14).

This claiming of the Sophia mother has to do in part with making a living distinction between strength and power, since the word *power* has the connotation of being driven by an unconscious complex. When the time is prepared, a woman—or a man like Dante—is able to choose to make real an individual strength and to know the palpable joy of claiming it. An active empathy arises for one's own family history, for the history of one's social matrix, and for the movement of the transpersonal powers from arbitrary judgment to loving compassion. In each case, there is a level of archaic unconscious chaos in the background out of which a conscious differentiation needs to develop.

It seems extraordinarily difficult and risky, as Beatrice implies in her question to Dante, "Did you not know that man is happy here?" (*Purgatorio* XXX, 75), to give up a negative view of oneself and to stop refusing one's life. That sacrifice would leave us too much exposed. We would have to trust the still small voice or image and lean on the everlasting arms. This submission to the trustworthy archetypal forces in one's psyche is most fully exemplified on the feminine side in Mary (and on the masculine in Christ) at this stage of development. They are not models of the literal slavery of women to men or men to women but signify a further life-giving breakthrough for the psyches of each. This goes beyond the Lucia advance in the responsibility to be conscious, toward an individual identity formed out of the ongoing exchange between ego and Self and the growing experience of being "intended" as a partner who must not only yield to, but choose, wrestle with, and insist on earthly limits.

The Beatrice-Lucia-Mary energies are not totally accepting, nor are they confined to a local or tribal group in the mode of the Earth Mother. As Beatrice makes obvious to Dante, when he is prepared at last to take responsibility for everything he has so far seen in his psyche, he is expected to "lift up [his] beard" (*Purgatorio*, XXXI, 68), to let go of his last shreds of self-pity and assent to the joyful condition he is approaching. Immersion in Lethe, forgetting the old bitternesses, requires the sacrifice of all sentimentality.

We might speculate that the three levels indicated by Dante in Beatrice, Lucia, and Mary represent the increasingly large perspectives that can be encompassed by the psyche as it learns to see and to live more and more wholly. If we can imagine looking through the eyes of each queenly woman in succession, we may understand the paradox of loving oneself and giving oneself in larger and larger contexts. Dante's three women also probably rest on the triune form in which many goddesses have been worshipped, symbolizing three levels of the development of an ego-Self connection in which ego takes as much responsibility as it can understand and realize at each level.

Dante communicates a genuinely worshipful sense of these three levels and the kinds of connection with each. Beatrice is on the most accessible, personally incarnated level, like a consistent dream figure (sometimes a life partner in reality) who shares the attitude of looking beyond, and she has a more comprehensive and objective perspective in certain important ways. Dante indicates that Beatrice, once manifested, continues to be present though separate; she remains until an even more developed sense of self-knowledge and centering occurs.

Lucia is the model of the rare and mysterious breakthroughs of consciousness, of dawning orientation, made with the help of an energy originating in another sphere entirely. This is extremely difficult for the ego to trust at first. More than that, Dante places Lucia where the traveler must fully shoulder his own responsibility for further progress by living the consequences of all former actions, whether they were made consciously or unconsciously. Now one has a different order of awareness and must live up to it by making hard choices and following them through.

Mary is found at the level of the most numinous, barely perceivable images, through which one intuits the "cloud of unknowing." Beatrice points her out as Rose; for Dante she is Crowned Flame and Eternal Fountain. The particularly feminine quality of this level resides in the experience of the person who receives images from there: these carry the extraordinary mix of huge receptive power and specific personal address that gives undeniable meaning to their manifestation. The experience is one of being touched and moved to respond from the most vulnerable places of heart and mind.

The movement of the compassionate energy downward at the beginning of the *Commedia*, from Mary through Lucia to Beatrice, turns upward through the person of Virgil and then in the final sphere is mediated by Bernard, whose life is known to have been an interchange between mystical contemplation and outer action and who is known for his restoration of the cult of Mary in the twelfth century. In the final canto Bernard prays to Mary for Dante. He asks that the presence of the light of the Love on which she gazes—the light that is beyond all categories—will not destroy this faithful pilgrim, who then discovers that he is able to bear the final vision.

251

In the final canto, Dante attempts to give words to his vision of the Eternal Light. Giovanni di Paolo chooses to illustrate something he can render visually. In lines 94–96, Dante compares what he cannot remember or describe here in this realm to all the forgetting that twenty-five centuries have caused since Jason's ship "startled Neptune with the *Argo's* shadow" (XXXIII, 96) above him in the sea. The image evokes the astonishment of an immortal god that a human being was able to venture across the ocean depths in search of the "golden fleece." This hero's quest for the central values of mortal experience is registered better in memory, after more than two millennia, than the poet's recollection of his rapture in the divine presence, which has only just occurred. Such is the impact of sacred vision. Giovanni di Paolo, making his own analogy, shows Beatrice and the pilgrim before a radiant Mary, on whose left the Argo and Neptune appear.

It is noteworthy that, by choosing to compare his own unrepresentable wonder before the divine light with Neptune's astonishment in the face of human achievement, the poet gives an example of the awesome effect of humankind on God, as well as of God on humanity.

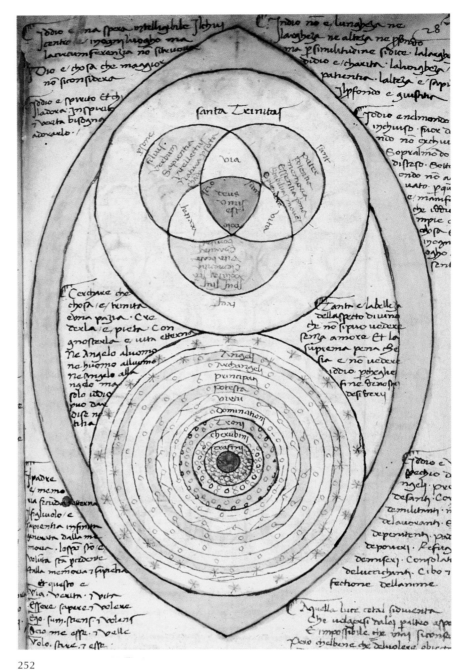

252

252   A Florentine
illuminator, ca. 1440, makes a
schematic version of the miraculous
wheeling rounds, emphasizing the
three circles of the Trinity. He con-
tains his image of ultimate whole-
ness and mystery in a mandorla,
the almond shape traditionally asso-
ciated with the ascension of Christ.
The uniting of segments of two cir-
cles seems to imply that the two
poles of matter and spirit have
become joined and to image in a
kind of sacred vulva the opening to
the material from the spiritual realm
that is the meaning of incarnation.

253   The Venetian illuminator of the late fourteenth century provides a more orthodox rendering of the Trinity in naturalistic figures. Here a faint dove of the Holy Spirit emanates from the mouth of the Father and touches the head of the Son. The artist makes his illustration notable within the manuscript by surrounding it with brilliant red instead of the usual paradisal blue, like the blare of a trumpet at the end. Dante kneels at the foot of the golden throne, now able to gaze steadily at the awesome sight.

253

254

254   In his unfinished final drawing, Botticelli sketches a tiny, far distant Virgin, Christ, and a third figure (usually taken to be the angel Gabriel), apparently just as much at a loss for descriptive power as Dante, as the poem concludes. It is striking that in so large a folio Botticelli has chosen to make his divine figures small, in contrast to his habit of enlarging the figures of Dante and Beatrice in almost all of his Paradisal drawings. Through this device, he emphasizes the otherness and distance of the divine.

There is something puzzling about this tiny drawing for, exceptionally here, Botticelli does not follow the imagery of the poem closely. Although Mary and Gabriel appear together in the last canto—and Botticelli seems to have written "33" beneath this folio—the figure of Christ does not accompany Mary in the poet's closing narrative. Yet his identification in the drawing seems more certain than Gabriel's, for we can see the marks of the stigmata in the raised hands of the central figure, and the small seated figure on the left is certainly Mary. To some eyes, the figure on the right looks more like Beatrice than Gabriel, feminine in appearance and lacking the wings that Botticelli gives his angels elsewhere (see fig. 238, for example). Perhaps, in his closing interpretation, Botticelli tentatively suggests the close affinity of Beatrice with Mary and Christ, reminding us again that it was Mary whose compassion sent Lucia to Beatrice so that Beatrice could become the mediator who intervenes, like Christ, to bring the poet to salvation. This ambiguity may be deliberate, for both Gabriel and Beatrice are mediators, Gabriel bringing the fertilizing word of incarnation to Mary, and Beatrice bringing the salvation this incarnation makes possible to the pilgrim. The conjunction of masculine and feminine figures in this image seems to suggest that Christ and Mary have together brought about personal access to the divine for humankind as a whole, for Beatrice and through her for Dante as the pilgrim in everyone. In any event, Botticelli leaves us with a small image of the union of human and divine, set in the vastness of his folio page as if to emphasize the unrepresentable mystery of the poem's conclusion. Leonard Baskin, in his contrasting final image (see fig. 255), conveys a modern preoccupation with the state of the artist as creator.

255   Baskin shows us Dante "at the end of all desiring," as he titles his illustration. He alludes to lines 46–48 of Canto XXXIII, where, as Allen Mandelbaum translates the passage, the poet says,

> And I, who now was nearing Him who is
> the end of all desires, as I ought,
> lifted my longing to its ardent limit.

It is notable that for this twentieth century artist all the light is in the figure of the pilgrim. Surrounded by darkness, he reveals his inner illumination.

Baskin's final illustration offers a concluding interpretation in which the artist's person, not his vision, is at the center. Interestingly, six hundred years earlier, Boccaccio described a legendary dream of Dante's son, Jacopo (some months after his father died), in which the poet appeared, in the dark before dawn, in very similar form: "clad in whitest garments, and his face shining with an unwonted light." Asked by Jacopo in the dream if "he were yet living," Dante replied "that he was, but in the true life, not in ours" (*Life of Dante*, 91). Baskin's image suggests that the artist's fulfilled work is a sacred completion (see "Exile and the Price of Completion," below).

The Human Image in God　　　In his final vision of Beatrice, the pilgrim sees her clearly, but from far away. In her intimate association of human and divine, Beatrice appears close to the central rays of deity, an apotheosis from which she smiles on her beloved with a care that is both personal and transpersonal. We are confident that the poet will rejoin her in Paradise, but there is no suggestion that his place will be as her companion. Rather, we know he will find that relationship to the divine center which is appropriate to his nature and that he will be satisfied to share with Beatrice the fulfilling contemplation of "the eternal fountain" (XXXI, 93), which is the blessing of all the souls at every level of the heavens.

Thus Dante makes it clear that blessedness for humankind is closeness to the source of love and life that derives from the unfathomable depths of the divine light. Among these mysteries is the vision of the triune nature of God with which the poet closes the poem. It is a vision, he insists, that barely reconstructs an experience he can recall only in its emotion, yet his words come closer to expressing the awe and wonder we feel in the presence of the divine mystery than anything else in Western literature.

Most mysterious of all is the appearance of the human form, "la nostra effige" (XXXIII, 131), contained within the second of the three circles that reflect the separate unity of Father, Son, and Holy Ghost:

> Eternal Light, You only dwell within
> Yourself, and only You know You; Self-knowing,
> Self-known, You love and smile upon Yourself!
> 　That circle—which, begotten so, appeared in
> You as light reflected—when my eyes
> had watched it with attention for some time,
> 　within itself and colored like itself,
> to me seemed painted with our effigy,
> so that my sight was set on it completely.
> 　As the geometer intently seeks
> to square the circle, but he cannot reach,
> through thought on thought, the principle he needs,
> 　so I searched that strange sight: I wished to see
> the way in which our human effigy
> suited the circle and found place in it—
> 　and my own wings were far too weak for that.
> But then my mind was struck by light that flashed
> and, with this light, received what it had asked. (XXXIII, 124–141)

Not only does the fulfillment of salvation bring individual souls where they can contemplate the wondrous Otherness of God, but the poet also depicts essential humanness itself as part of God's own being. Just as deity voluntarily descends into human flesh and finitude in the mystery of the Incarnation, so the human soul ascends to discover that the ultimate mystery of human nature is contained within God's essence. First we see that God is capable of becoming human and then we learn that archetypal humanness is already a part of God. This, "the way in which our human effigy / suited the circle and found place in it," is too heavy a mystery for the poet's wings to carry, yet it is at the core of the vision with which the poem closes.

The pathology depicted so vividly in the Inferno is never seen in Paradise to be a living aspect of the divine whole. Yet it is a part of the divinely ordained cosmos, symbolized most vividly by the figure of Dis split off and frozen into the center of Hell, which is also the center of the material universe. There is no dark side of the deity in heaven—though such dark emotions as Peter's rage at the condition of the Church (*Paradiso*, XXVII, 19–27) are vividly real—but the ultimate traitor to divine beneficence is built in structurally as the fulcrum whose hairy flank is the turning point on the journey of salvation. Thus Dante remains true to Christian theology, which proclaims the goodness of God, but his vision contains the dark side of both God and humankind within the totality we must know in order to become whole.

Each of the humans in Paradise carries there his or her lived-through experience of evil. In the narratives of every great mythic tradition the individual learns, precisely from the ills he or she induces or endures, the meanings of suffering and the opportunities for reconciliation with the sacred powers. And although these powers are known to be Wholly Other, as Rudolf Otto puts it in *The Idea of the Holy*, they are also elements of the human psyche: other to the ego but part of human nature, which in turn is part of God.

With a wisdom as ancient as the visions of mystics of every tradition and as modern as the symbolic perspective of archetypally oriented depth psychology, Dante insists that although God is infinitely larger, at crucial intersections God and humankind are one. Especially implicit in the Christian image of Incarnation is the recognition that interior reality as well as objective otherness is expressed symbolically by all the god-images reflected in sacred stories across the ages and around the world.

Writing with compassion in Tel Aviv after the horrors of the Second World War of a "new human standpoint which accepts darkness and the negative side," Erich Neumann concludes his *Depth Psychology and a New Ethic* with this bold image: "And yet, out of the midst of this circle of humanity . . . the same creative Godhead, unformed and manifold, is emerging within the human mind, who previously filled the heavens and spheres of the universe around us" (134, 135).

For Dante in his time, going beyond the accepted doctrine that in the Incarnation God chooses conception in human flesh, to perceive intuitively that human nature is an *original* aspect of the divine nature, is more than his imaginative wings can carry—but this is what he has seen in this final vision of the ultimate reality. His mind cannot grasp "the way in which our human effigy / suited the circle and found place in it," but it is "struck by light that flashed / and, with this light, received what it had asked." The grace of mystical vision confirms the reality of what he has seen—in a way that passes understanding but resolves the question:

> Here force failed my high fantasy; but my
> desire and will were moved already—like
> a wheel revolving uniformly—by
> the Love that moves the sun and the other stars. (142–145)

Even in this final attunement of the poet's desire and will with the sacred energy that activates the cosmos, we are reminded of how much emphasis Beatrice, in Canto XXVIII and elsewhere, has put on the lesson that "blessedness depends / upon the act of vision, not upon / the act of love—which is a consequence" (XXVIII, 109–111). And yet, as Beatrice also implies, we are here in the mystery of paradox, for, as she points out in discussing angelic virtue in Canto XXIX, "there is merit in receiving / grace, measured by the longing [l'affetto] to receive it" (65–66). That is, the profundity of one's desire for union with the divine is also essential to reception of "illuminating grace" (62) from the divine. And this desire has been evoked for Dante from the beginning by his passionate devotion to Beatrice, whose love has led him to his final vision.

The uniqueness of the conclusion of the Paradiso is that it conveys the poet's deep experience of being one with the divine light and love, even though this phenomenon can neither be understood fully nor articulated. Nevertheless, Dante's images touch the core of a sensitive reader to evoke a true spark of the experience itself and an awareness that in some mysterious way our humanness fits the circle of divinity. Yet his concluding images also remind us that no matter how sophisticated we may become in the language of modern science and depth psychology, the mystery endures in the symbolic realm where divine and human come together.

Conclusion   **Exile and the Price of Completion**

Writing a few decades after Dante's death, Boccaccio tells us of the poet's appointment in 1321 by his patron, Count Guido Novella of Ravenna (where Dante was living in a house supplied by the count), as one of his ambassadors to mediate a fierce dispute between Ravenna and Venice. Negotiations with the doge failed, and Dante returned to Ravenna by land rather than by ship, contracting a severe illness (probably malaria) as he passed through disease-infested territories along the shore. Shortly after his return, he died. Although he had completed the *Paradiso* just before he undertook this embassy, the final thirteen cantos of the poem could not be found after his death. Boccaccio reports that it was eight months later when Dante's son, Jacopo, had a dream in which his father showed him where the papers were hidden in the wall of the bedroom in which he had spent his last days. The concluding cantos, moldy and deteriorating, were secured for posterity in the nick of time. Boccaccio's uncorroborated account may be only legendary, but as we shall see, it appears to make psychological sense.

Exiled on pain of death should he return, Dante had grieved for his beloved homeland until the end of his life. We have seen the depth of his longing in *Paradiso* XXV in his unanswered prayer that his "sacred poem" might "overcome the cruelty / that bars me from the fair fold where I slept" (4–5). Writing in the *Convivio* earlier in his exile, perhaps after beginning but certainly before completing the *Inferno*, Dante calls his banishment "the stroke of fortune which is wont unjustly to be charged to the account of the stricken" and speaks of himself as "a ship without sail and without rudder, wafted to divers havens and inlets and shores, by the parching wind which woful poverty exhales" (*Dante's Convivio*, trans. William W. Jackson, 38). He never gave up the image of his exile as a wound, but in developing the design of the *Commedia* we know he was anything but an undirected and powerless vessel. Indeed, the composition of so great and sustained a work obviously requires resources of enormous energy, commitment, and control. We are led to wonder what displaced the poet's wounded sense of drift with the drive to undertake years of work on the *Commedia* even at the cost of leaving the *Convivio* unfinished.

More than one commentator has noted the irony that if Dante had not suffered exile, the poem as we know it would not exist. William Anderson observes that "Carducci thought that a statue should be put up in every Italian town to Conte de' Gabrielli for exiling Dante, and Carlyle makes play with a similar idea" (*Dante the Maker*, 165). We can join them in gratitude that the evil popes and political opponents he sprinkles liberally throughout the *Inferno* forced upon the poet the isolation for which he never forgave them. Only this provided him the essential freedom from the distractions of public life required for the detailed invention of his profoundly imagined journey. Yet for several years after being banished Dante could not give up his determined efforts to effect his return, as various epistles plotting for political and military recovery in the early years of exile make clear.

There is a substantial literature written in prison or isolation that depends for its depth on the forced separation of its authors from the world in which they had previously been active. One thinks of John Bunyan or Malcolm X or Piri Thomas in prison; of Milton and Beethoven cut off by blindness and deafness; or of the late-life themes of Sophocles' *Oedipus at Colonnus,* Shakespeare's *Tempest,* or Thomas Mann's *Holy Sinner,* in which old age provides detachment from the world. For Dante, the irony that his opponents have made possible the scale of his achievement is most vivid because their refusal to accommodate his return finally breaks his *own* preoccupation with place and power in the world.

But more than irony is involved in the intimate connection between Dante's exile and the scale of his creative opus. From a psychological perspective, enormous personal loss is a goad to the poet's creative development, from beginning to end. We know he lost his mother at a young enough age to affect his feeling life profoundly. Though we lack biographical confirmation, it is probable that this loss contributed greatly to his psychological projection onto Beatrice, from the age of nine forward, of the feminine value he lacked and needed for the fulfillment of his being. We do know that his fascination wed him to her image and nurtured his life as a child, binding him also to his poetic vocation from the moment he dreamed that she was held in the arms of the lord of his soul. From the hand of Amor she eats his heart, and the development of his poetic talent flows from the vicissitudes of his devotion.

When Beatrice dies, Dante suffers his second great loss, expressing his grief consciously as he could not have done for his mother; at last he determines to say no more until he can "compose concerning her what has never been written in rhyme of any woman." Thereupon he immediately concludes the *Vita Nuova* with the sentence, "And then may it please Him who is the Lord of courtesy that my soul may go to see the glory of my lady, that is of the blessed Beatrice, who now in glory beholds the face of Him *qui est per omnia secula benedictus*" (99). Noting these words after reading the *Paradiso,* we can see that they foreshadow the poet's final address to Beatrice many years later in Canto XXXI, when he places himself before her, still in life, and expresses his ultimate hope to keep her image within him in such a way that on his death he will deserve to share with her the presence of deity. There is vast poetic development between the end of his earliest work and the final vision of his last, but the intention to get from the one to the other has already been established.

However, the achievement of this goal was not to come without suffering the third great loss of his life. In the years following Beatrice's death and the writing of the *Vita Nuova,* Dante became engaged in the combative world of Florentine politics. He was sent to Rome to negotiate with Pope Boniface VIII, only to be betrayed while he was absent and then banished forever. We have seen in his poignant desire to return with honor how much he continued to feel that Florence was the matrix of his temporal life, the third great love from which separation is anguish. Orphaned once in the loss of his mother and in a feeling sense again in the loss of Beatrice, he is orphaned yet a third time in being cut off from the mother city to which he was so attached.

The alchemists have a saying that "the stone is an orphan," which baffles the rational mind until one sees that being truly orphaned means that we can no longer look for good-enough parenting at the concrete personal level but must turn instead to be healed from the transpersonal level. This is ultimately the function performed by the magnification of Beatrice's meaning to Dante through the lens of his multifold poem. His imagination of the meanings of suffering in human experience is the fruit of the author's quest for meaning in the heart of loss and betrayal.

Even though we know that Dante had a large creative undertaking in mind soon after Beatrice's death, we also know that subsequently enforced loneliness was not at first sufficient to activate his grand intention. For several years after his exile in 1302, he spent his time in study, writing in Latin and plotting with other exiles to find a way out of banishment and back to Florence. Only after several marked failures did he withdraw from most of his political associations and declare himself a "party of one." Even then, he did not at once take up the *Commedia*.

Most commentators see the writing of the *Inferno* commencing in about 1308, six years into exile, when the unfinished *Convivio* breaks off. William Anderson argues for a later date, about 1311, after Dante's attempts to further the accession to the imperial throne of Henry VII, for whom he campaigned vigorously in letters and tracts. Whatever year he actually began the *Inferno*, its commencement appears to have been strongly influenced by an experience on the banks of the Arno, reported in a letter to Lord Moruello, Marquis Malaspina, as a vision, a vision that recalls the dream of Beatrice in the arms of Amor.

In this epistle, numbered III in *The Portable Dante*, the poet describes what happened:

> No sooner had I set my feet by the streams of the Arno, in security and carelessness, than straightway behold a woman appeared to me, descending like a lightning flash, strangely harmonious with my condition both in character and in person. Oh, how was I struck dumb at her apparition! But my stupor yielded to the terror of the thunder that followed. For like as thunders straightway follow flashes from heaven, so when the flame of this beauty had appeared, Love [Amor] laid hold of me, terrible and imperious; raging, moreover, like a lord banished from his fatherland returning after long exile to what is all his own! For he slew or banished or enchained all opposition in me. He slew that praiseworthy determination in the strength of which I held aloof from women, those instruments of his enchantment; and the unbroken meditations wherein I was pondering on things both of heaven and of earth, he relentlessly banished as things suspected; and finally, that my soul might never again rebel against him, he chained my free will; so that I needs must turn not whither I would, but whither he wills. (649–650)

What is impressive about Dante's report of this encounter is its vivid description of the object of a new love and the appearance of Amor in "the terror of the thunder." Amor lays hold of him "terrible and imperious," much as the Eagle does in the first Purgatorial dream, conveying the transpersonal authority of a divinity who insists on surrender to his rule. Because Dante was engaged in fruitless political activity for a few years still after 1308, especially around the potential ascendancy of Henry VII to the imperial throne, it seems quite likely that Anderson is right in preferring the later date.

Either way, the point is that Amor interjects himself into the poet's life and calls him to his sacred task. No more than the papacy he castigates for betrayal to worldly power and wealth can he be preoccupied by political activism, or even with philosophic study and writing. The images are nearly as bold as in the early dream of Amor feeding his heart to Beatrice or, later, in the encounter with Beatrice on the banks of Lethe. Anderson asserts convincingly that this is the conversion experience that forces Dante finally to undertake his life-fulfilling task.

That such an overwhelming experience is necessary even after so many preparatory insights and visions indicates great tension in the poet's psyche between his ambition for personal knowledge, fame, and power and his inner call to create and honor a whole new image of divine authority—one framed within a Christian theology but also revealing the divine feminine and the "human effigy" as much at its center as the masculine Trinity. In the argument of the poem, he resolves this conflict by imagining a subordinate secular governance within the encompassing universe of sacred order, one in which the papacy attends to spiritual well-being but not to power, politics, and wealth.

Dante is isolated by his enemies in a way that enables him to fulfill his lifelong goal. But even after the opportunity is provided, he persists in political activity and writing that postpone his commitment for several years. It is then the less surprising that, when he gets to it, his treatment of the enemies he locates in the Inferno is so fierce and unforgiving: he must have felt himself threatened, both consciously and unconsciously, by the distractions of worldly power. Even in his image of ante-Purgatory, he condemns the basically virtuous but preoccupied rulers to many years of delay before they can begin to ascend the mountain. And most of all he condemns those who, like the great popes, failed to heed the explicit call to sacred duty. As he deferred that call himself, he punishes that failure savagely in those whose obligation was consciously and publicly pledged. We can see an almost paranoid rejection of the vice of worldliness by which he was himself most threatened.

No wonder then that he imagines Beatrice so angry with him in her first address, for she speaks on behalf of his long-frustrated soul. We are dramatically surprised, but it makes perfect psychic sense. What, indeed, might have happened if Henry VII had succeeded in claiming the emperor's throne and Dante had been able to return to Florence in honor and renewed authority? Either some other intervention of the teleological caller would have had to make him heed its voice or we would never have been given the *Commedia*.

It is as if the immutability of exile must wound him again and again with the "bitter taste / of others' bread, how salt it is," as Cacciaguida puts it (*Paradiso* XVII, 57–58), before the bitterness of salt can become its wisdom, the annealed detachment that derives from assimilated suffering and the education of feeling that accompanies it. Although the poet never fully accepts banishment from his worldly home and longs to the end that he might be restored to honor there, in time he puts to work in the service of his inner vision the relative freedom from activist politics that being stateless provides. He constructs an image of ideal temporal order to balance and complement the image of sacred order that is the glory of the poem, but few of his temporal hopes are ever realized.

In contemplating Dante's fate as a psychological event, one is reminded of Jung's observation that *the experience of the self is always a defeat for the ego*" (*CW* 14, para. 778, italics Jung's). He goes on to say, "The extraordinary difficulty in this experience is that the self can be distinguished only conceptually from what has always been referred to as 'God,' but not practically." By this he means that the forces at work in one's larger personality, often unconscious but having our wholeness, not our conscious image of ourselves, in mind, will thrust their purposes upon us in ways that painfully cross our conscious desires. Sometimes these crossings appear to be a malignant fate that has nothing to do with inner character or destiny—as we might well say of the death of Dante's mother, though it, too, plays a generative role in the poet's development. But many times they have the quality of tragedy, where personal character is largely responsible for unsought, and often disproportionate, suffering. Beatrice's death was not of Dante's making, but its lifelong impact on his psyche was forced on him by the power of his fascination combined with his determination to turn it to account. Her loss was a poignant suffering for his heart, but without it he would not have sustained his great ambition. So, too, without his passionate devotion to political life and his unbending refusal to submit to compromises that offended his integrity, he would not have suffered the permanent banishment that made possible the construction of his poem.

At one level, Dante's personal inclination to political activism conflicts with his deeper calling. For undertaking the embassy to Boniface, he suffers the dislocation of exile. Although that leads ultimately to the opportunity to create, it is a dangerous commitment that mortally threatens his life in this world. Moreover, it is again ironic that at the close of his life a political mission brings on his final illness. It is as if, having completed his poem, he believes he can reenter the political arena with impunity. But the trip is fatal, and almost a disaster for his readers if we believe Boccaccio, for it requires intervention by the sender-of-dreams to rescue the decaying manuscript from its damp hiding place in the wall. This new attempt to mediate between worldly cities seems to flow from a shadow element in Dante's character for which he must pay the ultimate price.

Yet the shadow he has conquered sufficiently to create his poem is also the source of his grand, albeit frustrated, vision of a worldly order in service to the divine. Tampering with the affairs of the cities of this world proves first nearly and later actually fatal to the poet's person. Even so, his passionate concern for the secular as well as the spiritual well-being of humankind gives rise to an image of the Holy Roman Empire as a kind of New Jerusalem in which incarnate life may be lived for its duration with the many instruments of human diversity united in harmonious accord. As the increasing generosity of the poem's vision unfolds, we see affirmations of the separation of church and state, of Joachim's era of the Holy Spirit with its implicit freedom of worship, that speak loudly from seven centuries ago to our condition today.

Thus the inner power-shadow that the poet must overcome in order to create the *Commedia* is also in part a source of its greatness. For Dante, the price of vision is sacrifice, sacrifice of a normal human life in time, sacrifice of the living honor that fidelity to so large a vision deserved. What, we may wonder, would have been the result had the poet declined the embassy to Venice and lived on while his poem gradually garnered the repute that might have brought him home to Florence as a revered citizen, wearing "the laurel crown" he imagines in *Paradiso* XXV? We cannot know, but it seems unlikely his final years would have been unperturbed by the political passions that had so stirred his heart.

What seems probable is that his life became complete precisely as the call to his fulfillment required. Amor worked in his psyche as the agent of the poetic calling that both competed with and was extended by his drive to political leadership and worldly honor. In reluctantly accepting separation from his homeland and ancestral roots, he endures his crucifixion between the opposites of incarnate flesh and timeless spirit. Mystified by "the way in which our human effigy / suited the circle and found place in it," he receives his final vision at the close of his great opus. Amor, the god who was the agent of his calling, has now become "l'amor," "the Love that moves the sun and the other stars." Having seen the human effigy in the second circle of the Trinity, his insight has not only prepared him for a return to the paradisal realm he has imagined but also moved him into a life that reaches beyond his own time, one that continues to serve our deepest sacred aspirations.

Works Cited

Anderson, William. *Dante the Maker*. New York, 1982.

Baskin, Leonard. *Illustrations to the Divine Comedy of Dante*, Graphic Arts Exhibition catalog, Introduction by Dale Roylance. New Haven, 1970. (The catalog contains selected illustrations from a 3-volume edition of *The Divine Comedy*, translated by T. G. Bergin, 124 plates [New York: Grossman, 1969], copy located in the Beinecke Rare Books and Manuscripts Library, Yale University.)

Bindman, David. *William Blake: His Art and Times*. London, 1982.

Boccaccio, Giovanni. *Life of Dante*. In *The Early Lives of Dante*, translated by Philip H. Wicksteed. London, 1904.

Bologna, Giulia. *Illuminated Manuscripts: The Book before Guttenberg*. New York, 1988.

Brieger, Peter H., Millard Meiss, and Charles S. Singleton. *Illuminated Manuscripts of the Divine Comedy*. 2 vols. Princeton, 1969.

Clark, Kenneth, ed. *The Drawings by Sandro Botticelli for Dante's Divine Comedy: After the Originals in the Berlin Museum and the Vatican*. Commentaries by George Robinson. London, 1976.

Cervigni, Dino S. *Dante's Poetry of Dreams*. Florence, 1986.

Dante Alighieri. *Dante's Convivio*, translated by William W. Jackson. Oxford, 1909.

———. *The Comedy of Dante Alighieri, the Florentine*, translated by Dorothy L. Sayers and Barbara Reynolds. 3 vols. New York, 1949, 1953, 1964.

———. *Divina Commedia: Codex Altonensis*, edited by Hans Haupt et al. Facsimile of the manuscript (and commentary, 2 vols.). Berlin, 1965.

———. *The Divine Comedy of Dante Alighieri*, translated by Allen Mandelbaum. 3 vols. Berkeley, 1980, 1982, 1984.

———. *The Divine Comedy*, translated by Charles S. Singleton. 3 vols. Princeton, 1970, 1973, 1975.

———. *L'Enfer de Dante Alighieri, avec les dessins de Gustave Doré*. Vol. 1. Paris, 1868.

———. *Le Purgatoire de Dante Alighieri, avec les dessins de Gustave Doré; Le Paradis de Dante Alighieri, avec les dessins de Gustave Doré*. Vol. 2. 2 vols. in 1. Paris, 1868.

———. *The Inferno, The Purgatorio, The Paradiso*, translated by J. A. Carlyle et al. Temple Classics edition. 3 vols. London, 1954.

———. *The Inferno, The Purgatorio, The Paradiso*, translated by John Ciardi. 3 vols. New York, 1954, 1957, 1961.

———. *La vita nuova*, translated by Barbara Reynolds. London, 1969.

———. *The Portable Dante*, edited by Paolo Milano. New York, 1977.

De Tolnay, Charles Q. *Michelangelo*. 6 vols. Vol. 5: *The Final Period*. Princeton, 1960.

Eliot, T. S. *Selected Essays*. New York, 1950.

Flaxman, John. *La divina commedia di Dante Alighieri*. Rome, 1802.

Fuseli, Henry. *L'opera completa di Fuseli*. Milan, 1977.

Guttuso, Renato. *Il Dante di Guttuso: Cinquantasei tavole dantesche disegnate da Renato Guttuso*. Milan, 1970.

Harding, M. Esther. *Women's Mysteries*. New York, 1955.

Huyghe, René. *Delacroix*. New York, 1963.

Jaffe, Irma B. *The Sculpture of Leonard Baskin*. New York, 1980.

Jung, Carl G. *The Collected Works of C. G. Jung*, edited by Herbert Read et al. 20 vols. New York, 1953–1979.

Klonsky, Milton. *Blake's Dante: The Complete Illustrations to the Divine Comedy*. New York, 1980.

Lebrun, Rico. *Drawings for Dante's Inferno*. Kanthos Press, n.p., 1963.

Lehman-Haupt, Helmut. *The Terrible Doré*. New York, 1943.

Luca Signorelli's Illustrationen zu Dante's Divina Commedia. Freiberg, 1892.

Luke, Helen. *Dark Wood to White Rose*. New York, 1989.

Neumann, Erich. *Depth Psychology and a New Ethic*, translated by Eugene Rolfe. New York, 1969. Originally published in German: Zurich, 1949.

———. *The Great Mother*. New York, 1955.

———. "Stages of Religious Experience and the Path of Depth Psychology." *Quadrant* (Spring 1988).

Otto, Rudolf. *The Idea of the Holy*. London, 1923.

Pope-Hennessy, John. *Paradiso: The Illuminations to Dante's Divine Comedy by Giovanni di Paolo*. New York, 1993.

Roe, Albert S. *Blake's Illustrations to the Divine Comedy*. Princeton, 1953.

Rose, Millicent. *Gustave Doré*. London, 1946.

Samek-Ludovici, Sergio, ed. *Dante's Divine Comedy: Illuminated Manuscripts of the Fifteenth Century, with Commentaries on the Miniatures*. New York, 1979.

Wilhelm, Richard, trans. *The I Ching*, English translation by Cary F. Baynes. Princeton, 1967.

Yeats, William Butler. *Essays and Introductions*. New York, 1961.

Acknowledgments

This book could not have been published in its present form without the assistance of a grant to Yale University Press from Robert A. Lawrence, who saw the need unasked—friend of Yale and a friend indeed.

We wish also to thank Donald Raiche and others exposed to early presentations for their encouragement. To Maynard Mack we owe especial thanks for a careful primary reading and wise counsel. One reader for Yale University Press, unknown to us, made a number of constructive suggestions. For assistance in the complex pursuit of images and permissions we are grateful to Gerhard Gruitrooy and Joseph Szazfai. And we owe much to the staff of Yale University Press, particularly Judy Metro, Laura Jones Dooley, Mary Mayer, and Sonia Scanlon.

Illustrations and Credits

For the selection and identification of illustrations we have depended on the illustrated books included in "Works Cited" but wish to acknowledge a special debt to Peter Brieger, Millard Miess, and Charles Singleton for the detailed scholarship in their two-volume study of "all important more or less fully illustrated codices of Dante's poem" (1, vi). The catalog in volume 1 by Peter Brieger, giving locations and including manuscript and folio numbers, was crucial to our search for transparencies. We would also like to extend our appreciation to permitters located throughout the Western world, in Amherst, Mass., Auckland, Berlin, Birmingham, Cambridge, Mass., Chantilly, Copenhagen, Florence, Hamburg, Imola, London, Melbourne, Naples, New York, Oxford, Padua, Paris, Perugia, Rome, Vatican City, Venice, and Zurich. Without the goodwill of the keepers of valuable manuscripts and collections this book would not have been possible. The specific libraries, museums, and creditors to whom we are indebted are cited below.

Each illustration is listed in order of appearance as a frontispiece or by figure number. If a title is specified for the illustration, it is in italics; often, we provide a short title to assist identification. These are followed by canticle and canto in parentheses, and the known or estimated date of the illustration. The source and credits for the illustration follow, including folio numbers for manuscripts when available.

Frontispiece: Pisan, title page for "L'Alta Comedya del Sommo Poeta Dante," ca. 1385. Codex Altonensis, cat. no. R 7², Historische Bibliothek des CHRISTIANEUMS, Hamburg.

Opposite "On the Illustrations": John Flax-man, title page, 1793. The artist imagines the poet creating his work in the middle world between the paradisal and infernal realms. From *Drawings for Dante's Divine Comedy* (pf MS Typ 26.4). The original pencil drawings for Flaxman's Italian engravings. By permission of The Houghton Library, Harvard University.

1. Gustave Doré, The Dark Wood (*Inf.* 1), 1868. From Dante Alighieri, *L'Enfer de Dante Alighieri, avec les dessins de Gustave Doré*, vol. 1 (Paris, 1868). Page size ca. 31 x 43 cm. Photo: Yale University Audio-Visual Dept.

2. Renato Guttuso, The Dark Wood (*Inf.* 1), 1970. Watercolor, from *Il Dante di Guttuso: Cinquantasei tavole dantesche disegnate da Renato Guttuso* (Milan: Mondadori, 1970). © 1997 Estate of Renato Guttuso / Licensed by VAGA, New York, N.Y. Photo: Yale University Audio-Visual Dept.

3. Sandro Botticelli, Chart of Hell, ca. 1495. Reg. Lat. 1896, fol. 101v, Biblioteca Apostolica Vaticana. Photo: Biblioteca Vaticana.

4. Dorothy Sayers's translation, Diagram of Hell. From *The Comedy of Dante Alighieri, the Florentine*, vol. 1, trans. Dorothy L. Sayers and Barbara Reynolds (vol. 3), 3 vols. (New York, 1949, 1953, 1964). Photo: Yale University Audio-Visual Dept.

5. Sienese, The Three Beasts (*Inf.* 1), ca. 1340. MS L. 70, Biblioteca Comunale Augusta, Perugia.

6. William Blake, *Dante Running from the Three Beasts* (*Inf.* 1), 1824–27. Pen, ink, and watercolor over pencil. 37.0 x 52.8 cm. Felton Bequest, 1920. National Gallery of Victoria, Melbourne.

7. Neapolitan, The Three Beasts (*Inf.* 1), ca. 1370. By permission of The British Library, London. Add. MS 19587, fol. 2r.

8. Pisan, The Three Beasts (*Inf.* 1), ca. 1385. Codex Altonensis, cat. no. R 7², Historische Bibliothek des CHRISTIANEUMS, Hamburg.

9. Pisan, Beatrice, Lucia, Mary (*Inf.* 2), ca. 1385. Codex Altonensis, cat. no. R 7², Historische Bibliothek des CHRISTIANEUMS, Hamburg.

10. Pisan, Hellgate (*Inf.* 3), ca. 1345. MS 597/1424, fol. 48r, Musée Condé, Chantilly, France. Giraudon/Art Resource, N.Y.

11. William Blake, *The Inscription over the Gate*, 1824–27. Hellgate (*Inf.* 3). Watercolor, 52.7 x 37.4 cm. Tate Gallery, London/Art Resource, N.Y.

12. Pisan, The Uncommitted (*Inf.* 3), ca. 1385. Codex Altonensis, cat. no. R 7², Historische Bibliothek des CHRISTIANEUMS, Hamburg.

13. William Blake, *The Vestibule of Hell and the Souls Mustering to Cross the Acheron* (*Inf.* 3), 1824–27. Ink and watercolor over pencil. 52.7 x 37.1 cm. Felton Bequest, 1920. National Gallery of Victoria, Melbourne.

14. Michelangelo Buonarroti, *Last Judgment*, detail of Charon's boat and the Damned (*Inf.* 3), completed 1541. Sistine Chapel, Vatican Palace, Vatican State. Scala/Art Resource, N.Y.

15. Gustave Doré, Crossing the Acheron (*Inf.* 3), 1868. From Dante Alighieri, *L'Enfer de Dante Alighieri, avec les dessins de Gustave Doré*, vol. 1 (Paris, 1868). Page size ca. 31 x 43 cm. Photo: Yale University Audio-Visual Dept.

16. Renato Guttuso, Crossing the Acheron (*Inf.* 3), 1970. Watercolor, from *Il Dante di*

Guttuso: Cinquantasei tavole dantesche disegnate da Renato Guttuso (Milan: Mondadori, 1970). © 1997 Estate of Renato Guttuso / Licensed by VAGA, New York, N.Y. Photo: Yale University Audio-Visual Dept.

17. William Blake, *Homer and the Ancient Poets*, 1824–27. Limbo (*Inf.* 4). Watercolor, 37.1 x 52.8 cm. Tate Gallery, London/Art Resource, N.Y.

18. Vecchietta, Limbo (*Inf.* 4), ca. 1445. By permission of The British Library, London. Yates-Thompson MS 36, fol. 7v.

19. William Blake, *Minos* (*Inf.* 5), 1824–27. Pen and watercolor over pencil and black chalk. 37.4 x 52.8 cm. Felton Bequest, 1920. National Gallery of Victoria, Melbourne.

20. Renato Guttuso, Minos (*Inf.* 5), 1970. Watercolor, from *Il Dante di Guttuso: Cinquantasei tavole dantesche disegnate da Renato Guttuso* (Milan: Mondadori, 1970). © 1997 Estate of Renato Guttuso / Licensed by VAGA, New York, N.Y. Photo: Yale University Audio-Visual Dept.

21. Vecchietta, Paolo and Francesca (*Inf.* 5), ca. 1445. By permission of The British Library, London. Yates-Thompson MS 36, fol. 10r.

22. William Blake, *The Circle of the Lustful: Paolo and Francesca* (*Inf.* 5), 1824–27. Engraving. 26.8 x 35.0 cm. Courtesy of the Fogg Art Museum, Harvard University Art Museums. Anonymous gift, in honor of Jakob Rosenberg.

23. Gustave Doré, Paolo and Francesca (*Inf.* 5), 1868. From Dante Alighieri, *L'Enfer de Dante Alighieri, avec les dessins de Gustave Doré*, vol. 1, (Paris, 1868). Page size ca. 31 x 43 cm. Photo: Yale University Audio-Visual Dept.

24. Pisan, Cerberus (*Inf.* 6), ca. 1385. Codex Altonensis, cat. no. R 7², Historische Bibliothek des CHRISTIANEUMS, Hamburg.

25. William Blake, *Cerberus* (*Inf.* 6), 1824–27. Pen, ink, and watercolor over pencil and black chalk. 37.3 x 52.7 cm. Felton Bequest, 1920. National Gallery of Victoria, Melbourne.

26. Vecchietta, The Avaricious (*Inf.* 7), ca. 1445. By permission of The British Library, London. Yates-Thompson MS 36, fol. 12v.

27. Florentine, The Wheel of Fortune (*Inf.* 7), ca. 1400. MS Lat. 4776.22, Biblioteca Apostolica Vaticana. Photo: Biblioteca Vaticana.

28. William Blake, *The Stygian Lake, with the Ireful Sinners Fighting*, 1824–27. The Wrathful and Sullen (*Inf.* 7). Pen, ink, and watercolor over pencil. 52.7 x 37.1 cm. Felton Bequest, 1920. National Gallery of Victoria, Melbourne.

29. Eugène Delacroix, *Dante and Virgil*, 1822. The Wrathful and Sullen (*Inf.* 8). Oil on canvas, 189 x 241.5 cm. Louvre, Paris. Erich Lessing/Art Resource, N.Y.

30. Gustave Doré, The Wrathful and Sullen (*Inf.* 8), 1868. From Dante Alighieri, *L'Enfer de Dante Alighieri, avec les dessins de Gustave Doré*, vol. 1 (Paris, 1868). Page size ca. 31 x 43 cm. Photo: Yale University Audio-Visual Dept.

31. William Blake, *Dante and Virgil in the Skiff of Phlegyas Are Hailed by Fillipo Argenti*, 1824–27. The Wrathful and Sullen (*Inf.* 8). Watercolor, black ink, and graphite on off-white antique laid paper. 37.0 x 52.2 cm. Courtesy of the Fogg Art Museum, Harvard University Art Museums.

32. Venetian, The Gate of Dis (*Inf.* 9), ca. 1440. MS 1035, fol. 17r, Biblioteca Riccardiana, Florence. Photo: Donato Pineider.

33. Sandro Botticelli, The Gate of Dis (*Inf.* 9), ca. 1495. Reg. Lat. 1896, fol. 97r, Biblioteca Apostolica Vaticana. Photo: Biblioteca Vaticana.

34. *Vitae Imperatorum* Master, The Heavenly Messenger (*Inf.* 9), ca. 1440. MS 76, Biblioteca comunale di Imola, Imola, Italy. Photo: Isola Press.

35. William Blake, *The Angel at the Gate of Dis* (*Inf.* 9), 1824–27. Pen and watercolor over pencil and black chalk. 37.2 x 52.8 cm. Felton Bequest, 1920. National Gallery of Victoria, Melbourne.

36. Gustave Doré, The Heretics, Farinata (*Inf.* 10), 1868. From Dante Alighieri, *L'Enfer de Dante Alighieri, avec les dessins de Gustave Doré*, vol. 1 (Paris, 1868). Page size ca. 31 x 43 cm. Photo: Yale University Audio-Visual Dept.

37. Henry Fuseli, *Dante und Vergil vor Cavalcanti und Farinate*, 1774. The Heretics (*Inf.* 10). Pen and brush. 25.9 x 27.1 cm. 1996, Kunsthaus, Zurich, Switzerland.

38. Gustave Doré, The Minotaur (*Inf.* 12), 1868. From Dante Alighieri, *L'Enfer de Dante Alighieri, avec les dessins de Gustave Doré*, vol. 1 (Paris, 1868). Page size ca. 31 x 43 cm. Photo: Yale University Audio-Visual Dept.

39. Renato Guttuso, The Minotaur (*Inf.* 12), 1970. Watercolor, from *Il Dante di Guttuso: Cinquantasei tavole dantesche disegnate da Renato Guttuso* (Milan: Mondadori, 1970). © 1997 Estate of Renato Guttuso / Licensed by VAGA, New York, N.Y. Photo: Yale University Audio-Visual Dept.

40. Sandro Botticelli, Violent Against Others (*Inf.* 12), ca. 1495. Reg. Lat. 1896, fol. 103r, Biblioteca Apostolica Vaticana. Photo: Biblioteca Vaticana.

41. Renato Guttuso, Violent Against Others (*Inf.* 12), 1970. Watercolor, from *Il Dante di Guttuso: Cinquantasei tavole dantesche disegnate da Renato Guttuso* (Milan: Mondadori, 1970). © 1997 Estate of Renato Guttuso / Licensed by VAGA, New York, N.Y. Photo: Yale University Audio-Visual Dept.

42. Florentine, Violent Against Others (*Inf.* 12), ca. 1400. MS Lat. 4776.42v, Biblioteca Apostolica Vaticana. Photo: Biblioteca Vaticana.

43. Guglielmo Giraldi, Violent Against Others (*Inf.* 12), ca. 1480. MS Urb. Lat. 365.30v, Biblioteca Apostolica Vaticana. Photo: Biblioteca Vaticana.

44. Vecchietta, Violent Against Themselves (*Inf.* 13), ca. 1445. By permission of The British Library, London. Yates-Thompson MS 36, fol. 23r.

45. Sandro Botticelli, Violent Against Themselves (*Inf.* 13), ca. 1495. Reg. Lat. 1896, fol. 102r, Biblioteca Apostolica Vaticana. Photo: Biblioteca Vaticana.

46. William Blake, *The Wood of the Self-Murderers: The Harpies and the Suicides*, 1824–27. Violent Against Themselves (*Inf.* 13). Watercolor, 37.2 x 52.7 cm. Tate Gallery, London/Art Resource, N.Y.

47. Gustave Doré, Violent Against Themselves (*Inf.* 13), 1868. From Dante Alighieri, *L'Enfer de Dante Alighieri, avec les dessins de Gustave Doré*, vol. 1 (Paris, 1868). Page size ca. 31 x 43 cm. Photo: Yale University Audio-Visual Dept.

48. Venetian, Violent Against God (*Inf.* 14), late 14th c. Cod. It. IX, 276 (=6902), fol. 10r, Biblioteca Nazionale Marciana, Venice.

49. Renato Guttuso, Violent Against God (*Inf.* 14), 1970. Watercolor, from *Il Dante di Guttuso: Cinquantasei tavole dantesche disegnate da Renato Guttuso* (Milan: Mon-

dadori, 1970). © 1997 Estate of Renato Guttuso / Licensed by VAGA, New York, N.Y. Photo: Yale University Audio-Visual Dept.

50. Pisan, Old Man of Crete (*Inf.* 14), ca. 1385. Codex Altonensis, cat. no. R 7², Historische Bibliothek des CHRISTIANEUMS, Hamburg.

51. Leonard Baskin, Violent Against Nature (*Inf.* 15), 1970. Drawing, from *Illustrations to the Divine Comedy of Dante*, Graphic Arts Exhibition catalog, Introduction by Dale Roylance (New Haven, 1970). Courtesy of R. Michelson Galleries, Amherst, Mass. Photo: Yale University Audio-Visual Dept.

52. Pisan, Violent Against Nature (*Inf.* 15), ca. 1345. MS 597/1424, fol. 113v–114r, Musée Condé, Chantilly, France. Giraudon/Art Resource, N.Y.

53. Pisan, Violent Against Nature (*Inf.* 15), ca. 1385. Codex Altonensis, cat. no. R 7², Historische Bibliothek des CHRISTIANEUMS, Hamburg.

54. Neapolitan, Violent Against Art, Geryon (*Inf.* 17), ca. 1370. By permission of The British Library, London. Add. MS 19587, fol. 28r.

55. Bolognese, Violent Against Art, Geryon (*Inf.* 17), ca. 1400. Biblioteca Angelica, Rome, MS 1102. Photo: Humberto N. Serra.

56. Sandro Botticelli, Geryon (*Inf.* 17), ca. 1495. Kupferstichkabinett, Staatliche Museen zu Berlin, Cod. Ham. 201, Cim. 33. Photo: Jörg P. Anders.

57. Italian, Geryon (*Inf.* 17), 15th c. MS XIII C4, fol. 6v, Biblioteca Nazionale, Naples. Photo: Massimo Velo.

58. Pisan, Geryon (*Inf.* 17), ca. 1385. Codex Altonensis, cat. no. R 7², Historische Bibliothek des CHRISTIANEUMS, Hamburg.

59. William Blake, *Geryon Conveying Dante and Virgil Down Towards Malebolge* (*Inf.* 17), 1824–27. Pen, ink, and watercolor over pencil and chalk. 37.2 x 52.7 cm. Felton Bequest, 1920. National Gallery of Victoria, Melbourne.

60. Gustave Doré, Geryon (*Inf.* 17), 1868. From Dante Alighieri, *L'Enfer de Dante Alighieri, avec les dessins de Gustave Doré*, vol. 1 (Paris, 1868). Page size ca. 31 x 43 cm. Photo: Yale University Audio-Visual Dept.

61. Guglielmo Giraldi, Geryon (*Inf.* 17), ca. 1480. MS Urb. Lat. 365.46r, Biblioteca Apostolica Vaticana. Photo: Biblioteca Vaticana.

62. Henry Fuseli, *Virgil, Dante, and Geryon* (*Inf.* 17), 1811. Pen and brown ink, 19.8 x 29.3 cm. Auckland Art Gallery collection, New Zealand.

63. Sandro Botticelli, Panderers and Seducers (*Inf.* 18), ca. 1495. Kupferstichkabinett, Staatliche Museen zu Berlin, Cod. Ham. 201, Cim. 33. Photo: Jörg P. Anders.

64. Rico Lebrun, Panderers and Seducers (*Inf.* 18), 1963. From Lebrun, *Drawings for Dante's Inferno* (Kanthos Press, 1963). Photo: Yale University Audio-Visual Dept.

65. Pisan, The Simonists (*Inf.* 19), ca. 1385. Codex Altonensis, cat. no. R 7², Historische Bibliothek des CHRISTIANEUMS, Hamburg.

66. William Blake, *The Simoniac Pope* (*Inf.* 19), 1824–27. Watercolor, 52.7 x 36.8 cm. Tate Gallery, London/Art Resource, N.Y.

67. Rico Lebrun, The Simonists (*Inf.* 19), 1963. From Lebrun, *Drawings for Dante's Inferno* (Kanthos Press, 1963). Photo: Yale University Audio-Visual Dept.

68. Rico Lebrun, The Diviners (*Inf.* 20), 1963. From Lebrun, *Drawings for Dante's Inferno* (Kanthos Press, 1963). Photo: Yale University Audio-Visual Dept.

69. Bartolomeo di Fruosino, The Diviners (*Inf.* 20), ca. 1420. MS It. 74, fol. 59, Bibliothèque Nationale de France, Paris. Photo: Bibliothèque Nationale de France.

70. Renato Guttuso, The Diviners (*Inf.* 20), 1970. Watercolor, from *Il Dante di Guttuso: Cinquantasei tavole dantesche disegnate da Renato Guttuso* (Milan: Mondadori, 1970). © 1997 Estate of Renato Guttuso / Licensed by VAGA, New York, N.Y. Photo: Yale University Audio-Visual Dept.

71. Pisan, The Grafters (*Inf.* 21), ca. 1385. Codex Altonensis, cat. no. R 7², Historische Bibliothek des CHRISTIANEUMS, Hamburg.

72. William Blake, *The Devils Setting Out with Dante and Virgil*, 1824–27. The Grafters (*Inf.* 21). Pen, ink, and watercolor over pencil. 37.2 x 52.8 cm. Felton Bequest, 1920. National Gallery of Victoria, Melbourne.

73. Gustave Doré, The Grafters (*Inf.* 21), 1868. From Dante Alighieri, *L'Enfer de Dante Alighieri, avec les dessins de Gustave Doré*, vol. 1 (Paris, 1868). Page size

ca. 31 x 43 cm. Photo: Yale University Audio-Visual Dept.

74. Luca Signorelli, *The Damned in Hell*, ca. 1500. The Grafters (*Inf.* 22). Fresco, Duomo, Orvieto, Italy. Scala/Art Resource, N.Y.

75. William Blake, *The Baffled Devils Fighting*, 1824–27. The Grafters (*Inf.* 22). Watercolor. By permission of Birmingham Museums and Art Gallery, Birmingham, England.

76. William Blake, *Virgil Rescues Dante from the Evil Demons* (*Inf.* 23), 1824–27. Pencil, chalk, pen, ink, and watercolor on antique laid paper. Watermark: "W. Elgar, 1796." 52.3 x 36.9 cm. Courtesy of the Fogg Art Museum, Harvard University Art Museums.

77. Pisan, The Hypocrites (*Inf.* 23), ca. 1385. Codex Altonensis, cat. no. R 7², Historische Bibliothek des CHRISTIANEUMS, Hamburg.

78. John Flaxman, The Hypocrites (*Inf.* 23), 1793. From *Drawings for Dante's Divine Comedy* (pf MS Typ 26.4). The original pencil drawings for Flaxman's Italian engravings. By permission of The Houghton Library, Harvard University.

79. Pisan, The Thieves (*Inf.* 25), ca. 1345. MS 597/1424, fol. 170r, Musée Condé, Chantilly, France. Giraudon/Art Resource, N.Y.

80. Rico Lebrun, The Thieves (*Inf.* 25), 1963. From Lebrun, *Drawings for Dante's Inferno* (Kanthos Press, 1963). Photo: Yale University Audio-Visual Dept.

81. Leonard Baskin, The Thieves (*Inf.* 25), 1970. Drawing, from *Illustrations to the Divine Comedy of Dante*, Graphic Arts Exhibition catalog, Introduction by Dale Roylance (New Haven, 1970). Courtesy of R. Michelson Galleries, Amherst, Mass. Photo: Yale University Audio-Visual Dept.

82. William Blake, *The Six-Footed Serpent Attacking Agnello dei Brunelleschi*, 1824–27. The Thieves (*Inf.* 25). Pen, ink, and watercolor over black chalk. 37.2 x 52.7 cm. Felton Bequest, 1920. National Gallery of Victoria, Melbourne.

83. Pisan, Fraudulent Counselors (*Inf.* 27), ca. 1385. Codex Altonensis, cat. no. R 7², Historische Bibliothek des CHRISTIANEUMS, Hamburg.

84. *Vitae Imperatorum* Master, Fraudulent Counselors (*Inf.* 27), ca. 1440. MS 76,

Biblioteca comunale di Imola, Imola, Italy. Photo: Isola Press.

85. Bartolomeo di Fruosino, Fraudulent Counselors (*Inf.* 27), ca. 1420. MS It. 74, fol. 80, Bibliothèque Nationale de France, Paris. Photo: Bibliothèque Nationale de France.

86. John Flaxman, Guido da Montefeltro (*Inf.* 27), 1793. From *Drawings for Dante's Divine Comedy* (pf MS Typ 26.4). The original pencil drawings for Flaxman's Italian engravings. By permission of The Houghton Library, Harvard University.

87. Rico Lebrun, Sowers of Discord (*Inf.* 28), 1963. From Lebrun, *Drawings for Dante's Inferno* (Kanthos Press, 1963). Photo: Yale University Audio-Visual Dept.

88. William Blake, *The Schismatics and Sowers of Discord: Mosca de' Lamberti and Bertrand de Born* (*Inf.* 28), 1824–27. Pen, ink, and watercolor over pencil. 37.0 x 52.7 cm. Felton Bequest, 1920. National Gallery of Victoria, Melbourne.

89. Pisan, Sowers of Discord (*Inf.* 28), ca. 1385. Codex Altonensis, cat. no. R 7², Historische Bibliothek des CHRISTIANEUMS, Hamburg.

90. Renato Guttuso, Sowers of Discord (*Inf.* 28), 1970. Watercolor, from *Il Dante di Guttuso: Cinquantasei tavole dantesche disegnate da Renato Guttuso* (Milan: Mondadori, 1970). © 1997 Estate of Renato Guttuso / Licensed by VAGA, New York, N.Y. Photo: Yale University Audio-Visual Dept.

91. Vecchietta, The Falsifiers (*Inf.* 30), ca. 1445. By permission of The British Library, London. Yates-Thompson MS 36, fol. 55r.

92. Bartolomeo di Fruosino, The Falsifiers (*Inf.* 30), ca. 1420. MS It. 74, fol. 89, Bibliothèque Nationale de France, Paris. Photo: Bibliothèque Nationale de France.

93. Renato Guttuso, The Falsifiers (*Inf.* 30), 1970. Watercolor, from *Il Dante di Guttuso: Cinquantasei tavole dantesche disegnate da Renato Guttuso* (Milan: Mondadori, 1970). © 1997 Estate of Renato Guttuso / Licensed by VAGA, New York, N.Y. Photo: Yale University Audio-Visual Dept.

94. Neapolitan, The Giants (*Inf.* 31), ca. 1370. By permission of The British Library, London. Add. MS 19587, fol. 52v.

95. *Vitae Imperatorum* Master, The Giants (*Inf.* 31), ca. 1440. MS It. 2017, fol. 361r,

96. Sandro Botticelli, The Giants (*Inf.* 31), ca. 1495. Kupferstichkabinett, Staatliche Museen zu Berlin, Cod. Ham. 201, Cim. 33. Photo: Jörg P. Anders.

97. Gustave Doré, The Giant Antaeus (*Inf.* 31), 1868. From Dante Alighieri, *L'Enfer de Dante Alighieri, avec les dessins de Gustave Doré*, vol. 1 (Paris, 1868). Page size ca. 31 x 43 cm. Photo: Yale University Audio-Visual Dept.

98. Gustave Doré, Cocytus, Traitors to Kin (*Inf.* 32), 1868. From Dante Alighieri, *L'Enfer de Dante Alighieri, avec les dessins de Gustave Doré*, vol. 1 (Paris, 1868). Page size ca. 31 x 43 cm. Photo: Yale University Audio-Visual Dept.

99. William Blake, *Dante Seizing the Traitor Bocca by the Hair*, 1824–27. Traitors to Homeland, Bocca (*Inf.* 32). Watercolor, pen, black ink, and graphite on off-white antique laid paper. 37.0 x 52.3 cm. Courtesy of the Fogg Art Museum, Harvard University Art Museums.

100. Henry Fuseli, *Dante und Vergil auf dem Eis des Kozythus*, 1774. Bocca (*Inf.* 32). Pen and brush, brown ink, 39.0 x 27.4 cm. Kunsthaus, Zurich, Switzerland.

101. Rico Lebrun, Ugolino and Ruggieri (*Inf.* 32), 1963. From Lebrun, *Drawings for Dante's Inferno* (Kanthos Press, 1963). Photo: Yale University Audio-Visual Dept.

102. Vecchietta, Ugolino's Story and Fra Alberigo (*Inf.* 33), ca. 1445. By permission of The British Library, London. Yates-Thompson MS 36, fol. 61r.

103. Gustave Doré, Traitors to Masters and Benefactors (*Inf.* 34), 1868. From Dante Alighieri, *L'Enfer de Dante Alighieri, avec les dessins de Gustave Doré*, vol. 1 (Paris, 1868). Page size ca. 31 x 43 cm. Photo: Yale University Audio-Visual Dept.

104. Pisan, Plan of Hell (*Inf.* 34), ca. 1385. Codex Altonensis, cat. no. R 7², Historische Bibliothek des CHRISTIANEUMS, Hamburg.

105. John Flaxman, Faces of Dis (*Inf.* 34), 1793. From *Drawings for Dante's Divine Comedy* (pf MS Typ 26.4). The original pencil drawings for Flaxman's Italian engravings. By permission of The Houghton Library, Harvard University.

106. Sandro Botticelli, Faces of Dis (*Inf.* 34), ca. 1495. Kupferstichkabinett,

Staatliche Museen zu Berlin, Cod. Ham. 201, Cim. 33. Photo: Jörg P. Anders.

107. Sandro Botticelli, Figure of Dis (*Inf.* 34), ca. 1495. Kupferstichkabinett, Staatliche Museen zu Berlin, Cod. Ham. 201, Cim. 33. Photo: Jörg P. Anders.

108. Vecchietta, Close Encounter with Dis (*Inf.* 34), ca. 1445. By permission of The British Library, London. Yates-Thompson MS 36, fol. 62v.

109. Pisan, Close Encounter with Dis (*Inf.* 34), ca. 1385. Codex Altonensis, cat. no. R 7², Historische Bibliothek des CHRISTIANEUMS, Hamburg.

110. Pisan, Close Encounter with Dis (*Inf.* 34), ca. 1385. Codex Altonensis, cat. no. R 7², Historische Bibliothek des CHRISTIANEUMS, Hamburg.

111. Lombard, Emergence from Hell (*Inf.* 34), ca. 1400. MS B. R. 39, fol. 141r, Biblioteca Nazionale Centrale, Florence.

112. Temple Classics, Chart of the Journey, 1954. From *The Inferno of Dante Alighieri*, trans. J. A. Carlyle et al., vol. 1 of 3, Temple Classics edition (London, 1954). Photo: Yale University Audio-Visual Dept.

113. Renato Guttuso, Shore of Purgatory (*Purg.* 1), 1970. Watercolor, from *Il Dante di Guttuso: Cinquantasei tavole dantesche disegnate da Renato Guttuso* (Milan: Mondadori, 1970). © 1997 Estate of Renato Guttuso / Licensed by VAGA, New York, N.Y. Photo: Yale University Audio-Visual Dept.

114. William Blake, *Virgil Girding Dante's Brow with a Rush*, 1824–27. Shore of Purgatory (*Purg.* 1). Watercolor, 52.7 x 37.1 cm. Tate Gallery, London/Art Resource, N.Y.

115. Neapolitan, Cato (*Purg.* 1), ca. 1370. By permission of The British Library, London. Add. MS 19587, fol. 62r.

116. Vecchietta, The Angel Pilot (*Purg.* 2), ca. 1445. By permission of The British Library, London. Yates-Thompson MS 36, fol. 68r.

117. Gustave Doré, The Angel Pilot (*Purg.* 2), 1868. From Dante Alighieri, *Le Purgatoire de Dante Alighieri, avec les dessins de Gustave Doré; Le Paradis de Dante Alighieri, avec les dessins de Gustave Doré*, vol. 2 (2 vols. in 1; Paris, 1868). Page size ca. 31 x 43 cm. Photo: Yale University Audio-Visual Dept.

118. Leonard Baskin, The Angel Pilot (*Purg.* 2), 1970. Drawing, from *Illustrations to the*

Divine Comedy of Dante, Graphic Arts Exhibition catalog, Introduction by Dale Roylance (New Haven, 1970). Courtesy of R. Michelson Galleries, Amherst, Mass. Photo: Yale University Audio-Visual Dept.

119. Sandro Botticelli, The Late Repentant, Excommunicates (*Purg.* 3), ca. 1495. Kupferstichkabinett, Staatliche Museen zu Berlin, Cod. Ham. 201, Cim. 33. Photo: Jörg P. Anders.

120. Dorothy Sayers's translation, Diagram of Purgatory. From *The Comedy of Dante Alighieri, the Florentine*, vol. 2, trans. Dorothy L. Sayers and Barbara Reynolds (vol. 3), 3 vols. (New York, 1949, 1953, 1964). Photo: Yale University Audio-Visual Dept.

121. John Flaxman, The Excommunicates (*Purg.* 3), 1793. From *Drawings for Dante's Divine Comedy* (pf MS Typ 26.4). The original pencil drawings for Flaxman's Italian engravings. By permission of The Houghton Library, Harvard University.

122. John Flaxman, The Indolent (*Purg.* 4), 1793. From *Drawings for Dante's Divine Comedy* (pf MS Typ 26.4). The original pencil drawings for Flaxman's Italian engravings. By permission of The Houghton Library, Harvard University.

123. Sandro Botticelli, The Indolent (*Purg.* 4), ca. 1495. Kupferstichkabinett, Staatliche Museen zu Berlin, Cod. Ham. 201, Cim. 33. Photo: Jörg P. Anders.

124. Pisan, The Steep Climb (*Purg.* 4), ca. 1385. Codex Altonensis, cat. no. R 7², Historische Bibliothek des CHRISTIANEUMS, Hamburg.

125. William Blake, *The Ascent of the Mountain of Purgatory*, 1824–27. The Steep Climb (*Purg.* 4). Watercolor, 52.8 x 37.2 cm. Tate Gallery, London/Art Resource, N.Y.

126. Luca Signorelli, *The Difficult Mountain Climb, Explanation of the Position of the Sun, the Slothful* (*Purg.* 4), ca. 1500. Fresco, Duomo, Orvieto, Italy. Scala/Art Resource, N.Y.

127. William Blake, *The Souls of Those Who Only Repented at the Point of Death*, 1824–27. Late Repentant Who Died by Violence (*Purg.* 5). Pen, ink, and watercolor over pencil and black chalk. 37.2 x 52.7 cm. Felton Bequest, 1920. National Gallery of Victoria, Melbourne.

128. Venetian, Late Repentant Seeking Prayers (*Purg.* 5), late 14th c. Cod. It. IX, 276 (=6902), fol. 30r, Biblioteca Nazionale Marciana, Venice.

129. Gustave Doré, Sordello (*Purg.* 7), 1868. From Dante Alighieri, *Le Purgatoire de Dante Alighieri, avec les dessins de Gustave Doré; Le Paradis de Dante Alighieri, avec les dessins de Gustave Doré*, vol. 2 (2 vols. in 1; Paris, 1868). Page size ca. 31 x 43 cm. Photo: Yale University Audio-Visual Dept.

130. William Blake, *The Lawn with the Kings and Angels*, 1824–27. The Preoccupied Rulers (*Purg.* 8). Pen, ink, and watercolor over pencil. 37.3 x 52.7 cm. Felton Bequest, 1920. National Gallery of Victoria, Melbourne.

131. Luca Signorelli, *Dante and Virgil Come upon Two Angels Guarding Purgatory*, ca. 1500. The Angels and the Serpent (*Purg.* 8). Fresco, Duomo, Orvieto, Italy. Scala/Art Resource, N.Y.

132. Neapolitan, The Angels and the Serpent (*Purg.* 8), ca. 1370. By permission of The British Library, London. Add. MS 19587, fol. 73r.

133. Sandro Botticelli, The Dream of the Eagle (*Purg.* 9), ca. 1495. Kupferstichkabinett, Staatliche Museen zu Berlin, Cod. Ham. 201, Cim. 33. Photo: Jörg P. Anders.

134. Gustave Doré, The Dream of the Eagle (*Purg.* 9), 1868. From Dante Alighieri, *Le Purgatoire de Dante Alighieri, avec les dessins de Gustave Doré; Le Paradis de Dante Alighieri, avec les dessins de Gustave Doré*, vol. 2 (2 vols. in 1; Paris, 1868). Page size ca. 31 x 43 cm. Photo: Yale University Audio-Visual Dept.

135. Vecchietta, The Dream, the Gate, and the Proud (*Purg.* 9–10), ca. 1445. By permission of The British Library, London. Yates-Thompson MS 36, fol. 84r.

136. William Blake, *Lucia Carrying Dante in His Sleep* (*Purg.* 9), 1824–27. Watercolor, black ink, and graphite on cream modern laid paper. 37.4 x 52.7 cm. Courtesy of the Fogg Art Museum, Harvard University Art Museums. Bequest of Grenville L. Winthrop.

137. William Blake, *Dante and Virgil Approaching the Angel Who Guards the Entrance of Purgatory* (*Purg.* 9), 1824–27. Watercolor, 52.7 x 37.3 cm. Tate Gallery, London/Art Resource, N.Y.

138. Italian, The Gate of Purgatory (*Purg.* 9), ca. 1365. MS Holkham Misc. 48, p. 74, The Bodleian Library, Oxford.

139. Italian, First Terrace, the Proud (*Purg.*

10–12), ca. 1365. MS Holkham Misc. 48, p. 78, The Bodleian Library, Oxford.

140. Pisan, Examples of Humility (*Purg.* 10), ca. 1385. Codex Altonensis, cat. no. R 7², Historische Bibliothek des CHRISTIANEUMS, Hamburg.

141. Sandro Botticelli, Examples of Humility (*Purg.* 10), ca. 1495. Kupferstichkabinett, Staatliche Museen zu Berlin, Cod. Ham. 201, Cim. 33. Photo: Jörg P. Anders.

142. Pisan, Examples of Pride (*Purg.* 12), ca. 1385. Codex Altonensis, cat. no. R 7², Historische Bibliothek des CHRISTIANEUMS, Hamburg.

143. Italian, Examples of Pride (*Purg.* 12), 15th c. The Royal Library, Copenhagen, MS Thott 411.2.

144. Pisan, The Envious (*Purg.* 13), ca. 1385. Codex Altonensis, cat. no. R 7², Historische Bibliothek des CHRISTIANEUMS, Hamburg.

145. Sandro Botticelli, The Envious (*Purg.* 13), ca. 1495. Kupferstichkabinett, Staatliche Museen zu Berlin, Cod. Ham. 201, Cim. 33. Photo: Jörg P. Anders.

146. Renato Guttuso, The Envious (*Purg.* 13), 1970. Watercolor, from *Il Dante di Guttuso: Cinquantasei tavole dantesche disegnate da Renato Guttuso* (Milan: Mondadori, 1970). © 1997 Estate of Renato Guttuso / Licensed by VAGA, New York, N.Y. Photo: Yale University Audio-Visual Dept.

147. Italian, The Envious (*Purg.* 13), ca. 1365. MS Holkham Misc. 48, p. 81, The Bodleian Library, Oxford.

148. Italian, The Wrathful (*Purg.* 16), ca. 1365. MS Holkham Misc. 48, p. 87, The Bodleian Library, Oxford.

149. Vecchietta, The Wrathful (*Purg.* 16), ca. 1445. By permission of The British Library, London. Yates-Thompson MS 36, fol. 93v.

150. Gustave Doré, The Wrathful (*Purg.* 16), 1868. From Dante Alighieri, *Le Purgatoire de Dante Alighieri, avec les dessins de Gustave Doré; Le Paradis de Dante Alighieri, avec les dessins de Gustave Doré*, vol. 2 (2 vols. in 1; Paris, 1868). Page size ca. 31 x 43 cm. Photo: Yale University Audio-Visual Dept.

151. Renato Guttuso, The Wrathful (*Purg.* 16), 1970. Watercolor, from *Il Dante di Guttuso: Cinquantasei tavole dantesche disegnate da Renato Guttuso* (Milan: Mon-

dadori, 1970). © 1997 Estate of Renato Guttuso / Licensed by VAGA, New York, N.Y. Photo: Yale University Audio-Visual Dept.

152. Sandro Botticelli, The Slothful (*Purg.* 18), ca. 1495. Kupferstichkabinett, Staatliche Museen zu Berlin, Cod. Ham. 201, Cim. 33. Photo: Jörg P. Anders.

153. Vecchietta, The Slothful and the Siren (*Purg.* 19), ca. 1445. By permission of The British Library, London. Yates-Thompson MS 36, fol. 98v.

154. Pisan, The Angel of Zeal (*Purg.* 19), ca. 1385. Codex Altonensis, cat. no. R 7², Historische Bibliothek des CHRISTIANEUMS, Hamburg.

155. Pisan, The Image of the Falconer (*Purg.* 19), ca. 1385. Codex Altonensis, cat. no. R 7², Historische Bibliothek des CHRISTIANEUMS, Hamburg.

156. Venetian, Angel of Purgatory (*Purg.* 15), late 14th c. Cod. It. IX, 276 (=6902), fol. 37v, Biblioteca Nazionale Marciana, Venice.

157. Venetian, Angel of Purgatory (*Purg.* 17), late 14th c. Cod. It. IX, 276 (=6902), fol. 41r, Biblioteca Nazionale Marciana, Venice.

158. Gustave Doré, The Avaricious and Prodigal (*Purg.* 19), 1868. From Dante Alighieri, *Le Purgatoire de Dante Alighieri, avec les dessins de Gustave Doré; Le Paradis de Dante Alighieri, avec les dessins de Gustave Doré*, vol. 2 (2 vols. in 1; Paris, 1868). Page size ca. 31 x 43 cm. Photo: Yale University Audio-Visual Dept.

159. Venetian, Hugh Capet (*Purg.* 20), late 14th c. Cod. It. IX, 276 (=6902), fol. 41v, Biblioteca Nazionale Marciana, Venice.

160. Sandro Botticelli, The Prodigal and Statius (*Purg.* 20–22), ca. 1495. Kupferstichkabinett, Staatliche Museen zu Berlin, Cod. Ham. 201, Cim. 33. Photo: Jörg P. Anders.

161. Italian, The Gluttonous (*Purg.* 22), late 14th c. The Pierpont Morgan Library, New York. M. 676, fol. 75v. Photo: David A. Loggie.

162. Sandro Botticelli, The Gluttonous (*Purg.* 23), ca. 1495. Kupferstichkabinett, Staatliche Museen zu Berlin, Cod. Ham. 201, Cim. 33. Photo: Jörg P. Anders.

163. Vecchietta, The Gluttonous (*Purg.*

23), ca. 1445. By permission of The British Library, London. Yates-Thompson MS 36, fol. 107r.

164. Renato Guttuso, The Gluttonous (*Purg.* 23), 1970. Watercolor, from *Il Dante di Guttuso: Cinquantasei tavole dantesche disegnate da Renato Guttuso* (Milan: Mondadori, 1970). © 1997 Estate of Renato Guttuso / Licensed by VAGA, New York, N.Y. Photo: Yale University Audio-Visual Dept.

165. Sandro Botticelli, The Lustful (*Purg.* 26–27), ca. 1495. Kupferstichkabinett, Staatliche Museen zu Berlin, Cod. Ham. 201, Cim. 33. Photo: Jörg P. Anders.

166. William Blake, *The Angel Inviting Dante to Enter the Fire* (*Purg.* 27), 1824–27. Pen, ink, and watercolor over pencil and black chalk. 52.7 x 37.3 cm. Felton Bequest, 1920. National Gallery of Victoria, Melbourne.

167. William Blake, *Dante at the Moment of Entering the Fire* (*Purg.* 27), 1824–27. Pen, ink, and watercolor over black chalk and pencil. 52.8 x 36.9 cm. Felton Bequest, 1920. National Gallery of Victoria, Melbourne.

168. William Blake, Dante's Dream of Leah (*Purg.* 27), 1824–27. The Ashmolean Museum, Oxford.

169. Sandro Botticelli, Virgil Crowns the Pilgrim (detail, *Purg.* 27), ca. 1495. Kupferstichkabinett, Staatliche Museen zu Berlin, Cod. Ham. 201, Cim. 33. Photo: Jörg P. Anders.

170. Sandro Botticelli, The Sacred Wood (*Purg.* 28), ca. 1495. Kupferstichkabinett, Staatliche Museen zu Berlin, Cod. Ham. 201, Cim. 33. Photo: Jörg P. Anders.

171. William Blake, *Beatrice in Procession* (*Purg.* 29), 1824–27. The British Museum, London.

172. Italian, The Pageant (*Purg.* 29), late 14th c. MS XIII C1, fol. 120r, Biblioteca Nazionale, Naples. Photo: Massimo Velo.

173. Emilian, The Pageant (*Purg.* 29), ca. 1340. By permission of The British Library, London. Egerton MS 943, fol. 117v.

174. William Blake, *Beatrice Addressing Dante from the Car* (*Purg.* 30), 1824–27. Watercolor, 37.2 x 52.7 cm. Tate Gallery, London/Art Resource, N.Y.

175. Neapolitan, The Pageant (*Purg.* 30), ca. 1370. By permission of The British Library, London. Add. MS 19587, fol. 111v.

176. Sandro Botticelli, Crossing Lethe (*Purg.* 31), ca. 1495. Kupferstichkabinett, Staatliche Museen zu Berlin, Cod. Ham. 201, Cim. 33. Photo: Jörg P. Anders.

177. Paduan, The Pilgrim Swoons (*Purg.* 31), early 15th c. MS 67, fol. 208r, Biblioteca del Seminario Vescovile, Padua. (This illustration actually occurs at *Par.* 3 in the manuscript, as noted in the commentary at fig. 177.) Photo: Romanin Alessandro.

178. John Flaxman, Matilda Immerses the Pilgrim (*Purg.* 31), 1793. From *Drawings for Dante's Divine Comedy* (pf MS Typ 26.4). The original pencil drawings for Flaxman's Italian engravings. By permission of The Houghton Library, Harvard University.

179. Sandro Botticelli, Transfiguration of the Chariot (*Purg.* 32), ca. 1495. Kupferstichkabinett, Staatliche Museen zu Berlin, Cod. Ham. 201, Cim. 33. Photo: Jörg P. Anders.

180. William Blake, *The Harlot and the Giant* (*Purg.* 32), 1824–27. Pen, ink, and watercolor over pencil and black chalk. 37.2 x 52.7 cm. Felton Bequest, 1920. National Gallery of Victoria, Melbourne.

181. John Flaxman, The Giant and the Whore (*Purg.* 32), 1793. From *Drawings for Dante's Divine Comedy* (pf MS Typ 26.4). The original pencil drawings for Flaxman's Italian engravings. By permission of The Houghton Library, Harvard University.

182. Italian, The Spring of Lethe and Eunoe (*Purg.* 33), late 14th c. The Pierpont Morgan Library, New York. M. 676, fol. 89v. Photo: David A. Loggie.

183. Sandro Botticelli, Immersion in Eunoe (*Purg.* 33), ca. 1495. Kupferstichkabinett, Staatliche Museen zu Berlin, Cod. Ham. 201, Cim. 33. Photo: Jörg P. Anders.

184. Giovanni di Paolo, Dante and Beatrice Ascending (*Par.* 1), ca. 1445. By permission of The British Library, London. Yates-Thompson MS 36, fol. 130r.

185. Venetian, Dante Prays to Apollo (*Par.* 1), late 14th c. Cod. It. IX, 276 (=6902), fol. 53r, Biblioteca Nazionale Marciana, Venice.

186. Venetian, Heaven of the Moon (*Par.* 2), late 14th c. Cod. It. IX, 276 (=6902), fol. 53v, Biblioteca Nazionale Marciana, Venice.

187. Giovanni di Paolo, Heaven of the

Moon (*Par.* 2), ca. 1445. By permission of The British Library, London. Yates-Thompson MS 36, fol. 132r.

188. Sandro Botticelli, Heaven of the Moon (*Par.* 2), ca. 1495. Kupferstichkabinett, Staatliche Museen zu Berlin, Cod. Ham. 201, Cim. 33. Photo: Jörg P. Anders.

189. John Flaxman, Heaven of the Moon: Piccarda (*Par.* 3), 1793. From *Drawings for Dante's Divine Comedy* (pf MS Typ 26.4). The original pencil drawings for Flaxman's Italian engravings. By permission of The Houghton Library, Harvard University.

190. Venetian, Piccarda's Story (*Par.* 3), late 14th c. Cod. It. IX, 276 (=6902), fol. 54v, Biblioteca Nazionale Marciana, Venice.

191. Sandro Botticelli, Piccarda Disappears (*Par.* 4), ca. 1495. Kupferstichkabinett, Staatliche Museen zu Berlin, Cod. Ham. 201, Cim. 33. Photo: Jörg P. Anders.

192. Sandro Botticelli, Beatrice's Discourse (*Par.* 5), ca. 1495. Kupferstichkabinett, Staatliche Museen zu Berlin, Cod. Ham. 201, Cim. 33. Photo: Jörg P. Anders.

193. Gustave Doré, Heaven of Mercury (*Par.* 5), 1868. From *Dante Alighieri, Le Purgatoire de Dante Alighieri, avec les dessins de Gustave Doré; Le Paradis de Dante Alighieri, avec les dessins de Gustave Doré,* vol. 2 (2 vols. in 1; Paris, 1868). Page size ca. 31 x 43 cm. Photo: Yale University Audio-Visual Dept.

194. Giovanni di Paolo, Heaven of Mercury: Justinian (*Par.* 6), ca. 1445. By permission of The British Library, London. Yates-Thompson MS 36, fol. 139r.

195. John Flaxman, Justinian (*Par.* 6), 1793. From *Drawings for Dante's Divine Comedy* (pf MS Typ 26.4). The original pencil drawings for Flaxman's Italian engravings. By permission of The Houghton Library, Harvard University.

196. Venetian, Heaven of Venus: Cunizza (*Par.* 9), late 14th c. Cod. It. IX, 276 (=6902), fol. 58v, Biblioteca Nazionale Marciana, Venice.

197. John Flaxman, Cunizza (*Par.* 9), 1793. From *Drawings for Dante's Divine Comedy* (pf MS Typ 26.4). The original pencil drawings for Flaxman's Italian engravings. By permission of The Houghton Library, Harvard University.

198. Giovanni di Paolo, Cunizza with

Folco (*Par.* 9), ca. 1445. By permission of The British Library, London. Yates-Thompson MS 36, fol. 145r.

199. Venetian, Heaven of the Sun (*Par.* 10), late 14th c. Cod. It. IX, 276 (=6902), fol. 59v, Biblioteca Nazionale Marciana, Venice.

200. Italian, Heaven of the Sun (*Par.* 10), 15th c. The Royal Library, Copenhagen, MS Thott 411.2.

201. Sandro Botticelli, Heaven of the Sun (*Par.* 10), ca. 1495. Kupferstichkabinett, Staatliche Museen zu Berlin, Cod. Ham. 201, Cim. 33. Photo: Jörg P. Anders.

202. Lombard, Heaven of the Sun (*Par.* 12), ca. 1400. Ms B. R. 39, fol. 353v, Biblioteca Nazionale Centrale, Florence.

203. Italian, Heaven of the Sun (*Par.* 12), late 14th c. The Pierpont Morgan Library, New York. M. 676, fol. 106r. Photo: David A. Loggie.

204. Gustave Doré, Heaven of the Sun (*Par.* 12), 1868. From *Dante Alighieri, Le Purgatoire de Dante Alighieri, avec les dessins de Gustave Doré; Le Paradis de Dante Alighieri, avec les dessins de Gustave Doré,* vol. 2 (2 vols. in 1; Paris, 1868). Page size ca. 31 x 43 cm. Photo: Yale University Audio-Visual Dept.

205. Giovanni di Paolo, Heaven of the Sun: Bonaventure (*Par.* 12), ca. 1445. By permission of The British Library, London. Yates-Thompson MS 36, fol. 151r.

206. Venetian, Heaven of the Sun: Solomon (*Par.* 14), late 14th c. Cod. It. IX, 276 (=6902), fol. 63r, Biblioteca Nazionale Marciana, Venice.

207. Italian, Heaven of Mars: The Cross (*Par.* 14), mid-14th c. MS 8530, Bibliothèque de l'Arsenal, Paris. Photo: Bibliothèque Nationale de France, Paris.

208. Venetian, Heaven of Mars: The Cross (*Par.* 14), late 14th c. Cod. It. IX, 276 (=6902), fol. 63r, Biblioteca Nazionale Marciana, Venice.

209. Gustave Doré, Heaven of Mars: The Cross (*Par.* 14), 1868. From *Dante Alighieri, Le Purgatoire de Dante Alighieri, avec les dessins de Gustave Doré; Le Paradis de Dante Alighieri, avec les dessins de Gustave Doré,* vol. 2 (2 vols. in 1; Paris, 1868). Page size ca. 31 x 43 cm. Photo: Yale University Audio-Visual Dept.

210. Paduan, Heaven of Mars: Cacciaguida (*Par.* 15), early 15th c. MS 67, fol.

252v, Biblioteca del Seminario Vescovile, Padua. Photo: Romanin Alessandro.

211. Giovanni di Paolo, Cacciaguida Names the Lights (*Par.* 18), ca. 1445. By permission of The British Library, London. Yates-Thompson MS 36, fol. 160r.

212. Sandro Botticelli, Beatrice Grows in Brilliance (*Par.* 18), ca. 1495. Kupferstichkabinett, Staatliche Museen zu Berlin, Cod. Ham. 201, Cim. 33. Photo: Jörg P. Anders.

213. Gustave Doré, Heaven of Jupiter (*Par.* 18), 1868. From Dante Alighieri, *Le Purgatoire de Dante Alighieri, avec les dessins de Gustave Doré; Le Paradis de Dante Alighieri, avec les dessins de Gustave Doré,* vol. 2 (2 vols. in 1; Paris, 1868). Page size ca. 31 x 43 cm. Photo: Yale University Audio-Visual Dept.

214. John Flaxman, Heaven of Jupiter (*Par.* 18), 1793. From *Drawings for Dante's Divine Comedy* (pf MS Typ 26.4). The original pencil drawings for Flaxman's Italian engravings. By permission of The Houghton Library, Harvard University.

215. Giovanni di Paolo, Heaven of Jupiter: The Eagle (*Par.* 19), ca. 1445. By permission of The British Library, London. Yates-Thompson MS 36, fol. 162r.

216. Gustave Doré, The Eagle (*Par.* 19), 1868. From Dante Alighieri, *Le Purgatoire de Dante Alighieri, avec les dessins de Gustave Doré; Le Paradis de Dante Alighieri, avec les dessins de Gustave Doré,* vol. 2 (2 vols. in 1; Paris, 1868). Page size ca. 31 x 43 cm. Photo: Yale University Audio-Visual Dept.

217. Italian, The Eagle (*Par.* 19), late 14th c. The Pierpont Morgan Library, New York. M. 676, fol. 112r. Photo: David A. Loggie.

218. Giovanni di Paolo, Heaven of Saturn (*Par.* 21), ca. 1445. By permission of The British Library, London. Yates-Thompson MS 36, fol. 165r.

219. Gustave Doré, Heaven of Saturn (*Par.* 21), 1868. From Dante Alighieri, *Le Purgatoire de Dante Alighieri, avec les dessins de Gustave Doré; Le Paradis de Dante Alighieri, avec les dessins de Gustave Doré,* vol. 2 (2 vols. in 1; Paris, 1868). Page size ca. 31 x 43 cm. Photo: Yale University Audio-Visual Dept.

220. Italian, Heaven of Saturn: Benedict (*Par.* 22), ca. 1365. MS Holkham Misc. 48, p. 140, The Bodleian Library, Oxford.

221. Venetian, Heaven of Saturn: Benedict (*Par.* 22), late 14th c. Cod. It. IX, 276 (=6902), fol. 68v, Biblioteca Nazionale Marciana, Venice.

222. Sandro Botticelli, Ascent to Heaven of the Fixed Stars (*Par.* 22), ca. 1495. Kupferstichkabinett, Staatliche Museen zu Berlin, Cod. Ham. 201, Cim. 33. Photo: Jörg P. Anders.

223. Venetian, Prayer to Gemini (*Par.* 22), late 14th c. Cod. It. IX, 276 (=6902), fol. 69r, Biblioteca Nazionale Marciana, Venice.

224. Giovanni di Paolo, Looking Back Toward Earth (*Par.* 22), ca. 1445. By permission of The British Library, London. Yates-Thompson MS 36, fol. 169r.

225. Venetian, Heaven of Fixed Stars (*Par.* 23), late 14th c. Cod. It. IX, 276 (=6902), fol. 69v, Biblioteca Nazionale Marciana, Venice.

226. Sandro Botticelli, Heaven of Fixed Stars (*Par.* 23), ca. 1495. Kupferstichkabinett, Staatliche Museen zu Berlin, Cod. Ham. 201, Cim. 33. Photo: Jörg P. Anders.

227. Giovanni di Paolo, Heaven of Fixed Stars: Saint Peter (*Par.* 24), ca. 1445. By permission of The British Library, London. Yates-Thompson MS 36, fol. 173r.

228. John Flaxman, Saint Peter (*Par.* 24), 1793. From *Drawings for Dante's Divine Comedy* (pf MS Typ 26.4). The original pencil drawings for Flaxman's Italian engravings. By permission of The Houghton Library, Harvard University.

229. Venetian, Saint Peter (*Par.* 24), late 14th c. Cod. It. IX, 276 (=6902), fol. 70r, Biblioteca Nazionale Marciana, Venice.

230. Giovanni di Paolo, Saints James and John (*Par.* 25), ca. 1445. By permission of The British Library, London. Yates-Thompson MS 36, fol. 174r.

231. William Blake, Dante Interrogated by Saint John (*Par.* 26), 1824–27. The British Museum, London.

232. Gustave Doré, Dante Interrogated by Saint John (*Par.* 26), 1868. From Dante Alighieri, *Le Purgatoire de Dante Alighieri, avec les dessins de Gustave Doré; Le Paradis de Dante Alighieri, avec les dessins de Gustave Doré*, vol. 2 (2 vols. in 1; Paris, 1868). Page size ca. 31 x 43 cm. Photo: Yale University Audio-Visual Dept.

233. Sandro Botticelli, Dante blinded (*Par.* 26), ca. 1495. Kupferstichkabinett, Staatliche Museen zu Berlin, Cod. Ham. 201, Cim. 33. Photo: Jörg P. Anders.

234. Giovanni di Paolo, Adam (*Par.* 26), ca. 1445. By permission of The British Library, London. Yates-Thompson MS 36, fol. 176r.

235. Venetian, Peter's Anger (*Par.* 27), late 14th c. Cod. It. IX, 276 (=6902), fol. 72r, Biblioteca Nazionale Marciana, Venice.

236. Venetian, Primum Mobile (*Par.* 28), late 14th c. Cod. It. IX, 276 (=6902), fol. 73r, Biblioteca Nazionale Marciana, Venice.

237. Giovanni di Paolo, Primum Mobile: The Point of Light (*Par.* 28), ca. 1445. By permission of The British Library, London. Yates-Thompson MS 36, fol. 179r.

238. Sandro Botticelli, Primum Mobile: Angelic Hierarchies (*Par.* 28), ca. 1495. Kupferstichkabinett, Staatliche Museen zu Berlin, Cod. Ham. 201, Cim. 33. Photo: Jörg P. Anders.

239. Gustave Doré, Primum Mobile: Angelic Hierarchies (*Par.* 28), 1868. From Dante Alighieri, *Le Purgatoire de Dante Alighieri, avec les dessins de Gustave Doré; Le Paradis de Dante Alighieri, avec les dessins de Gustave Doré*, vol. 2 (2 vols. in 1; Paris, 1868). Page size ca. 31 x 43 cm. Photo: Yale University Audio-Visual Dept.

240. Giovanni di Paolo, Fallen Angels (*Par.* 29), ca. 1445. By permission of The British Library, London. Yates-Thompson MS 36, fol. 181r.

241. Sandro Botticelli, Empyrean: The River of Light (*Par.* 30), ca. 1495. Kupferstichkabinett, Staatliche Museen zu Berlin, Cod. Ham. 201, Cim. 33. Photo: Jörg P. Anders.

242. Giovanni di Paolo, The River of Light (*Par.* 30), ca. 1445. By permission of The British Library, London. Yates-Thompson MS 36, fol. 183r.

243. Emilian, The River of Light (*Par.* 30), ca. 1340. By permission of The British Library, London. Egerton MS 943, fol. 179v.

244. William Blake, *Dante in the Empyrean, Drinking at the River of Light* (*Par.* 30), 1824–27. Watercolor, 37.1 x 52.8 cm. Tate Gallery, London/Art Resource, N.Y.

245. Giovanni di Paolo, Celestial City in the Rose (*Par.* 30), ca. 1445. By permission of The British Library, London. Yates-Thompson MS 36, fol. 184r.

246. Giovanni di Paolo, The Saints in the Rose (*Par.* 31), ca. 1445. By permission of The British Library, London. Yates-Thompson MS 36, fol. 185r.

247. Gustave Doré, The Celestial Rose (*Par.* 31), 1868. Dante Alighieri, *Le Purgatoire de Dante Alighieri, avec les dessins de Gustave Doré; Le Paradis de Dante Alighieri, avec les dessins de Gustave Doré*, vol. 2 (2 vols. in 1; Paris, 1868). Page size ca. 31 x 43 cm. Photo: Yale University Audio-Visual Dept.

248. William Blake, *The Queen of Heaven in Glory*, 1824–27. The Rose (*Par.* 31). Pen and watercolor over pencil and black chalk. 37.1 x 52.8 cm. Felton Bequest, 1920. National Gallery of Victoria, Melbourne.

249. Italian, The Virgin Enthroned in the Rose (*Par.* 32), ca. 1365. MS Holkham Misc. 48, p. 145, The Bodleian Library, Oxford.

250. Venetian, The Virgin Enthroned (*Par.* 32), late 14th c. Cod. It. IX, 276 (=6902), fol. 76r, Biblioteca Nazionale Marciana, Venice.

251. Giovanni di Paolo, The Virgin, the Argo, and Neptune (*Par.* 32), ca. 1445. By permission of The British Library, London. Yates-Thompson MS 36, fol. 190r.

252. Florentine, Diagram of Paradise, ca. 1440. MS 1122, fol. 28r, Biblioteca Riccardiana, Florence. Photo: Donato Pineider.

253. Venetian, A Vision of God (*Par.* 33), late 14th c. Cod. It. IX, 276 (=6902), fol. 77v, Biblioteca Nazionale Marciana, Venice.

254. Sandro Botticelli, Virgin, Christ, and Angel(?) (*Par.* 33), ca. 1495. Kupferstichkabinett, Staatliche Museen zu Berlin, Cod. Ham. 201, Cim. 33. Photo: Jörg P. Anders.

255. Leonard Baskin, *The End of All Desiring* (*Par.* 33), 1970. Drawing, from *Illustrations to the Divine Comedy of Dante*, Graphic Arts Exhibition catalog, Introduction by Dale Roylance (New Haven, 1970). Courtesy of R. Michelson Galleries, Amherst, Mass. Photo: Yale University Audio-Visual Dept.

Index

. . . (continued)